COLONIZING CHRISTIANITY

ORTHODOX CHRISTIANITY AND CONTEMPORARY THOUGHT

SERIES EDITORS
Aristotle Papanikolaou and Ashley M. Purpura

This series consists of books that seek to bring Orthodox Christianity into an engagement with contemporary forms of thought. Its goal is to promote (1) historical studies in Orthodox Christianity that are interdisciplinary, employ a variety of methods, and speak to contemporary issues; and (2) constructive theological arguments in conversation with patristic sources and that focus on contemporary questions ranging from the traditional theological and philosophical themes of God and human identity to cultural, political, economic, and ethical concerns. The books in the series explore both the relevancy of Orthodox Christianity to contemporary challenges and the impact of contemporary modes of thought on Orthodox self-understandings.

COLONIZING CHRISTIANITY

Greek and Latin Religious Identity in the Era of the Fourth Crusade

GEORGE E. DEMACOPOULOS

FORDHAM UNIVERSITY PRESS
New York • 2019

Fordham University Press has no responsibility for the persistence or accuracy of URLs for external or third-party Internet websites referred to in this publication and does not guarantee that any content on such websites is, or will remain, accurate or appropriate.

Fordham University Press also publishes its books in a variety of electronic formats. Some content that appears in print may not be available in electronic books.

Visit us online at www.fordhampress.com.

Library of Congress Cataloging-in-Publication Data available online at https://catalog.loc .gov.

Printed in the United States of America

21 20 19   5 4 3 2 1

First edition

CONTENTS

INTRODUCTION

This book began as (and remains) a thought experiment. Its animating question is what happens if we apply the resources of colonial and postcolonial critique to texts about Christian difference that were produced in the context of the Fourth Crusade? It proposes that treating the Fourth Crusade as a colonial experience helps us to understand more fully the ways in which Latin Christians authorized the subjugation of Greek Christians, the establishment of Latin settlement in the Christian East, and the exceptional degree of resource extraction—both material and religious—from the region. It also explores in detail the ways in which the experience of colonial subjugation not only transformed the way that Eastern Christians viewed themselves and the Western Christian Other but also how the same experience opened permanent fissures within the Orthodox community, which struggled to develop a consistent response to aggressive demands for submission to the Roman Church. This internal fracturing has done more lasting damage to the modern Orthodox Church than any material act perpetrated by the crusaders.

This book is not a history of the Fourth Crusade. Nor does it propose to be any kind of comprehensive study of Eastern Christian/Western Christian relations during the Middle Ages. In these regards, historiographers are likely to be disappointed. Rather, *Colonizing Christianity* offers a close reading of a handful of texts from the era of the Fourth Crusade in the hope of illuminating the mechanisms by which Western Christians authorized and exploited the Christian East and, concurrently, the ways

1

in which Eastern Christians understood and responded to this dramatic shift in political and religious fortunes.

Although the book employs methodological resources that might appear unconventional, even esoteric to some readers, the argument of the book is straightforward. Namely, *Colonizing Christianity* maintains that the statements of Greek and Latin religious polemic that emerged in the context of the Fourth Crusade should be interpreted as having been produced in a colonial setting and, as such, reveal more about the political, economic, and cultural uncertainty of communities in conflict than they offer genuine theological insight. Given that it was in the context of the Fourth Crusade— and not the so-called Photian Schism of the ninth century, the so-called Great Schism of 1054, or any other period of ecclesiastical controversy— that Greek and Latin apologists developed the most elaborate condemnations of one another, it behooves historians (and those who care about Christian unity) to investigate anew the conditions that give rise to the most deliberate efforts to forbid Greek and Latin sacramental unity in the Middle Ages and to ask whether those arguments reveal genuine theological insight or simply convey political or cultural animosity in the guise of theological disputation.

The Fourth Crusade: A Very Quick History

There is, of course, no shortage of scholars who have studied the crusades either as a whole or individually.[1] Indeed, new books about the Fourth Crusade or the subsequent Latin Empire of Byzantium appear regularly.[2] In the chapters that follow, we will explore a variety of historical events and personalities in detail but, for now, we can sketch the general historical parameters of the Fourth Crusade, even though it is a rather complex story.[3]

When Pope Innocent III ascended Peter's throne in 1198, he almost immediately began planning for what was supposed to be the largest crusade to date.[4] Whereas many previous expeditions had been bogged down by proceeding along a land route through Central Europe and Byzantium, Innocent and the crusade leaders devised a plan to contract with the Republic of Venice and to set sail for Egypt, hoping to march from Egypt to Jerusalem. This was an expensive undertaking and Innocent did something no previous pope had done, which was to levy a tax against every diocese in the Christian West. But Innocent's plans were stymied from the start—not only was he unable to raise the number of soldiers that he had hoped, but he and the crusade leaders also failed to obtain sufficient funding to meet their contractual arrangement with the Venetians. The Venetians refused to acquiesce without payment.

Against Innocent's explicit warnings, the Venetians and the crusaders hatched a plan wherein the soldiers would lay siege to the Christian city of Zara (a break-away Venetian colony on the coast of modern-day Croatia) and the Venetians would agree to accept a delayed payment on the debt owed to them. Pope Innocent III had previously demanded that the crusaders not attack any Christian city. Furious with what had happened, Pope Innocent excommunicated the crusade leaders and all of their soldiers and sailors. It looked like the entire project might fall apart.

Meanwhile in Constantinople, in 1195, the Byzantine emperor, Isaac II Angelos was deposed, blinded, and imprisoned by his brother, Alexius III, in a palace coup. Isaac's son, the eventual Alexius IV, managed to escape the city and in 1201 made his way to the West where he took shelter with his sister and brother-in-law, Philip of Swabia, one of the eventual leaders of the Fourth Crusade. Upon his arrival, the younger Alexius, attempted to convince Philip and other Western aristocrats to help him restore his father's throne. But it was not until the ill-fated expedition to Zara and the uncertainty that it unleashed that Alexius was able to convince the crusade leadership to support his claim in Constantinople. But that support also came with a price—Alexius not only promised the crusade leaders a significant monetary payment, but he also promised to provide soldiers for their eventual attack on Egypt.

Despite the repeated warnings of further papal condemnation, the crusaders arrived on the outskirts of Constantinople in June of 1203. After a few weeks of sparring on the plains outside of the city and at the city's harbor walls, Alexius III took flight in the middle of the night and the Byzantine aristocracy decided to restore the aged and blind Isaac II to the throne. By August, Alexius IV was crowned coemperor and he began the process of paying his debts to the crusaders. Alexius IV soon proved unable to provide everything that he promised and the crusaders grew frustrated with their situation.[5] When Alexius IV was murdered in yet another palace coup, the crusaders decided to take matters into their own hands.

On April 13, 1204, the crusaders defeated a demoralized Byzantine guard and seized the city for themselves. The scale of looting and rapine that is said to have followed is unlike anything else in the Orthodox Christian imagination.[6] The surprise and extent of the plunder deeply alienated local attitudes toward the Latins. But perhaps of equal importance to the present study is the fact that the crusaders transformed the very structure of Byzantine society by seizing control of both church and state and by often imposing a Western feudal structure throughout the Balkans that would serve as a beachhead for further Frankish and papal aspirations in the Christian East.

As we will see in the chapters that follow, the Franks carved the Byzantine Empire into a series of lesser kingdoms, principalities, duchies, and fiefdoms. Although remnants of the Byzantine political power would coalesce in independent Greek successor states—in Nicaea, in Epiros, and in Trebizond—those successor states were as likely to war with one another as they were to resist the crusaders. And, as we will see, in a great number of places, including Thrace, Thessaly, and the especially the Peloponnese, local Greek aristocrats were just as likely to swear allegiance to Frankish lords as they were to fight under the banner of the Greek leaders of Epiros or Nicaea. Even though the Nicaeans were able to reclaim Constantinople and its immediate vicinity in 1261, some of the Frankish and Venetian colonies lasted longer in the eastern Mediterranean than the Byzantine Empire, which ended in 1453.[7]

Not to be lost in this brief sketch of events are the efforts of Pope Innocent III and his successors to use the capture of Constantinople in 1204 as a means to govern the Greek Church on the papacy's own terms. As we will see in Chapter 3, Innocent was quick to pardon the sins of the crusaders when he learned of the startling turn of events of 1204. And, as we will see in several chapters, the efforts of the Roman Church to force subservience to the papacy were met with stiff resistance not only from some of the indigenous Greek population but also from Frankish leaders in the East who were typically willing to tolerate religious independence of their subjects so long as that did not translate into political or economic independence.[8] Indeed, the interplay and tension between the expectations of those who remained in the West versus the reality of shared experience of Franks and Greeks in the East is one of the most fascinating dynamics of the history of the Latin Empire of Byzantium. But an even more important dynamic of Greek religiosity in the wake of the Fourth Crusade—and, frankly one of the reasons that postcolonial analysis is so appropriate to this history—is that the Greek Church fractured internally with respect to how best to respond to the demands placed upon it by Innocent III and his successors.

The Crusades as Colonialism and the
Use of Postcolonial Critique

In his extensive introduction, *Postcolonialism: A Historical Introduction*, Robert Young boldly asserts that the "colonial" era belongs exclusively to the period between 1492 and 1945 and that it is structurally distinctive from imperialism.[9] In large part, this insistence is grounded in a commitment to a very specific set of contemporary political and economic causes, all of which relate to the aftereffects of the decolonial process in Africa, Asia, and South America.[10] And, in this way, Young's assertions about the technical categories of colonialism, decolonialism, and postcolonialism reflect many of the assumptions of the most influential postcolonial theorists of the twentieth century, including Fanon, Said, Spivak, and Bhabha.[11]

While a framework that situates colonialism strictly within the confines of Western European settlement in the tricontinental region in the age after Columbus may help to illuminate current political and economic structural injustices, there are substantial historical reasons for seeing the crusades as an essential precursor of later European colonial networks, if not an actual expression of colonialism as defined by Young and others.[12] Indeed, some of the very characteristics that Young associates with the distinctiveness of colonization vis-à-vis imperialism—its peripheral nature, its economic emphasis, and its moral justification—were essential to the early crusader kingdoms in the eastern Mediterranean. As we will see in many chapters of this book, these aspects of colonialism were definitively operative for the Franks and Venetians who occupied Byzantium during the thirteenth century.

Given the fragmented nature of medieval political structures, including those of the Roman Church, it would be a gross mischaracterization to suggest that the Frankish involvement in various crusading expeditions was some kind of centralized expansion of authority (i.e., what Young labels "imperialism"). Even Venice, which did conduct its business in a more coherent and directed fashion, developed a system of operation in the Orient that was based upon trading partnerships rather than imperialism. What is more, the development of deposit and merchant banking (critical preconditions for colonial and modern capitalism) underwent key structural changes during the crusade era in order to fund expeditions and to accommodate the financial needs of soldiers in the crusader colonies. Even some Byzantine authors described Western settlers and merchants in the East as "colonists."[13] In sum, there are a great number of reasons to view the crusades as a kind of protocolonial endeavor that served as a model for subsequent European colonial expansion.

Perhaps just as important as the structural patterns of colonial activity, an analysis of thirteenth-century crusade discourse indicates a series of key components of a subsequent colonial discourse. For example, several chapters in *Colonizing Christianity* will investigate the ways that our texts attempt to counter those Western European voices who were critical of the (colonial) endeavor.[14] Moreover, we will see how other aspects of crusader discourse, including orientalism and sexuality, anticipate the colonial discourse of later centuries. In short, there is little doubt that the Western European experience in the eastern Mediterranean from the eleventh century onward provided both the conceptual and the practical models for the European colonial expansion to the tricontinental regions in subsequent eras.[15]

As early as the 1970s, the eminent crusade historian Joshua Prawer was arguing that the best way to understand the crusades was to see them within the framework of subsequent European colonialism.[16] Prawer, like all successful historians, spurred a number of responses and revisions but his willingness to treat the crusades as a colonial encounter has had a profound impact not only on the scholarship of the crusades, but on scholarship of the Middle Ages more generally.[17] For example, it is now customary for elite scholars of Byzantine history such as Averil Cameron and Anthony Kaldellis to describe the Fourth Crusade as a colonial encounter.[18] And, perhaps even more significantly, Kaldellis and Cameron have also turned to some of the insights of postcolonial critique to identify inherent biases such as "orientalisms" in Western historiography about Byzantium.[19] In this way, they follow other scholars of the Middle Ages who have successfully appropriated postcolonial critique to illuminate medieval encounters and discourses of Otherness.[20]

As much as possible, this book will seek to avoid an overly technical or overly theoretical use of postcolonial analysis. Rather, by framing the events of the Fourth Crusade as a kind of colonial encounter, it will draw from some of the basic insights of postcolonial critique to look in new ways at the discourse of Orthodox/Roman Catholic difference that took its mature form in the thirteenth century. As such, one of the most important conclusions of this study is that the development of the most vitriolic statements of Orthodox/Catholic religious polemic in the Middle Ages were based in political and cultural alienation, not theological development.[21] Not only is this an important historical insight, it has genuine significance for those in the present day who are concerned with the cause of Christian unity.

Put another way, this book is designed to be something of a three-way bridge between ecclesiastical historians who adhere to more traditional historical-critical methods; scholars who believe that the resources of critical theory (including discourse analysis and postcolonial analysis) have much to offer our understanding of the past; and theologians and Christian leaders who believe that an honest accounting of history is directly relevant to the contemporary Church. To these ends, the initial chapters will engage a variety of well-tread postcolonial insights to ease the reader into the ideas and opportunities offered by postcolonial scholarship. Later chapters will delve into more complicated categories of analysis, such as ambivalence and hybridity, and engage individual theorists, like Homi Bhabha and Robert Young, to offer deeper layers of investigation.

At this point, allow me to identify three aspects of postcolonial insight upon which this book will frequently turn. First, drawing upon Edward Said's contention that the "Orient" functions for Western authors as an epistemological system of representations that originates within the political, cultural, and economic imagination of the West,[22] several chapters will explore the dimensions of colonial discourse of crusader texts that sexualized the encounter with the Greek East, and authorized and/or celebrated its conquest. In other words, when the crusaders and bishops of Rome wrote about the Christian East in ways that licensed its domination, the Christian East they described was largely a construction of the Western imagination that served narrative and rhetorical purposes. It was never an objective accounting of Eastern Christian people or Eastern Christian theology.

Second, I will frequently draw upon Said's contention that there is an intrinsic link between sexuality and the colonial condition, not only in terms of the power dimensions intrinsic to military conquest but also in the wide variety of narrative formulae employed by Western authors, including sexual fantasy, sexual threat, and the emasculation of Eastern men.[23] Some scholars of Byzantium, such as Charis Messis, have begun to identify the ways in which anti-Greek religious polemics in the period relied upon accusations of Eastern effeminacy.[24] I will take this analysis further (and include concerns over the production of "hybrid" children) to show how Latin and Greek authors in the era of the Fourth Crusade fixated on issues of sexual politics not only to authorize colonial exploitation but also to resist it. As we will see, the production of children of "mixed race," which resulted from Latin settlement in the East, generated a great deal of concern but few consistent responses from writers of the period.

Third, an important insight of postcolonial critique concerns the question of whether or not a discursive opportunity exists for a colonized community.[25] In other words, does a community in a colonial or postcolonial condition possess its own, distinctive epistemic possibilities or are those possibilities forever framed by the shadow of its master? As we will see, through complicated and overlapping responses of acquiescence, assimilation, and resistance, Greek authors in the era of the Fourth Crusade not only renegotiated the boundaries of their political and religious communities, they simultaneously (but not always consistently) recalibrated ethical priorities in order to account for both the practical and the conceptual realities of Western settlers and the heavy hand of the Roman Church. Not only was the Orthodox narration of Self and Other that resulted an innovative narration, this narration varied considerably, with each voice longing in its own way for a return to the before. The fourth and fifth chapters, especially, will look at the ways by which Eastern Christian identity narratives not only account for the Latin Other but indirectly recognize the formation of ecclesiastical factionalism animated by alternative responses to the Western Christian Other.

Building on this final aspect of postcolonial critique, let me conclude my methodological overview with the recognition that we should not treat a society like Byzantium as a typical colonial "subaltern." Although the term "subaltern" originated in a different analytical context, during the 1970s postcolonial theorists began to apply it to those peripheral populations whose lives were governed by hegemonic colonial power structures beyond their control.[26] For many theorists, one of the great tragedies of the colonial condition is the fact that the subaltern is so marginalized in the world of the colonial master that they come to embrace the colonizer's outlook, including the notion that the colonizing civilization is more "advanced" or "modern" than the indigenous one.[27] While this phenomenon might adequately describe many examples of early-modern colonialism, it does not reflect the Byzantine situation in the wake of the Fourth Crusade, at least not without considerable clarification.

Unlike most of the tricontinental societies colonized by Western European powers in the early-modern era, Byzantium was a more "advanced" civilization than its colonial masters (i.e., the petty baronies of the Western Europe). It was not only more culturally sophisticated in terms of its art, literature, and politics, it was also the most powerful and most wealthy state in the Christian world. To be sure, it had fallen on hard times, but it was within living memory that the emperor Manuel II had manipulated the kings of Europe like pawns as he bought them off with his superior wealth.[28] Indeed, Byzantium had been until very recently the gold standard of Christian empire and Christian society. It is no wonder that Western leaders had, since the time of Charlemagne, aspired to see themselves as the equals of the Byzantines. The uniqueness of the Byzantine/crusader dynamics requires us to think carefully about the ways in which postcolonial critique does and does not prove fruitful in our analysis of the Fourth Crusade. Among other things, we must be cognizant of the fact that the Byzantine sense of cultural and religious superiority did not simply evaporate with the arrival of the crusaders. Moreover, we must also be alert to the fact that the crusader experience in Byzantium was rather different than what the British may have experienced in India centuries later.

Nevertheless, it is precisely because of these dynamics that a postcolonial examination of the texts surrounding the Fourth Crusade offers so much potential, not only for understanding the events and the transformation of Orthodox/Catholic religious identity, but also for understanding how a key example of premodern colonialism largely does (but partially does not) map onto the templates of subsequent colonial, decolonial, and postcolonial experiences. In Chapters 4 and 5, especially, we will explore how Greek authors in the wake in the Fourth Crusade never cede cultural, political, or religious superiority to the "barbarians" of the West but, at the very same time, these same authors desperately seek to narrate what it means to be Orthodox and Byzantine in the wake of the cataclysmic events of 1204. Indeed, these chapters demonstrate that the conditions, experience, and destructiveness of colonialism are powerfully operative in a society even when the elite members of that society appear to maintain an air of indignation and superiority.

The Chapters That Follow

In each of the chapters that follow, I connect what the text says about the Christian "Other" to the colonial, decolonial, or postcolonial conditions that frame the perspective. Each chapter focuses on a different author, typically a single text, and my choice of texts has been carefully selected so that I can engage as many different genres of medieval Christian writing as possible, including chronicle, hagiography, epistolary, and canonical interpretation. Chapters 1, 2, 3, and 6 engage texts that supported the Fourth Crusade in one way or another. Chapters 4 and 5 scrutinize Greek texts that provide alternative positions vis-à-vis the Roman Church in the wake of the Fourth Crusade.

Chapter 1 explores *The Conquest of Constantinople* by Robert de Clari, which is the lone surviving firsthand account of the Fourth Crusade composed by a rank-and-file Frankish soldier who participated in the endeavor. Chapter 2 examines the *Hystoria Constantinopolitana* by Gunther of Pairis, which is a hagiography celebrating the theft of Constantinopolitan religious treasure. Chapter 3 turns to the correspondence of Pope Innocent III, his interlocutors, and his successors in order to understand more fully the conditions that gave rise to the first papal pronouncements asserting that Greek theological error was so egregious that it warranted violence, occupation, and larceny. As we will see, that determination came only after the siege of Constantinople in 1204, and it was used to authorize new violence against those Greeks who refused to accept the authority of the Roman bishop. But we will also observe and interrogate the ways in which this discursive turn conveyed a deep ambivalence.

Chapters 4 and 5 turn to two very different kinds of Greek texts. Chapter 4 explores a pair of canonical opinions written by Demetrios Chomatianos, the archbishop of Ohrid in the 1220s. These texts draw sharp sacramental boundaries not only between Greek and Latin Christians, but more notably, between Greek Christians who hold differing opinions about the standing of Latins within the Church. Chomatianos opined, for the first time in history, that Greek Christians who failed to acknowledge the threat posed by Latin Christians should be barred from the sacramental rites of the Orthodox community. Chapter 5 explores aspects of George Akropolites's *History*, which was a chronicle of the Byzantine successor state in Nicaea covering the years 1204–61. More than anything else, what we learn from Akropolites with respect to the concerns of this investigation is that there were a great number of Greek Christians who did not believe that the Latin Church should be sacramentally isolated from the Greek Church even if the Latins were an inferior race and their presence in the East had caused devastation to the Byzantine community.

Perhaps it is in Chapter 6, with an analysis of *The Chronicle of Morea*, where we find some of the most intriguing aspects of the colonial encounter of the Fourth Crusade. Although it has a very complicated textual history, *The Chronicle of Morea* tells the multigenerational story of the Frankish Villehardouin dynasty, which ruled the Peloponnese in the centuries after the conquest of 1204. This text reveals not only the way that colonizer and colonized eventually came to work alongside one another but also the way that the prolonged encounter between Greeks and Franks transformed the means by which both understood their sense of identity and religious commitments. It is precisely because of these aspects of this text—and the others on offer—that the insights of postcolonial analysis help us to understand the many complexities that they convey.

A Note about Translations and Terminology

Because this study is meant to reach an audience well beyond experts in the crusades or Byzantine ecclesiastical history, I have made every effort possible to put my analysis to texts that already have printed English translations. This was mostly but not entirely possible. At present, there is no English translation of Demetrios Chomatianos (the subject of Chapter 4), and while most of the papal letters referenced in Chapter 3 have an English translation, not all of them do. Wherever possible, references in the notes point to both the primary language edition and the modern English translation.

All scholars of "Byzantium" are confronted with the challenge of what to do about political and cultural nomenclature when they write about their field. As is generally well known, the "Byzantines" never self-described as Byzantines and they only very rarely referred to themselves as Greeks, *Graeci*. The inhabitants of the medieval Eastern Roman Empire always described themselves as Romans. The Latin term "Greek," *Graeci*, was typically employed by Westerners as a derogatory term designed to undermine the East Roman claim of Roman-ness. For a variety of reasons well explained by Anthony Kaldellis in his magisterial *Hellenism in Byzantium*, the Byzantines began to (re-)appropriate the category of "Hellene" at roughly the same time as the crusades, but the reader should understand that their appropriation of "Hellene" was, to their understanding, very different from the Latin smear of *Graeci*.[29]

Today, most scholars as well as popular opinion regularly use the terms "Byzantine" and "Byzantium" to refer to the post-Constantinian Eastern Roman Empire. Those words were first routinely employed by nineteenth-century Western European historians who sought to differentiate the "real" Roman Empire from what was, to their minds, an Eastern and Christian aberration of empire that came afterwards. The decision to introduce those new terms was not an apolitical one, nor was it innocent. But it remains the common parlance. And, for that reason, this book will repeatedly use the words Byzantine and Byzantium, except in those instances when it becomes important to convey the precise claim of Roman-ness in a cited text or when there is a need to differentiate between those Greek-Romans who were loyal to the successor state of Epiros from those who were loyal to the successor state of Nicaea. Moreover, for convenience, I will routinely employ the word Greek and Greeks to refer to the indigenous population in the region. I, of course, do so in a nonderogatory fashion, similar to the way that it is used in contemporary speech.

1

ROBERT DE CLARI

There are several reasons why Robert de Clari's *Conquest of Constantinople* is an important source for the Fourth Crusade.[1] It offers an eyewitness account of nearly every stage of the expedition in a chronological order—its planning, the detour to Zara, the decision to travel to Constantinople, and, of course, the siege and plunder of the city.[2] The narrative continues for approximately one year beyond the conquest of the city, likely the duration of Robert's stay in the East, offering an account of the unexpected decline in crusader fortunes. Throughout the chronicle, Robert provides a running commentary about his sojourn in the East that includes biting criticisms of both the local population and the crusade leaders who exploited their soldiers.

Robert is one of two Western chroniclers of the Fourth Crusade, both of whom composed their work in French vernacular—the other is Geoffrey de Villehardouin. Whereas Geoffrey provides an insider's view of the debates and attitudes within the French aristocracy (he was one of the key organizers of the crusade),[3] Robert offers a rare rank-and-file soldier's account, which is often critical of the crusade leaders who fail to share the spoils of conquest equitably.

In addition to its significance vis-à-vis the political and military developments of the crusade, Robert's account is also important because it includes lengthy descriptions of the majestic sites and artifacts of Constantinople. His record and descriptions of these items are, in fact, more complete than any other contemporary account (including the Byzantines who simply took the existence of their monuments for granted).[4]

It is generally assumed that Robert was illiterate and that he dictated his story to a scribe sometime after his return to northern France in 1205.[5] While Robert's modern interpreters have not been flattering—they tend to prefer Geoffrey's "reliability" and view Robert's travelogue approach as too "childish" and "literary" (as opposed to "historical")—more recent assessments have been positive, suggesting Robert's account might contain aspects of great mental ingenuity.[6] For scholars such as Sharon Kinoshita, Robert's narrative limits do not reflect an uncertain command of historical events but rather reveal the paucity of discursive structures adequate for the unpredictable turns of the Fourth Crusade.[7] In other words, Robert's text reflects a cleavage between his ideological commitments (e.g., noble lineage, Christian piety, feudal honor), and his experience as a crusader in the East, which consistently betrayed those commitments. Thus, for Kinoshita, the exoticisms in Robert's text are no mere digression of fancy but encode the lived experience of a feudal society undergoing a major transition.[8]

Robert's text is one of the earliest examples of Old French prose.[9] For our purposes, what is perhaps most significant about the emergence of vernacular prose is the way that it presents more complex, more multifaceted, and often more tolerant alternatives to the religious Other than the "official culture" mediated by Latin texts, typically in control of the Western clerical establishment.[10] Indeed, this chapter will conclude with an analysis of the remarkable fact that Robert's constructed "Greek"—Othered and dehumanized in multiple ways—is not a religious Other. As we will see, Robert's presentation of French/Greek difference is multilayered and highly charged, but even though the Greeks are seen as shameful in so many ways, Greek Otherness is typically not established on theological grounds.[11]

Proceeding to that analysis, this chapter offers a careful reading of key aspects of Robert's text that underscore its colonial condition. It begins with a lengthy examination of the ways that Robert attempts to assert the moral superiority of the crusaders. Robert's assertion of crusader virtue, coupled with the denigration of Greek wickedness, serves as the primary mechanism for justifying the subjugation and humiliation of fellow Christians. The second section of the chapter analyzes the sexual politics undergirding Robert's account. More than a mere repetition of tropes juxtaposing Greek effeminacy to French virility, Robert ignores stories of crusader rapine found in other contemporary accounts and, instead, transfers that moral failing to Greek leaders whom he presents as serial rapists. The same section analyzes French/Greek marriage through the lens of colonial conquest as a feature that simultaneously names but undoes French superiority. The final segment of the chapter scrutinizes Robert's description of Constantinople as a wealthy and exotic land in need of subdual. While the *Conquest of Constantinople* is one in a long line of Western texts viewing the Orient as an opulent and dangerous land, Robert's outsized emphasis on the mystery and majesty of the city and its objects structure the whole of his account.

Moral Superiority

While Robert's stated purpose for composing the *Conquest of Constantinople* is to tell the "truth" about the conquest of Constantinople and how his lord, Baldwin of Flanders, became its emperor, the underlying strategy of Robert's account centered on the moral justifications for these surprising developments. More than simply tell his tale, Robert seeks to explain why the crusaders abandoned their initial quest (an assault on Muslim Egypt) and why the expedition has led to a permanent thinning of the local aristocracy, who have decided to remain in Byzantium rather than return home.

As we would expect, the framework within which Robert establishes this moral authorization aligns with early thirteenth-century Frankish notions of Christian moral purpose, chivalry, feudal hierarchy, and so forth. Throughout, Robert enunciates his examples of moral superiority through a juxtaposition of the virtuous French and the wicked Greek. Based on the principles of his cultural horizon, the French would have had no moral standing to seize and loot Christian Constantinople—the conquest of Constantinople should have failed the tests of Christian purpose, chivalry, and feudal loyalty. But Robert presents the moral failings of the Greeks in such stark ways that the pursuit of the moral good required the crusaders to liberate the city and to extract its resources.

Latin Virility versus Greek Cowardice

Given the knightly culture in which Robert lived, one of the easiest ways for him to establish the moral superiority of the French is to contrast crusader courage at arms to Greek cowardice and effeminacy.[12] Robert, of course, was neither the first Western author nor the first crusade chronicler to assign cowardice and effeminacy to the Greeks/Byzantines—the trope stretches back to the Roman world and is incorporated into Odo of Deuil's account of the Second Crusade.[13] But Robert's use of the trope is particularly important for his justification of crusader action.

Early in the text, as Robert narrates the political crises that brought the crusaders to Constantinople, he twice provides lengthy discussions regarding the cowardice of Greek soldiers. In the first example, he claims that the Francophile emperor, Manuel II (1143–80), relied almost exclusively on Latin troops. When evil advisors corrupt the emperor and convince him to have the Westerners dismissed, the Greeks show themselves to be cowards by comparison. Manuel, being a good ruler, restores Western troops to his battalions and publicly professes his love for and dependence upon the French, a pledge that is followed by a commitment to "pay them more than before" for their military service.[14] In a subsequent backstory designed to explain why Boniface of Montferrat (the leader of the crusade) was particularly ill-deposed to the usurper Alexius III, Robert tells the story of Boniface's older brother, Conrad, who had been in Constantinople years earlier. When a Greek aristocrat, Alexius Branas, started a rebellion against Isaac II, it was Conrad, rather than the Byzantines themselves, who suppressed the revolt. In fact, during the confrontation, the emperor and his troops fled the field, leaving Conrad alone to restore honor to Alexius's throne.[15]

And, of course, the examples continue. During the first encounter between Byzantine soldiers and the crusaders, the Byzantines quickly retreat in fear behind the shelter of the city's walls.[16] In the months that followed, most of the skirmishes that occur between the Byzantines and French/Venetians follow the same pattern—initial confrontation in the open, followed by the Byzantines fleeing for the safety of the city. Even the French cooks and horse boys strike fear into the hearts of the Greek soldiers.[17] At one point, a skirmish occurs close enough to the city that the women of Constantinople observe the cowardice of the Greeks. Not only are these women said to be enamored by the machismo of the French, they scold their countrymen when they shamefully retreat behind the walls.[18]

Individual Byzantine rulers are singled out for their spinelessness, especially Murzuphlus, the short-termed emperor who usurped the throne from Alexius IV in 1204, prompting the crusader assault on the city. For

Robert, Murzuphlus's every political action is unmanly: he murders Alexius IV and his father Isaac while they are sleeping, he drops a miracle-working icon on the battlefield (an icon that had until that point always assured victory to its holder), and when the assault of the crusaders appears imminent, he flees the city under the cloak of night.[19] Abandoned, the Greeks hastily raise a new emperor, Theodore I Laskaris, but he too flees the city before dawn, thus affirming the characterization of Greek cowardice.[20]

In many ways, Robert's presentation of French virility conforms to what scholars have found elsewhere regarding the culture of masculinity in contemporary Western literature. For example, Ruth Karras has examined the ways in which men asserted their masculinity through conflict, through the visible mastery over others, whether on the battlefield, in the university forum, or in the sexual conquest of women.[21] What is more, the juxtaposition between French virility and Greek effeminacy in Robert's account is especially noteworthy given William Burgwinkle's argument that the transformation of masculine subjectivity in French literature in this period was increasingly tied, in one way or another, to the specter of sodomy.[22]

Indeed, Robert's view of Greek weakness is all the more striking when we compare his presentation of Greek soldiering to his account of the other "Other" described in the text—the Cumans, who were a nomadic tribe from the Asian steppe and who fight on behalf the Bulgarian Vlachs. Whereas Greek men are consistently portrayed as cowardly, effeminate, and unskilled in military tactics, the Cumans are fearless soldiers of exceptional horsemanship and archery (two traits highly praised in French knightly culture). Even though Robert presents the Cumans as completely uncivilized (they do not know how to farm, they live in tents, they worship idols, and their native land is infested with insects), they are more skilled at the art of war than the French themselves.[23] In fact, it is the Cumans, not the Greeks, who humble the French at the Battle of Adrianople in 1205, killing Baldwin, the first Latin emperor of Constantinople.[24] Robert's distinction between Greek and Cuman is all the more surprising when we look to Geoffrey de Villehardouin, whose presentation of the Cumans lacks any similar estimation of their martial talent.[25] While Robert's Greeks are a more familiar "Other" than the Cumans—they are both Christian and share in the cultural inheritance of ancient Rome—they are for Robert, nonetheless, insufficiently manly, requiring the French to take matters into their own hands.

The True Romans

A second way that Robert establishes the moral superiority of the French over and against the Greeks is by framing the French, rather than the Byzantines, as the true Romans. On this score, it is important to note that the very naming of the Byzantines as "Greek" was an explicit rejection of the Byzantine claim that they were "Roman"—as noted in the introduction, the people we call Byzantines never employed the term Byzantine (it is a modern categorization), never used the Latin *Graecus,* and only began to employ the Greek word "Hellene" around the time of the Fourth Crusade.[26] Rather, they almost always self-identified as Romans.[27] Robert not only rejects their Roman identity by referring to them as *Graeci,* he repeatedly asserts that it is the French, not the Byzantines, who adhere to the "law of Rome."

One of the most intriguing ways that Robert establishes the "Romanness" of the French in contrast to the Byzantines is with the expression "the law of Rome" (*lei de Rome* in Old French). In Robert's hands, *lei de Rome* is likely a shorthand for "the law of the Roman Church," which would mean those who adhere to the Latin canon law tradition.[28] As such, it serves as a stand-in for saying Latin Christians and as a way to differentiate between the Byzantines and the crusaders. Indeed, in the first use of the expression, Robert notes that the Byzantines employ the word "Latins" for all those of the "law of Rome."[29] Thus, just as the Greeks do not define themselves by the same cultural modifier that their proximate Other applies to them, so too it would appear that even though the Greeks use "Latins" as a stand-in for Western European Christians, Robert understands "Latins" to be an awkward or uncommon designation for his community broadly conceived. Instead, Robert prefers to distinguish between those who do and those who do not adhere to the judicial apparatus of Rome. Most importantly, this is one of the most significant means of discerning moral superiority: Crusaders are good because they adhere to law of Rome; Greeks are wicked because they do not.

The phrase is repeated a few times after its first instance but its most detailed gloss appears precisely at the moment that the crusaders have made the final decision to take the city. In order to establish once and for all that the conquest of the city was a righteous act, Robert says that the crusaders sought the opinion of their bishops.

Finally, the bishops and the clergy of the host consulted together and gave judgment that the battle was a righteous one and they were right to attack them. For anciently they of the city had been obedient to the *law of Rome*, but now they were disobedient to it, saying that the *law of Rome* was worth nothing and that all who believed in it were dogs. And the bishops said that on this account they were right to attack them, and that it was not at all a sin, but rather a righteous deed.[30]

Robert then names some of the bishops who were most zealous, adding that they "showed the pilgrims that the battle was righteous, for the others were traitors and murderers and disloyal, since they had murdered their rightful lord, and they were worse than the Jews."[31] The bishops, arbiters of the law of Rome, offer moral authorization for the siege of Constantinople, but their authorization is expressed as a political not a theological verdict.

While the expression would typically imply a measurement of religious orthodoxy (those who adhere to church law and those who do not), in Robert's hands it also functions as a way to distinguish those whose claim to the legacy of ancient Rome is legitimate from those for whom it is not. Nowhere is this interpretation more explicit than the encounter between the French nobleman Pierre of Bracheux and John the Vlach, which occurs during an arranged truce between the two sides after the Vlachs had killed the first Latin emperor. John the Vlach professes his respect for French chivalry and military prowess but inquires why the crusaders would have ventured so far away from home. Pierre responds, "Have you not heard how Troy the great was destroyed by what trick? Well, Troy belonged to our ancestors and those who escaped from it came and settled in the country we come from; and because it belonged to our ancestors, we are come here to conquer land."[32]

Long before the crusaders, the ancient Romans had asserted themselves as the descendants of ancient Troy (most famously expressed in Virgil's *Aeneid*). And whereas Odysseus's cunning, which led to the destruction of Troy, had been celebrated among the ancient Greeks, for the Romans and their Western European cultural inheritors, the destruction of Troy gave birth to a long-running trope that warned about the duplicitous Greek. Robert's presentation of French moral superiority over the Byzantines on the basis of the legacy of ancient Rome (via Troy) fits within that discursive

tradition and simply reaffirms one of the longest-running cultural asper-
sions against Eastern Christians—that they are not genuine inheritors
of the Roman tradition (Christian or otherwise).[33]

The "Duplicitous" Greek

Robert justifies the conquest, settlement, and plunder of Constantinople
most forcefully on the basis of the wickedness of Byzantine rulers.[34] And,
in doing so, he enumerates their shortcoming according to a taxonomy that
most reflects his own cultural standards of aristocratic virtue—hereditary
succession, feudal oaths, and chivalric honor. Thus, for Robert, it is not
just that Byzantine rulers are cowardly on the battlefield and do not own
a legitimate share in the legacy of ancient Rome; they are, in every way,
bereft of those qualities that most befit the nobility. Even the way in which
they engage in battle is duplicitous—rather than confront the enemy in
the open, they rely on deception, trickery, and ambush.[35]

According to Robert, Byzantine rulers since the reign of the Francophile
Manuel I have been duplicitous, fratricidal, and prone to sexual debauchery.[36] His first excoriation of Greek leadership is directed at the usurper
Andronicus, relative of the noble Manuel. After murdering his cousin,
emperor Alexius II in 1183, Andronicus is said to go on a killing and raping
spree.[37] From Robert's perspective, Andronicus's greatest crime is his treatment of the murdered emperor's wife, sister to the king of France: "He did
so many great villainies [to her] that never did any traitor or murderer
do as many as he did."[38]

It is intriguing that Robert chooses to frame Andronicus's evil in this
way. It was, in fact, during the short reign of Alexius II in 1182, with
Andronicus serving as a behind-the-scenes power broker, that eighty
thousand Latin residents in Constantinople were murdered by orchestrated
mob violence. Even though the massacre forced a genuine sea-change in
Western attitudes toward the Byzantines, Robert does not mention it. Why
would he emphasize Andronicus's usurpation and sexual debauchery rather
than his role in the mass slaughter of those who adhere to the "law of
Rome?" Perhaps he does not know of Andronicus's role in the massacre. But
it is also possible that Robert prefers to emphasize those moral shortcomings that most differentiate Andronicus from the crusader leaders (his frat-
ricide, his lack of chivalry, etc.), precisely because he cannot differentiate
Andronicus and the crusade leaders simply on the basis of mass slaughter.

Additional examples of Greek duplicity abound. Robert offers a detailed account of the ways in which the emperor Alexius III wronged Boniface, Marquis of Montferrat and leader of the Fourth Crusade.[39] Alexius III is also shown to be traitorous to his people, first by shrinking from the field of battle and later by slipping away from the city in the dark of night.[40] Perhaps the only person more maligned than Andronicus and Alexius III is the short-termed emperor Murzuphlus, mentioned above. For Robert, Murzuphlus's defining sin was his murder of Alexius IV and his father while they were sleeping.[41]

There is little doubt that Robert's emphasis on Greek duplicity, like his presentation of Greek cowardice and his rejection of Byzantine claims to the Roman legacy, was designed to authorize both the permanent presence of the Latin ruling class in Byzantium and the extraction of material and religious resources from the conquered land. And, of course, Robert builds upon earlier Western accounts that had laid the shortcomings of previous crusades at the feet of the duplicitous Greeks.[42] It is precisely because the Greeks do not respect the laws of inheritance and the political structures of feudal loyalty that Robert asserts the righteousness of the crusaders who break their own feudal vows to the Byzantines.[43] And, indeed, in Robert's telling the siege and exploitation of Constantinople is not only permissible, it is demanded by the moral code governing French society.[44]

In every conceivable way, Greek rulers and Greek society are shown to be less than French. To be sure, the Greek is not wholly Other—he is not unrecognizable. Rather, it is precisely because the Greeks are knowable and especially because they are familiar with but reject the French moral order through their cowardice, their rejection of the law of Rome, and their duplicitous behavior that the crusader conquest of the city emerges as the only, if unanticipated, moral response to the murder of Alexius IV in the spring of 1204. But the moral inferiority of the Greeks, an inferiority affirmed by crusader bishops (albeit in decidedly political rather than theological language), offers the discursive enabling of far more than a military or political act—it authorizes the dehumanization, subordination, colonization, and deprivation of the Eastern Christian.

The Sexual Politics of Conquest

In his groundbreaking book *Orientalism*, Edward Said identified the connection between sexuality and the colonial condition, not only in terms of the power dimensions intrinsic to conquest, but also in the narrative formulae employed by Western authors to assert their superiority over Eastern men. While it is true that sexual objectification and sexual threat vis-a-vis a foreign Other routinely occur outside of a colonial context, Said's insights help us to understand the ways that sexuality functions in the colonial setting. Indeed, an examination of crusader accounts often reveals just how much these same formulae were operative in the imagination of Western men who traveled to Byzantium.

With these considerations in mind, it is rather telling that one of the most consistent aspects of Robert's account is the suggestion that Greek leaders, especially the most nefarious ones, are sexually deviant. The most culpable in this regard is the emperor Andronicus whose greatest crimes are sexual in nature. He has an illicit relationship with the widow of the Frankish king of Jerusalem and he marries the widow of Emperor Alexius II (who happens to be sister to the king of France) with whom he "did so many great villainies that never did any traitor or murderer do as many as he did."[45] By contrast, on the eve before the final assault of the city, the crusaders are so morally self-conscious that they send the women (i.e., the prostitutes) away from their camp in order to be properly prepared for the moral good they are about to perform.[46] Given Robert's complete silence about crusader rapine during the conquest of the city, his fixation on Andronicus's sexual crimes, particularly those against French women, is noteworthy. Not only does it evince a deliberate effort to frame his account in such a way as to authorize the conquest of the Christian Orient, but it also helps to explain a set of cultural assumptions about French moral superiority vis-à-vis their Greek counterparts that is entirely embedded within a discourse of sexual behavior.

Another obvious, if brief, example of the sexual dimensions of Robert's account occurs during one of the presiege skirmishes. In this particular scene, a medium-sized battalion of French knights finds itself on the plain to the west of Constantinople, and aligned against a much larger force led by the new emperor, Murzuphlus. As Robert begins to recount the consternation of the crusaders who are so outnumbered, he digresses to note:

And the ladies and maidens of the palace were mounted to the windows, and the other people of the city, both ladies and maidens, were mounted on the walls of the city, and were watching this battle ride forward and the emperor on the other side. And they were saying to one another that our men seemed like angels, they were so beautiful, because they were so finely armed and their horses so finely accoutered.[47]

As in other presiege skirmishes, the emperor and his troops are said to flee the battle to the safety of their walls, even though they greatly outnumbered their opponent and even though the crusaders were at a particular disadvantage because of the way that the city's aqueduct crossed the potential field of battle. Robert tells us that, upon returning, the emperor was "harshly blamed by the ladies and maidens, and by one and all, because he had not fought against so few people as the French were, with so great a force as he had had with him."

We have already discussed Robert's penchant to juxtapose Greek cowardice against French virility. In this particular passage, however, Robert takes the extraordinary additional step of reinforcing that juxtaposition through a pair of passages that appear to speak for the sexual desire and repulsion of Byzantine women. As constructed by Robert, Greek women desire French men because their own men are not sufficiently manly—at least not with respect to the cultural markers with which Robert is writing, which places knightly virility and chivalry at the pinnacle of the pantheon of masculinity.

The very fact that Robert would engage female desire in his chronicle demonstrates the extent to which Byzantine women function as a kind of commodity that attracts the crusaders' colonial interest. One implication is that a crusader need not rape or abscond with Byzantine women, one merely needs to go to the East and fight like a Frenchmen in order to trigger the sexual desire of the natives. Not only does this passage reinforce the discursive framing of French manliness versus Greek effeminacy, it authorizes so much of what is to come—namely, the string of Latin noblemen who will take Byzantine brides as they settle permanently into the region.

One of the most politically significant marriages in the wake of the crusader conquest of Constantinople was that between Boniface, Marquis of Montferrat, and the widow of Emperor Isaac II (Alexius IV's father) who married shortly after the conquest of the city. Noteworthy is the fact that the unnamed woman in question is not wholly Greek/Byzantine. She was, in fact, sister to the king of Hungary.[48] But she was sufficiently well accepted by the Byzantines as a royal personage that Boniface leveraged her standing (and that of her hybrid children) to expand his personal share in the division of territory by attempting to annex additional land in Adrianople.

A more remarkable marriage alliance was contracted between the second Latin emperor, Henry, and the unnamed daughter of Boris, the king of the Vlachs.[49] The Vlachs and their Cuman soldiers had, in fact, shattered expectations of crusader invincibility by routing them near Adrianople in 1205 and killing the first emperor, Baldwin (Henry's brother) in the process. The proposed alliance was designed to neutralize the threat to the new empire and to give the crusaders ample opportunity to establish their rule over the region. Robert's account is worth investigating in full:

> So this Boris became king of Vlachia, and he had a beautiful daughter. Then it happened that the emperor, Henry, who was a right and good emperor, took counsel with his barons as to what he should do about the Vlachs and Comans, who were thus making war on the empire of Constantinople, and who had slain the emperor Baldwin, his brother. Finally the barons advised him to send to this Boris who was king of Vlachia, and ask him to give him his daughter to wife. The emperor answered that he would never take a wife of such low lineage. And the barons said: "Sire, you should do so. We urge you to make peace with them, for they are the most powerful people and the most dread enemy of the empire and of the land." . . .
>
> Then Boris the king had his daughter attired very richly and very nobly, and many people with her. And he sent her to the emperor and he commanded sixty pack horses to be sent to him all loaded with treasure, with gold and silver and cloth of silk and precious jewels, and there was no horse that was not covered with a cloth of vermilion samite, so long that it trailed behind fully seven or eight feet, and never did they go through mud or by evil roads, so that onto one of the samite cloths was injured, all for daintiness and nobility.
>
> When the emperor knew that the maiden was coming, he went to meet her, and the barons with him, and the made great welcome for her and her people, and then afterwards the emperor married her.[50]

To be sure, marriage alliances with foreign powers were old hat for European powers, as was the commoditization of aristocratic daughters. But in a single passage, Robert gives voice to the repulsion/desire syndrome of crusader colonists. She is beautiful but low-born, she represents power but needs to be wrapped in gifts. She is a paradox—at once alluring but distant, desirable but unknown. Despite his initial objection to her low station, Henry comes to accept that taking her as wife, literally placing her in his bed, enables the fulfillment of his other desires—for land, power, and acclaim. There is never any hint that there is anything sacramentally problematic about their marriage. Nor is there ever a reminder for the reader that the girl's father had been responsible for the death of Henry's brother. All of these concerns are silenced in favor of the excessive ornamenting of her bridal train—sixty pack horses loaded with treasure all designed to make a "beautiful" young woman more alluring.[51] As Kinoshita observes, the ample dowry ultimately turns the barbarian princess into a Byzantine empress, "her [newfound] nobility inherent in her dress and baggage train."[52] Henry's initial reluctance followed by his sexual dominance of the Eastern girl serves as a metaphor for the entire Fourth Crusade—hesitation gives way to political expediency, which leads to defilement and plunder.

Of course, not all marriage alliances benefit the French, at least not those involving their daughters. An intriguing episode in the run-up to the siege of Constantinople is the (re-)discovery of a former child bride, Agnes/Anna, who had been sent to Constantinople decades earlier. Shortly after they install Alexius IV on the throne, the French barons ask the young emperor about a sister to the king of France who had been sent there as a child.[53] The barons learn that she is still alive and married to a local aristocrat by the name of Branas. But when the Frenchmen approach her, Anna shows nothing but disdain for them. Tellingly, she has lost the capacity to speak in French and must rely on an interpreter. Worse still, she reproaches them for having come to the East and for putting Alexius IV on the throne.[54] Discursively, all of these elements combine to demonstrate that the French bride has been tainted by her time among the Greeks: She has lost her cultural inheritance, she cannot distinguish between good and bad rulers, and she is rude to the valiant men who offer her assistance.[55] Although subtle, there are undercurrents of sexual disdain and sexual contamination—a woman who otherwise would have been one of the most desirable in French society (the sister of the king) has, through prolonged exposure to the beds of Byzantine men, become undesirable. When we compare this to

Robert's earlier claim that Greek women are, themselves, attracted to French men, we discover a logical gap in the author's effort to present a unified sexual politics for the women of the East.

The Allure of the East

When Robert dictated his *Conquest of Constantinople* sometime after his return to northern France in 1205, he engaged an audience that was already accustomed to thinking of the Orient as an exotic, rich, and alluring land. Mystery, barbarity, and opportunity for adventure were well-worn Orientalizing tropes that Western authors had been circulating and embellishing for centuries and these traditions had only expanded with the encounters of the first century of crusading.[56] Thus, Robert's use of these literary conceits not only helps us to understand the epistemic horizon of his audience and himself but, even more importantly, demonstrates one of the most important means by which he was able to justify the conquest, settlement, and pillage of Christian Constantinople. In order to analyze this aspect of Robert's text, I divide my analysis according to his comments about Byzantine wealth; Constantinople as a repository of majestic architecture and artifacts; and Constantinople as a meeting point for the truly exotic.

The first mention of "Greece" occurs in the aftermath of the siege of Zara, with the crusaders out of funds and struggling to identify their next course of action. Here, Dandalo, the aged Venetian doge, is reported to say: "Lords, in Greece there is a land that is very rich and plenteous in all good things. If we could only have a reasonable excuse for going there and taking provisions and others in the land until we were well restored, it would seem to me a good plan. Then we should be well able to go to [the holy land]."[57] As if foregrounding the crusader duplicities that are to come, Robert's doge seeks an excuse to liberate Greece of its great wealth. A few pages later, Robert offers his first backstory to the political turmoil that has engulfed the Byzantine Empire. In order to emphasize the depths of the current plight, Robert describes the efforts of the Francophile emperor, Manuel II, to arrange for a marriage alliance between his son and the sister of the king of France. In describing the ambassadors that Manuel sent to France, Robert notes, "Never were people seen to go more richly or more nobly than these did, so that the king of France and his people marveled greatly at the noble display the messengers made."[58] Once again, the Greeks are said to possess wealth beyond imagination.

Robert's most complete explication of Greek wealth concerns his description of Constantinople in the wake of the crusader siege and pillage of the city. Referring to the spoils gathered in a central place, he notes:

> Not since the world was made, was there ever seen or won so great a treasure or so noble or so rich, not in the time of Alexander nor in the time of Charlemagne nor before nor after. I do not think, myself, that in the forty richest cities in the world there had been so much wealth as was found in Constantinople. For the Greeks say that two thirds of the wealth of this world is in Constantinople and the other third is scattered throughout the world.[59]

Robert's goal, of course, is not to offer an exact accounting of what was obtained by the crusaders but to solicit the wonder and awe of his reader. In doing so, he would seem to achieve three goals. First, he establishes the magnitude of the crusader achievement—the acquisition of a treasure greater than anything obtained in recorded history. Second, he stretches Western assumptions about Eastern opulence—a move that no doubt inspires others to seek treasure in the East. Third, and perhaps most significantly, he masks the crimes perpetrated by the crusaders by blinding his readers' perception of right and wrong through a dazzling account of extraordinary wealth amassed by the duplicitous Greeks.

Robert's descriptions of the palaces, churches, relics, and monuments of Constantinople function in much the same way. Reporting on the palaces of Constantinople, Robert turns to the little details—such as the presence of silver rather than iron door hinges and columns that are made of jasper or porphyry rather than ordinary stone—to paint his picture of exorbitant wealth.[60] The churches, too, possess every possible opulence—the stonework, the gold, the jewels, the icons, etc. Hagia Sophia, of course, captures Robert's wonder:

> The master altar of the church was so rich that it was beyond price, for the table of the altar was made of gold and precious stones broken up and crushed all together, which a rich emperor had had made. This table was fully fourteen feet long. Around the altar were columns of silver supporting a canopy over the altar which was made just like

a church spire, and it was all of solid silver and was so rich that no
one could tell the money it was worth. The place where they read the
gospel was so fair and noble that we could not describe to you how
it was made. Then down through the church there hung fully a hundred chandeliers, and there was not one that did not hang by a great
silver chain as thick as a man's arm. And there were in each chandelier
full five and twenty lamps or more.[61]

Interestingly, the Church of Holy Apostles seems to have made an even
greater impression. Robert observes, "There was so much richness and nobility there that no one could recount to you the richness and nobility of this
church."[62] As he had in his account of the booty seized by the crusaders,
Robert pushes his readers to stretch their imaginations to a mythic sense
of material wealth contained within the mighty Constantinople.

Just as Constantinople was the epicenter for material wealth, so too was
it the storehouse for the greatest cache of miracle-working relics and icons
in the Christian world. Even though efforts had been underway since the
seventh century to identify Rome (not Constantinople) as the center of
Christian religious treasure and even though the Greeks were (theoretically)
schismatics, Robert presents Constantinople's religious riches in much the
same way he had presented its material resources—as a city/civilization in
possession of wealth beyond imagination. It is noteworthy that Robert
makes no effort to authorize the looting of religious treasure on the basis
of Greek theological error.[63] Nor does he ever suggest that the theological
power of these relics is in any way obscured by their being housed in Constantinople. As we will see in the next chapter, Gunther of Pairis framed his
entire account according to the theological error of the Greeks. But for
Robert there is no difference between, nor need for, a distinct authorization
for the acquisition of material and religious treasure. Indeed, the distance and mystery of the East is made recognizable through the appropriation of religious treasures that accord to Western Christian rituals of
veneration and translation.

Beyond the mere amazement with the scope of the wealth contained in
Constantinople, however, is an underlying current of exoticism that is most
manifest by Robert's description of the physical monuments in city. One
of the most revealing examples is his discussion of a pair of statues of
beautiful woman.

Now there was elsewhere in the city another marvel. There were two statues made of copper in the form of women, well and naturally made, and more beautiful than a good deal. And neither of them was less than a good twenty feet in height. One of these figures held its hand out toward the West, and it had letters written on it which said: "From the West will come those who will capture Constantinople," and the other figure held its hand out toward a vile place and said "Here," said the figure, "here is where they will throw them."[64]

The statue that Robert believes to gesture to the West is Athena, the ancient goddess, and she does not gesture to the West, but actually to the South. But it is telling of Robert's exoticizing and eroticizing of Byzantine women that he would describe a beautiful and naked statue as one that beckons soldiers of the West and even prophesizes that they will justifiably conquer the city.[65] The second statue, of course, functions for Robert as a symbolic rejection of the men of Constantinople in favor of the French.[66] Robert's interpretation of the two statues conforms to his previous speculation about the sexual desire that actual Byzantine women had for French men along with their disdain for Greek men. What is perhaps most interesting about his treatment of the ancient artifacts scattered throughout the city is the way that he co-opts the monuments of a glorious Byzantine/Greek past in such a way as to authorize the moral superiority of the French present. The Greek/Roman/Byzantine past rightly belongs to the French present. The current Greeks, through their effeminacy and treachery, have forfeited their claim to this past.

In addition to the monuments, the mysterious personalities that the city draws are a fascination for Robert. Nearly two-thirds of the way into the chronicle, Robert offers a lengthy digression about an exotic pilgrim, the king of Nubia, who is visiting the city on the eve of the invasion.[67] With deep dark skin and a cross tattooed on his forehead, the king represents a stark contradiction in Robert's conceptual imagination. In her analysis of the passage, Kinoshita argues that the king is both fully Other and strangely familiar.[68] His black skin stands as a symbol of his alterity but his Christianity (especially the level of his commitment to the faith) puts things into confusion.[69] Like the crusaders, he is a pilgrim. But, as Kinoshita observes, the crusaders are silent in his presence—they are unprepared for the variety of Christianity that proliferates in the eastern Mediterranean, "let alone for the black pilgrim king whose every trait simultaneously inverts and redoubles their own."[70]

The Cuman soldiers (described previously) offer a similar form of exotic doubling/troubling. They are exotic and savage. They are at once wholly foreign because of their strange behaviors and pagan practice but they are also familiar in their military prowess, horsemanship, and courage. Indeed, it is remarkable that the savage Cumans, who are a greater threat to the crusaders, are presented in a more positive light than the far more civilized Byzantines. Both fall outside of the Frankish normative order, but the Cumans also lie outside of the juridical field of the "law of the Romans," as Robert expresses it. Although they fail to adhere to it, the Greeks are a fixable category according to a Frankish narration of "Roman" but the Cumans are wholly Other. They run wild and they operate according to their own code of virtue.

Whereas the Nubian king challenges, even threatens, the crusaders' sense of Christian faith and practice, the Cuman soldiers present a challenge to crusader virility. And they are more than a symbolic threat—they shatter the crusader army and kill the first Latin emperor of Byzantium. It is worth noting that the Cumans were thought to originate in the same part of the world as the Scythians did for Herodotus and it is noteworthy that they share many of the same traits (both barbaric and martial).[71] Most importantly, the Cumans, like the Scythians of old, are a nomadic people who challenge the established patterns of fixed societies. For Robert's Franks, the Cumans "scramble the signifiers of chivalry as radically as the Nubian king had those of Christianity."[72]

Throughout his *Conquest of Constantinople*, Robert portrays the citizens, artifacts, monuments, and visitors to Constantinople according to an Orientalizing register that marks them as Other—exotic, strange, mysterious, and beautiful. As objects of a French gaze, their meaning is established according to measurements of French knightly culture—in terms of transportable wealth, Christian value, or martial valor. Like the moral authorization for crusader behavior and the implicit (often explicit) sexual interests employed throughout his chronicle, Robert's relies on the exotic qualities of narrative setting to frame his account of French superiority. At once foreign but familiar, conquered but dangerous, Constantinople and Byzantium offer an alluring topography upon which Robert maps his story of heroic adventure. And, in doing so, he invites his Western audience to picture themselves, in both fantasy and in reality, undertaking a similar journey.

Robert's Eastern Christian

As we might expect of any medieval chronicle, particularly one focused on the crusades, the *Conquest of Constantinople* offers a richly textured account of popular religion, both in terms of certain aspects of its belief structure as well as the ways in which it is expressed through behavior. Indeed, the text reflects a discursive framework that accepts as plausible, even noble, the idea that a midtier knight would undertake an extremely dangerous journey to an unknown Eastern world in order to fulfill a religious pledge. Throughout, Robert offers multiple examples of pious devotion as we might expect of a crusader: His fellow expeditionaries embrace the cross as an act of religious fervor; he affirms the miraculous power of relics and icons; and he attributes certain military turns of event to the direct intervention of God. Even the saints have their say in the fortunes of the crusaders (as we find in the oft-repeated tale that has St. Demetrios appearing in the night in order to kill John the Vlach for trespassing on Demetrios's home turf, Thessalonika).[73]

Given the widespread integration of popular religion and given the rampant condemnation of the Latin/Greek Other in other contemporary accounts, it thus quite remarkable that Robert's construction of Greek error is almost entirely based upon nontheological concerns and avoids any direct theological critique of Eastern Christianity. Never, for example, does Robert declare that the Greeks are in theological error, never does he link Greek moral failure to errant theological teaching, and never does he authorize the killing, colonization, or pillage of Byzantium on the basis of Christian theological difference. The Greeks are certainly in error, but their errors are enunciated according to the structures of French political ideology, which values manliness, hereditary succession, and a respect for feudal oaths.

As noted previously, Robert asserts several times that it is the French, not the Greeks, who adhere to the "law of Rome" (*lei de Rome*). And, as noted, this expression both derives from and connotes an ecclesiastical distinction between Western and Eastern Christians, which is predicated upon differentiating between those who do and those who do not adhere to the Roman canon law tradition. While there is little reason to contest either the origin or the implication of Robert's invocation of the "law of Rome" as a means to differentiate between Eastern and Western Christians, it is noteworthy that he never offers any kind of gloss on the phrase or what it might entail for him. Should we limit ourselves to the words he uses, just "law of Rome" and, if so, what does it mean that his expression offers no direct connection to theological belief or who defines it? Should we take the expression to the next plausible interpretive step and assume that he means that the Greeks are in error because they do not accept Roman canon law? If so, what canon law do they accept and how is it different in Robert's eyes? Might we take Robert's expression to mean that the Greeks do not accept the authority of the Church of Rome to compose, advance, or adjudicate the law of the Church? If so, why does Robert never mention the pope, his office, or his connection to the *lei de Rome*? In short, what, if anything, does Robert's use of this phrase tell us about his view of Eastern Christianity, beyond the fact that the Eastern Christian is "Other"?

Perhaps we should take our interpretive cues from the most extensive use of the expression, which Robert provides at the moment when the crusaders consult their bishops on the eve of the final assault and pillage of the city. As noted, the bishops encourage the crusaders go forward with their assault without any sense of compunction because the Greeks fail to adhere to the "law of Rome." Tellingly, the injunction is both framed and reinforced by examples of Greek political and moral disorder, not by theological error: "They showed the pilgrims that the battle was righteous, for the others were traitors and murderers and disloyal, since they had murdered their rightful lord, and they were worse than the Jews."[74]

The bishops go on to declare that the Greeks are the enemies of God (*enemi Damedieu* in the Old French), but even that is framed in terms of political and moral error, never on the basis theological belief or practice.[75] There is no mention of *filioque* or leavened bread, or disrespect of papal authority. There is no mention of schism or heresy at all. Not once does Robert imply that Greek churches or sacraments are off limits to the crusaders. On the contrary, during the months prior to the siege, crusaders and Venetians routinely go into the city to worship and venerate the miraculous relics and icons. And, after the siege, Robert completely omits any discussion of the papal efforts to bring the Greek Church under the pope's control or the various forms of resistance that the Greeks mount against those efforts. To be sure, Robert's Greek is duplicitous, murderous, cowardly, effeminate, and deserving of his fate. But the "othering" of Robert's Greek that authorizes his colonization is never based upon religious identity or practice.

To understand Robert's construction of the Eastern Christian we must further reflect upon his juxtaposition between French manliness and Greek effeminacy. In many ways, Constantinople and the Christian East more broadly provide a previously untapped space for Robert's crusaders to exhibit their masculinity more forcefully than is possible at home. Not only does the Christian East offer the opportunity to subjugate a mysterious new land, not only do the moral and political crimes of the Greeks authorize the unleashing of French manliness through feats of arms, but the incessant reminders of Greek cowardice and military failure offer further affirmations of French machismo. Thus, at every turn, Robert demasculinizes the Greek. More than just being cowardly on the field of battle, Robert's Greek leaders are expensively dressed, concern themselves with pomp and circumstance, and travel with a train of attendants, much like an aristocratic woman.[76] The portrayal of Greek effeminacy is all the more arresting when we compare it to the manliness of the Saracen and Slavic Other for whom Robert has great admiration. And the difference between the two might well lie in the fact that it is the Greeks who are forced into submission by the French, while the Saracens and Slavs remain untamed.

In her analysis of the text, Sharon Kinoshita argues that although Robert's chronicle is far more sophisticated than previous assessments have understood, ultimately, his narrative falls in upon itself because of the weight of its own inner contradictions. Despite Robert's best efforts to establish a contrary narrative, the text lays bare crusader greed and disdain for political loyalty (expressed most clearly in their demand for payment, the failure to divide spoil fairly, and their murder of Murzuphlus after his capture).[77] Thus, for Kinoshita, the moral failure of the crusaders that we find in the *Conquest of Constantinople* reflects transformations in political and social structures in France itself.

As compelling as Kinoshita's analysis is, I wonder if we might also interpret Robert's text as insinuating that prolonged exposure to the duplicitous and effeminate Greeks had, in fact, corrupted crusader valor. Indeed, by the time we arrive at the end of the text, the crusaders have themselves been profoundly transformed by their new role as masters of the East. We see this transformation in the vivid details Robert offers for the coronation ceremony—with its elaborate gestures and dainty clothing—when Baldwin of Flanders becomes the first Latin emperor.[78] Indeed, it is hard to imagine another setting in which the French military aristocracy might perform a ritual dressing of another man in silk and jewels as the ritual event authorizing his military or political ascendency. (Is it any wonder that Baldwin and his troops are defeated by the Cumans who do not even need saddles and can outride even the most talented French knight?)[79] And, of course, there are other ways that Robert describes the French aristocracy as adapting to their new land.[80] Although he never makes the explicit connection, if we look close enough we just might see a glimmer of Greek duplicity and love of money in his repeated accusations that the crusade leaders stole from the rank-and-file soldiers who had done the heavy lifting. Indeed, it is for this reason and this reason alone that Robert believes the Latin Empire experienced it greatest setbacks in the years immediately following the conquest. Thus, in the end, the French turned out to be only slightly better than the Greeks whom they had mastered.

CHAPTER

2

GUNTHER OF PAIRIS'S *HYSTORIA CONSTANTINOPOLITANA*

Whereas Robert de Clari's text conforms to the genre and structure of a medieval chronicle, Gunther of Pairis's *Hystoria Constantinopolitana* fits more neatly within the hagiographic subgenre of a *translation*, a sanctioned movement of relics.[1] Indeed, its primary purpose is to explain and justify the means by which an otherwise undistinguished monastery in the Rhineland came to acquire religious treasure that had been looted during the early days of the pillage of Constantinople in 1204.[2] The story's hero, Martin, is the abbot of the Cistercian monastery of Pairis (in the Orbey Valley in the Alsace region of modern-day Germany). Martin both recruited knights for the Fourth Crusade and then accompanied them to Constantinople. He returned home in 1205 with an incredible cache of religious treasures from the Christian East, including drops of Christ's blood, a sizeable piece of the Cross, as well as additional relics from more than three dozen saints.[3] The author of the *Hystoria*, Gunther of Pairis, did not witness the events he describes but rather serves as scribe to Martin's story.[4]

As David Perry explains, the flood of Eastern religious treasure that made its way into the monasteries and cathedrals of Western Europe in the months following the siege of Constantinople required authentication and memorialization. For Perry, the sophistication of Gunther's work was unprecedented.[5] Perhaps its most noticeable deviation from others in the genre is the fact that Gunther's text is a prosimetrum, a literary form that alternates between prose and poetry (like Boethius's *Consolation of Philosophy*). By all accounts, the *Hystoria* is the most urbane (and fascinating!) of

35

the numerous *translatio* texts that emerged in the wake of the Fourth Crusade.[6]

A careful analysis of the *Hystoria Constantinopolitana* demonstrates that the implementation of its hagiographic *topoi* is overlaid with what we might best describe as colonial or protocolonial discursive features. Following a brief summary of the text, this chapter will analyze these elements of the work in order to gain greater access to the epistemic horizon within which Gunther and his monastic community made sense of the theft of religious treasures from the largest Christian city in the world. Specifically, it will examine the ways in which Gunther justifies the violence enabling colonial settlement as a moral good; defends the extraction of Eastern Christian religious treasure; employs effeminacy and homoerotic sexual fantasy as rhetorical instruments; and describes Eastern topography according to exotic and erotic registers.

Structure and Content of the *Hystoria Constantinopolitana*

Like many other hagiographies and, especially, *translationes*, Gunther's *Hystoria Constantinopolitana* begins with a defense of its historical reliability. Gunther notes that even though the events he is about to reveal might seem extraordinary—and even scandalous—the careful reader will understand that they proclaim, celebrate, and explain God's mysterious intervention in the affairs of the world.[7] Chapters 2–5 follow additional literary conventions by establishing the credibility of the narrative's hero, Martin. Here, Gunther recounts Martin's ability to recruit crusaders and the official blessing he received from both Pope Innocent III and Martin's Cistercian masters at Citeaux prior to joining the crusade. Chapter 5 draws a favorable comparison between Abbot Martin and his namesake, St. Martin of Tours, in whom the connection between the military and monastic service had long been established.[8]

It is worth noting that Martin's advocacy for the crusade, contained in a sermon he is said to have delivered to Frankish soldiers, is largely an appropriation of the rhetorical arguments first put forth by Pope Urban II more than a century earlier.[9] The outsized emphasis on the Cross in Martin's sermon, of course, functions to authorize the abbot's eventual acquisition of the relic. What is so interesting in this respect is that the sermon specifically emphasizes the need for the crusaders to go to Jerusalem because that is the site of Christ's crucifixion and of the Cross. Martin, of course, will obtain his relic of the Cross in Constantinople, not Jerusalem. Thus, Gunther foreshadows the work of divine providence, which unfolds in ways unanticipated but, at the same time, Gunther cannot not escape the moral ambiguity of how Martin acquired his religious treasure.

Chapters 6–12 offer Gunther's explanation and justification of why the crusaders came to the decision to attack Zara and, then, from there determined to go to Constantinople rather than Alexandria. This section includes brief detours by Martin to Rome (as an ambassador of the crusaders to the Holy See following their excommunication) and then to Acre.[10] Both diversions allow Gunther to exonerate Martin from any mistakes the crusaders made and, at the same time, continue with the text's thesis that divine providence functions in ways unanticipated. These chapters also lay the initial groundwork for one of the most important aspects of the text— the moral authorization for the military seizure of Constantinople. Indeed, Chapters 10–12 offer a historical gloss of the political crises in Byzantium that led the crusade leadership to view Alexius IV as a victim of political intrigue. Chapters 13–18, then, chronicle the means by which the crusaders help Alexius IV reclaim his thrown, their patient waiting for him to fulfill his promises, their decision to take the city for themselves, and an account of the siege itself.

Chapter 19 is one of the longest and is, perhaps, the most significant. It begins with an account of the general plunder of the city but then quickly shifts to detail Martin's specific act of holy theft. We are told that Martin went deliberately to the monastery of Christ Pantocrator. While others ransacked the monastery for its gold and jewels, Martin searches for more secretive and sacred spaces. Stumbling upon an old and "beautiful" Greek priest, Martin threatens the man with violence if he will not yield secret treasures. The monk relents, becomes Martin's servant, and even helps him obtain suitable accommodation in the city. Martin remains in Constantinople for the duration of the summer, enraptured by a heretofore unknown religious elation made possible by his secretive devotion to his new treasures.

Chapters 20 and 21 detail the political division of the city and its resources by the crusaders. This historical account is accompanied by several Orientalizing reflections on the topography and riches of the city. Chapter 22 recounts a quick excursion by Martin to Acre, where he has a rather curious encounter with the very "manly" Werner. Chapter 23 reminds its readers that while the Orient might be alluring and mysterious, it is also dangerous. It is not a place of tranquility nor is it suited to permanent spiritual reflection. For these reasons, Martin returns home. Chapter 24 provides a full list of relics that Martin brings to his monastery and Chapter 25 offers a closing exhortation defending the monastery's ownership of the relics.

A great number of nineteenth- and twentieth-century scholars concerned themselves with trying to ascertain whether and to what extent the historical details provided by Gunther reflect a reliable history of the Fourth Crusade, particularly when his description is at odds with other sources such Geoffrey de Villehardouin and Robert de Clari.[11] While such examinations are historically interesting, our concerns lie with what Gunther's text reveals about Western Christian attitudes toward the Christian East, the discourse of moral superiority that enables conquest and extraction, and the subtle sexual innuendo that accompanies each of these aspects.

Moral Superiority

Like Robert de Clari's account of the Fourth Crusade, Gunter's *Hystoria Constantinopolitana* employs multiple means to present the crusader invasion of Constantinople as a moral good that benefitted both the crusaders and the local inhabitants of Constantinople. Gunther repeats many of the rhetorical conventions for the authorization of the crusades in general, including the notion that infidels have defiled the land of Christ's passion and that this land belongs to the Christians (specifically, Frankish Christians).[12] But the unanticipated outcomes of the Fourth Crusade—both its destruction of the Christian sea town of Zara and its eventual occupation of Constantinople—required unprecedented rhetorical maneuvering in order to claim that the crusaders' aims remained virtuous, despite the turn of events. It is precisely because there were contemporary Latin-Christian critics of the Fourth Crusade and its pillaging of Eastern Christian religious treasure that Gunther and others like him had to recalibrate the rhetorical conventions that had previously authorized crusading in order to construct a moral justification for the seizure and pillaging of a Christian land.[13]

To this end, Gunther develops a series of moral justifications, beginning with the basic assertion that everything that transpired was, in fact, in fulfillment of divine providence. As evidence of God's intervention, Gunther insists that the crusaders were not only greatly outnumbered (implying that success could have only been achieved because of God's favor) but also that, despite such great odds, only one soldier died in the siege—a miracle, indeed.[14] Then shifting from providence to prophecy, Gunther interprets a marble relief on the base of the Obelisk of Theodosius as predicting that the city would fall to the crusaders.[15] As we saw in the previous chapter, Robert de Clari had similarly employed Constantinopolitan statues to presage the crusader victory over the Greeks.

Another important way that Gunther establishes the moral superiority of the crusaders vis-à-vis the Greeks is the assertion that the decision to take Constantinople was, in fact, a defensive measure.[16] According to Gunther, after the murder of Alexius IV and the continued deprivation of the crusader army, which was short on supplies, the crusade leadership attacked the great city not because they coveted its treasures or even because they expected to be successful, but because they saw themselves as having no other alternative.

> For what could the pilgrims do, or what hope could they have at such a moment, trapped as they were, with no secure haven in which for even an hour they could catch their breath? Should they declare war on those whom they knew to be their enemies and who previously had been secretly so, thereby inciting them to open attack? Yet the number of Greeks was endless and grew daily through reinforcements.[17]

Along the same lines, Gunther insists that the crusaders refrained from taking innocent life. And, anticipating a Western audience that might know differently, he suggests that any killing of innocent Greeks that did occur was perpetrated by foreign residents of Constantinople (not the crusaders) as revenge for past wrongs.[18]

Perhaps the most effective rhetorical stratagems, however, are those that most explicitly contrasted the righteousness of the crusaders against the perfidy of the Byzantines. The chivalrous, noble, and virtuous German ruling class is repeatedly juxtaposed to the duplicitous, murderous, and tyrannical "Greeks." As noted in the introduction and the previous chapter, the use of the word "Greek" in this context functions as a pejorative. Gunther and other Latin authors employ the term Greek specifically to undermine the "Roman" ancestry of the Byzantines.[19]

For Gunther, the Latins are honorable and pious Christians who withheld violence for so long that they put their lives at risk; the Greeks, by contrast, are "the most wicked race" (*pessime nacionis*) and incapable of adhering to the purity of an authentic Christianity.[20] Thus, Gunther asserts that moral clarity—the ability to discern between what is virtuous and what is not—is a characteristic belonging only to the crusade leaders.[21]

Set within this discursive binary, the conquest of Constantinople becomes, in Gunther's hands, an act of political and religious charity that rescues the native population from its heresies and political decay. In Gunther's framing, even the initial decision to support Alexius IV against his usurping uncle is an act of political honor (installing a rightful king in the place of a tyrannical one).[22] By intervening when they did, the crusaders achieved three moral goods on behalf of local Christians: They established a legitimate ruling class (themselves); they rescued Eastern Christians from their heresy by uniting them with the Church of Rome; and they prevented Eastern Christians from becoming the slaves of the Muslims, who would have surely capitalized on God's punishment of the Eastern Christians. He notes, "Divine goodness arranged through this sequence of events that this people, so proud because of its wealth, should be humbled by their very pride and recalled to the peace and concord of the Holy Catholic Church."[23] Underscoring these precise points, Gunther observes that God enabled the crusaders to march into Constantinople on Palm Sunday in imitation of the Lord's triumphal entry into Jerusalem on the same day.[24] Just as Christ brought salvation to the Jews, so too the crusaders offer the possibility of redemption to the citizens of Constantinople.

Whatever sins or mistakes may have happened along the way, the crusaders' sack and pillage of Constantinople is, on balance, a moral good, not only because the crusaders are morally superior to the Greeks but because they offer the Greeks the possibility to share in Latin Christian virtue. But to acquire the virtue of the crusaders, to benefit from their nobility, the Greeks must submit themselves in perpetuity to the Latin Christian. It is in this context that Gunther makes his case for the permanent settlement in and rule of Byzantium by the crusaders.[25] But Gunther is also clear that the Greeks must do more than submit themselves to the political rule of the crusaders; they must also submit to Latin Christian teaching. And, in this context, it is worth observing that Gunther resuscitates a series of papal legends connecting Emperor Constantine to Pope Sylvester (and through him to St. Peter) in order to show that the city of Constantinople had first been authorized by the pope himself and therefore, rightly belongs to the Roman Church and its soldiers.[26]

As we have already seen, it was a commonplace for chroniclers of the crusades to authorize violence against the Greeks according to a moral dualism in which Latins are good and Greeks are bad. And, to be sure, Gunther's presentation of the honorable Western soldier who is both juxtaposed to and a cure for the duplicitous Greek can be understood as existing within a historiographic topos that would become standard for Western European colonization of the eastern Mediterranean of later centuries. Indeed, for authors like Edward Said and Dipesh Chakrabarty, it was precisely this kind of prejudicial cultural outlook that authorized and sustained the colonial subjugation of much of the globe.[27] Christopher Johnson has examined nineteenth-century travelogues to the orient and identified a great number of ways that Western European Christians attempted to "save" Eastern Christians from themselves according a set of cultural hegemonic assumptions that are remarkably similar to those in play in Gunther's *Hystoria Constantinopolitana*.[28] Thus, what we find in Gunther's narrative of moral justification for the Fourth Crusade is an early articulation a system of cultural binaries that would one day be redeployed to authorize a global colonial network on the one hand and a concomitant Western Christian discourse of hegemonic superiority over its Eastern Christian counterparts on the other.

Resource Extraction and the Noble Savage

Building upon the moral authorization that Gunther provides not only for the conquest of the city but the permanent settlement of Latin Christians in Byzantium, we turn now to an analysis of the discursive presentation of Martin's holy theft—the primary purpose of Gunther's account. But our analysis will follow a rather unorthodox approach in that it treats Gunther's presentation of the Greek monk who assists Martin's theft from the literary perspective of a "noble savage," an exotic character whose deliberative actions authorize his subjugation and exploitation. To be sure, the scholarly examination of the noble savage conceit belongs to a different historical and cultural setting.[29] Thus, I use the phrase in this context provocatively in order to explore the ambivalent relationship between attraction and repulsion that seems to characterize Gunther's ambiguously eroticized description of the relationship between Martin and his unnamed Greek servant.[30]

According to Gunther, as the crusaders begin their pillage of the city, Martin makes haste to a richly adorned monastery, Christ Pantocrator, which had been the recipient of lavish gifts from the imperial family over the previous century and served as an imperial cemetery.[31] Whereas the soldiers concern themselves with the gold, silver, and precious stones that were kept in the monastery, Martin stealthily and instinctively locates a remote spot within the monastic complex where the sanctity of the location indicated the presence of religious treasure.[32] "There he found an old man, beautiful in appearance with a long and white beard. He was definitely a priest, but by the appearance of his body, he was very different from our priests."[33] The Greek is nameless and exotic.[34] He is physically attractive but in an unfamiliar and intriguing way.[35] He is simultaneously like but different from Gunther's readers. Martin accosts the exotic foreigner, annunciates his inadequacy, and demands that he release his treasure: "Come, you faithless old man. Show me the most powerful of the relics you preserve. Otherwise, know that you will be punished immediately with death."[36] The beautiful monk contemplates Martin's demand, but does not understand it, because it had been uttered in Latin.

What follows are a series of unanticipated events. First, the Greek responds to Martin's threats with acquiescence and then cultural imitation—a subtle narrative move by Gunther that underscores a master/slave relationship between the two clerics. Specifically, the Greek answers Martin in a "Roman language" (*romana lingua*).[37] Even though Martin, who has traveled to the East has not taken the time to learn Greek, the indigenous cleric has somehow already learned the language of his foreign master. Ironically, Martin barely understands the Western language that the Greek offers him.[38] So he angrily reinforces his demands.

Gunther's account continues, "examining Martin's face and dress and thinking it more tolerable that a man of religion violate the holy relics in awe and reverence, rather than worldly men should pollute them, with bloodstained hands, the old man opened for Martin an iron chest and showed him the desired treasure."[39] In other words, the Greek monk determines that Martin, rather than the soldiers, should be the one to "violate" (*contrectaret*) the relics, because he, at least, will do so with some respect.

In his English translation of this passage, Alfred Andrea noted the unusual choice of words that Gunther used to convey the Greek monk's mental calculus that led to the decision to surrender the relics to Martin. Rather than the neutral verb "caparet" (to seize or to possess), which is what we might expect, Gunther employs "contrectaret," which means explicitly "to touch illicitly," "to have sexual intercourse with," or "to dishonor."[40] For Andrea, Gunther has chosen a verb with explicit sexual overtones to heighten the passage's "ironic humor."[41] But I would like to propose that there is an alternative way of interpreting the sentence, which is to see Martin's violation of the relics not as irony but as a metaphor for the possibility of a sexual violation of the Greek monk specifically and the crusader violation of the Christian East more generally. In other words, the sentence does more than affirm that Martin's character is superior to that of ordinary soldiers, thereby authorizing Martin's theft. It also insinuates that the monk selects Martin, rather than the soldiers, as his personal violator. Such an interpretation seems consistent with what follows.

After determining that he will yield to Martin, the nameless priest, unlocks a secret iron chest containing the monastery's most precious relics, which Martin finds to be "more desirable than all of the riches of Greece."[42] Framed in this way, Martin's theft is not a theft at all because the Greek monk willfully gives him the sacred objects. Gunther's scene relies upon the subservience of the Greek priest—a native whose virtue is insufficient to overcome his Otherness but who is, nonetheless, sufficiently noble to recognize that Martin deserves to possess all that he could possibly offer.

After Martin ravenously seizes and then transports his sacred booty to a carefully selected hiding place aboard his ship, the native monk reappears in the narrative.[43] But in this second appearance, the exotic Easterner is now fully cast as Martin's subjugated partner, who "clings to him in a rather intimate manner."[44] In this new capacity, the dutiful oriental arranges suitable lodging for Martin in the city, enabling Martin to remain for the entirety of the summer to delight in his sacred spoils in a secretive, perhaps eroticized, display of piety that is known only to this mysterious oriental monk and one additional deputy: "There he lingered the entire summer, unceasingly cherishing those holy relics. To be sure, they were venerated in secret, but with great love. And by his respectful devotion, he made up for what was lacking externally."[45]

In a recent monograph on the exoticism of cross-Mediterranean encounters in Old French romance literature, Megan Moore draws upon Edward Said's insight concerning the narrative gendering of the colonial encounter, whereby the masculinized Westerner typically observes a feminized native man.[46] For Moore, crusader romances like the *Floire et Blancheflor* do more than align the oriental with the feminine—they figure masculinity (both positively and negatively) through exoticism. Thinking alongside Moore's observations about the French romances in this setting, what is so intriguing about the encounter between Martin and the unnamed Greek monk in the *Hystoria Constantinopolitana* is the not-so-subtle erotic elements of a narrative arc that begins with attraction, progresses to conquest, and ends in a kind of willful enslavement.

What is particularly noteworthy is this regard is Gunther's initial description of the Greek monk and his beard—that he was "beautiful in appearance with a long and white beard"—because Greek beards were a frequent source of "sexualized" disdain in Latin polemics against a constructed Byzantine effeminacy. As Charis Messis has demonstrated, Latin assaults on Greek cultural customs in this period routinely sought to undermine Byzantine masculinity by attacking a perceived feminized vanity that was reflected by the concern for the appearance of one's beard.[47] In this particular text, however, the beard functions as a source of beauty and exotic desire rather than of explicit disdain or to condemn effeminacy.

Perhaps, Gunther's fascination with the Greek priest's beard, like his multifunctional depiction of the monk's subservience to Martin, is more richly layered than other Latin condemnations of Byzantine beards precisely because it is set within the colonial context of the Fourth Crusade. The subtle insinuations of homoerotic attraction, like the more explicit enslavement of the Greek monk, are possible precisely because they are narrated against the backdrop of a seductive strangeness provided by a conquest of the Orient. Understood in this way, Martin's dominance of the nameless Greek monk functions as more than a metaphor for the military and religious conquest of the Greek East—it also conveys the ambivalence of attraction and repulsion that is often reflected in the idiom of sexual fantasy that is a common aspect of colonial discourse.

In *The Invention of Sodomy*, Mark Jordan offers a genealogy of the medieval Christian discourse prohibiting same-sex copulation. Among other things, Jordan describes the way in which geographical reference (such as "the city of Sodom" or "the land of Greece") could encode illicit sexual behavior without having to name that behavior.[48] He also demonstrates that some medieval theological texts that explicitly championed a particular form of sanctity could also convey a discourse of same-sex attraction, even if it is only the enemies of the saints who act on that desire.[49] Thinking alongside Jordan, it is interesting to note the ways in which Gunther repeatedly plays with the themes of religious fervor, secrecy, and master/slave domination as he describes Martin's encounter with the Greek monk. And it is also noteworthy that the very possibility of an illicit sexual longing is framed by the distance and evocation of the "land of the Greeks" conceit.

An Exotic and Erotic Land

Like Robert de Clari's chronicle, Gunther's text also employs a series of exoticisms in its account of Eastern topography but, more than Robert had, these exoticisms provide a broader discursive permissiveness that, in some cases, includes erotic fantasy.[50] For instance, in his own account for the unprecedented riches of Constantinople, Gunther offers an apocryphal story about why the Roman emperor Constantine built the city. Of significance are the multiple ways in which Gunther weaves Pope Sylvester into the narrative in order to establish the (Western) Catholic origins of a city that was, at the time of the Fourth Crusade, woefully astray from the correct faith.[51] Rhetorically, the connection between Sylvester, Constantine, and Constantinople allows Gunther to explain why it is that such a powerful city could simultaneously be so alien and, yet, rightfully belong to the Roman Church and its Frankish army. It is precisely because it does belong to the Western Church that its representatives (i.e., the crusaders) fulfill their historical obligation to subjugate the city's heretics and extract its religious resources.

In the pages that follow, Gunther continues to invite his readers to conceptualize Constantinople as a city more majestic than any other. Its conquest, therefore, is unlike anything in recorded or imagined history: "I confess that among everything recorded by historians or even by poets, I have read of nothing like it or of anything so splendid."[52] To this end, the concluding poem for Chapter 19 offers a kind of supersessionist critique of ancient poets who deliberately exaggerated the accounts of the conquest of Troy to impress their readers.[53] The comparison to the conquest of Troy was common among the chroniclers of the Fourth Crusade.[54] For Gunther's part, he asserts that his history is both true and even more magnificent than the ancient tales because, whereas it took thousands of men ten years to conquer Troy, Constantinople was subjugated in one day with the loss of only a single man.[55]

The conquest of the exotic capital is further elaborated in Chapter 21, where Gunther offers an extended and confused gloss on a famous architectural feature of Constantinople, the Obelisk of Theodosius.[56] Gunther offers an unusual level of detail concerning both its striking (phallic) appearance and the components of its construction.[57] He misinterprets the artistic reliefs from the base of the object, arguing that they describe a Sibylline prophecy about fall of the city. But it is the multilayered connection between the exotic object, its pagan omens, and the death of the most nefarious of the Greek leaders that allow Gunther to elaborate further on his view that it is Divine Providence that has allowed the subjugation of the Eastern capital. And it is precisely this link between the exotic topography of the Christian East and the thesis of Providence that illuminates the discursive space upon which Gunther maps the conquest of the distant but mighty Constantinople.

This summation of Constantinople's subjugation awkwardly transitions in the next chapter to an account of Martin's final escapade during his Eastern sojourn—a trip to Acre, which was at that time the best-fortified crusader outpost in the Muslim-controlled Near East.[58] Martin intends to keep secret his possession of religious treasure during this sojourn, but then changes his mind when he encounters Werner, "a strong and honorable man . . . a German by birth, indeed from the region of Alsace, of noble blood, who was, above all, admired for his manliness (*virtute conspicuus*)."[59] Werner and Martin had known each other in Germany, but here, in this exotic land surrounded by danger, Werner "embraced Martin with even greater affection" (*maiori dilectione amplexus*) and "honored him above all others" (*ceteris fere omnibus excolebat*).[60] Sensing a degree of intimacy with Werner he had not felt for any other Westerner in Constantinople, Martin divulges his secret. And the disclosure induces a profound but ambiguous religious ecstasy: "When the abbot showed him those gifts of God which he had borne with him, Werner immediately trembled, seized with a joyous fear, and began to marvel exceedingly [*ille statim leto timore corrptus expavit et cepit graciam illam*] at the favor which God had bestowed upon His servant."[61] Gunther's description could be read to blur the line between religious ecstasy and homoerotic taboo.[62] Werner is so overcome by Martin's sharing of his treasure that he makes every possible effort to convince him to remain permanently in the crusader colony as a kind of monastic settler.[63] But Martin chooses to bring his sojourn in Acre to a close and returns to Germany.

The encounter between Martin and Werner is unexpected and impossible to interpret unequivocally.[64] Nonetheless, there is little doubt that the discursive and interpretive possibilities of the passage are expanded by the opaqueness of distance that the Christian East provides. Indeed, although an explicit sexual pairing of Martin and Werner would have been unacceptable to his monastic circle, Gunther employs the exotic and dangerous setting of Acre to imply, if only through innuendo, an illicit encounter between Martin and the crusader colonist as a metaphor for the gratification of religious desire that is made possible by the conquest of the Christian East.

Exploiting the Cultural Gap

There are, of course, additional elements within Gunther's *Hystoria Constantinopolitana* that we might interpret within a colonializing register.[65] Given that Gunther's primary concern is the theological legitimation of Martin's theft, the text is not particularly illuminating of the ways in which Western rulers and their financial supporters orchestrated the political and economic domination of Byzantium.[66] But it does offer multiple clues as to how the cultural presumptions of colonial expansion and exploitation function within Gunther's Frankish monastic community.

At a most basic level, the *Hystoria Constantinopolitana* reflects the extent to which the discourse of crusader colonization of the Near East had taken root within the religious imagination of monastic communities in the Rhineland. While there were those Western voices that decried the conquest of a "Christian" Constantinople, the *Hystoria Constantinopolitana* reveals a discursive framework within which such a conquest not only makes sense but could be celebrated. Indeed, it is through a postcolonial reading of Gunther's chronicle of Martin's exploits in Christian East that we come to see the extent to which the text not only reflects but likely fueled the monastic appetite for the acquisition of Eastern religious treasure. To be sure, the *Hystoria Constantinopolitana* served as a kind of moral authorization for the subjugation of the indigenous Greek, whose religion was heresy and whose leaders were tyrants. And the story of the beautiful, white-bearded monk who became Martin's personal assistant and shared in his exotic secrets added to the allure of conquest and possession. Perhaps this was especially true because the genre enabled Gunther to insinuate multiple erotic encounters for his story's hero in a fashion that presages subsequent European accounts linking colonial expansion in the Orient to sexual gratification.

In multiple and overlapping ways, then, the *Hystoria Constantinopolitana* anticipates the colonial literature of a much later period, wherein the objects of colonial desire (both material and sexual) occupy a distant geographic space. To be sure, Latin West and Greek East had ancient practices (religious, political, economic, and even linguistic) that provided a fundamental cultural cohesion that did not exist for the colonists who settled in the tricontinental regions in the centuries that followed. Nevertheless, the gaps between Latin West and Greek East in the era of the crusades were sufficient to provide an opening for a colonial expedition that would last for centuries and provide the moral, economic, and religious precedents for eventual Western European conquest of the globe.

CHAPTER
3

INNOCENT'S AMBIVALENCE

Whereas previous chapters sought to apply the resources of postcolonial critique to contemporary accounts of the siege and plunder of Constantinople in 1204, this chapter turns its focus to the correspondence to and from the papal chancellery during the early part of the thirteenth century.[1] It also considers a parallel text, the *Gesta Innocentii III* (*Deeds of Innocent III*), by an anonymous source close to the papal chancery, which in the process of justifying Innocent's activity related to the Fourth Crusade rearranges the sequence of letters in the *Register* and provides additional letters not otherwise extant.[2] While Innocent's correspondence typically does not contain the imaginative sexual or Orientalizing dimensions of Robert or Gunther's accounts, it does evince many of the ways that the papacy managed the crusades as a protocolonial enterprise. It also suggests that the unexpected conquest of Constantinople forced a recalibration of crusader ideology from a papal perspective.

The subjugation of the schismatic Greeks may have provided certain opportunities for those eager to assert the supremacy of the papacy as the governing body of the Church, but the use of military force to achieve and sustain Greek subjugation also called into question the integrity of the crusading endeavor and, more importantly, it upended previous assumptions regarding the boundaries of the Christian community. The events surrounding the Fourth Crusade and the subsequent maintenance of the Latin territory in the Greek East triggered a striking ambivalence in papal articulations of whether and to what extent the Greeks were "Christian" in the proper sense. As papal rhetoric gradually moved toward a more

49

hostile characterization—eventually defining the Greeks as the "enemies of God,"—the papacy became more willing to authorize a number of colonial enterprises previously inconceivable, including violence against Greek Christians, the permanent settlement of Byzantine territory, and the extraction of Byzantine treasure (religious and otherwise).[3]

This chapter will not provide a comprehensive historical account of papal involvement in the Fourth Crusade or the subsequent maintenance of the Latin Empire. Rather, it will interpret the shifts in papal articulations of Greek Christians as a Christian Other through the lens of colonial discourse and it will interrogate the ensuing papal "ambivalence" through the theoretical resources provided by the postcolonial critic Homi Bhabha.

The chapter argues that the unexpected capture of Constantinople put Pope Innocent III into a rhetorical and practical double bind. On the one hand, the pontiff sternly criticized the crusaders for their brutality against fellow Christians and for compromising the military effort in the Holy Land.[4] On the other hand, Innocent saw the conquest of Constantinople as an opportunity to resolve the Greek schism on his own terms and, at least initially, he hoped that the accrual of Byzantium to the crusaders' eastern network might be beneficial to his larger objectives. But if Innocent was to capitalize on this, it meant that he would need to reformulate the very basis of crusading ideology so as to authorize the subjugation of a community that he had previously defined as Christian.

As we will see, it was only after the Latin Empire began to fail on both counts that Innocent and his successors amplified their rhetoric against the "pernicious" Greeks. Indeed, rather than retrench, the papacy doubled down on its efforts to colonize the heretical Greeks who were no longer seen as merely disobedient. The Greeks, in papal eyes, had rejected the true faith and they were unable to self-correct. As the fortunes of the Latin Empire went from bad to worse, the "othering" of the Greek Christian moved into unprecedented territory, a move from which it has never really recovered.

Colonial Management and the Dream of a Restored Christendom

The final decades of the twelfth century had been harsh for the Latin crusaders. In 1174, Saladin consolidated Muslim Egypt and Syria into a single dynastic power (the Ayyubid dynasty) and by 1187 he had achieved a decisive victory over the crusaders at the Battle of Hattin. The unexpected loss of the Holy Land prompted Pope Gregory VIII to issue the call for what would become known as the Third Crusade (1189–92), which succeeded in garnering the participation of Europe's three most powerful kings and reinforced crusader power in Cyprus and along the coast of Syria, but failed to recapture Jerusalem.[5] It was this continued occupation of Jerusalem by Islamic forces and the desire to reclaim it that animated Pope Innocent III's call for the Fourth Crusade and it was this same overarching concern for Jerusalem, as the center of the papacy's colonial project in the East, that would frame Innocent's shifting attitudes toward the Greeks and the Latin Empire of Byzantium.

Innocent issued the call for the Fourth Crusade on August 15, 1198, his first year as pope.[6] The pontiff hoped to inspire the largest crusading endeavor to date and to achieve this end he not only extended the customary indulgence and other privileges to those who took the cross but he also followed Pope Gregory IX by offering special indulgences to nonsoldiers who accompanied the army.[7] As time went on, Innocent would expand on this approach to recruitment, seeking permanent settlers for the Latin Empire of Byzantium.[8] Even more noteworthy, however, was Innocent's decision to embed two papal legates (Cardinal Soffredo and Cardinal Peter Capuano) within the army so as to enable the papal curia to maintain control of the entire endeavor.[9] In many respects, Innocent viewed both the new crusade and the entire European operation in the Near East as part of an ongoing colonial enterprise.

A careful examination of Innocent's edict reveals just how much had changed in the Western European orientation toward the Holy Land in the hundred years since the First Crusade. For example, whereas Urban II's call in 1095 had stressed the misfortunes of distant Christians—those of the holy sites and those of Byzantium—Innocent's call frames Jerusalem as domestic territory and its suffering Christians as Latin Christians.[10] "For behold, our inheritance has been turned over to strangers, our houses have gone to foreigners." And, "our glory . . . is held in hostile hands."[11] This shift is further elucidated by observing that Urban had, at least in part, portrayed the Holy Land as a distant but untapped reservoir of land, resources, and opportunity for glory. Such blatant optimism and opportunity is missing in Innocent's edict of 1198, which focused more squarely on the demise of Christian institutions and on the infighting among European leaders, which had courted contempt and ridicule from the Saracens.[12]

Another important shift in the rhetorical framing of the initial call for the Fourth Crusade is the cementing of the Apostolic See as the foundation of the crusader movement. It is the Apostolic See that is "alarmed." It is the Apostolic See that is "grieved." It is the Apostolic See that "cries out." And it is the Apostolic See—only the Apostolic See—that will harness the military power of Christian Europe to avenge the disasters perpetrated against Latin Christians in Jerusalem.

Both shifts in tone—the Holy Land as familiar and the gravitational force of the Apostolic See—indicate the extent to which the papacy had come to a new understanding of its own role in the century between the First and the Fourth Crusade. Innocent's edict in August of 1198 was no mere flight of aspirational fancy, as Urban's had been. The papacy was now at ground zero of the most significant international engagement of the European Middle Ages and Innocent was intent to maintain control of the operation in ways that none of his predecessors had.

For example, Innocent issued strict instructions regarding the preaching of the new crusade and the expansion of indulgences that were being offered as compensation to those who would take up the cross.[13] Any bishop, abbot, or priest who failed to preach the crusade and/or raise money for its success would be "punished as a transgressor against the sacred canons . . . [and] suspended from his office."[14] Subsequent letters to ecclesiastics in Europe reinforced Innocent's directives and, at times, reveal the pontiff's frustration with the slowness with which people were responding.[15]

Perhaps the most deliberate escalation of papal control of the colonial enterprise was the appointment of the two cardinal legates who would not only direct the crusade itself but also coordinate all European operations throughout the crusader's colonial network. Even the announcement of the cardinal legates' appointment indicates Innocent's deliberate rhetorical hand. Employing the royal "we," Innocent describes the enlistment of his legates as an example of shared burden, a sacrifice for the noble cause of the Holy Land, undertaken by all righteous Christians.[16] But there was no mistaking the significance of the assignment. The two clerics would "humbly and devoutly precede the army of the Lord."[17] Innocent immediately dispatched one legate to the royal courts of France and England and the other to Venice to ensure that proper measures would be undertaken at the highest levels and to make clear just who would be in charge. As events unfolded, it was Innocent's legates, more than the crusaders themselves, who received the lion's share of papal indignation.[18]

Of course, Innocent did not restrict his efforts to the work of his legates. He wrote repeatedly to the Frankish and Venetian leaders in order to inspire, direct, and criticize their actions.[19] As early as 1198, Innocent wrote to the doge and people of Venice threatening to excommunicate anyone who offered material assistance to the Saracens.[20] And once Innocent learned of the attack on Zara, he unleashed a series of scathing letters and bulls of excommunication against the crusaders, their leaders, and the Venetians who had concocted the disastrous affair.[21] What these letters, in particular, reveal is just how quickly Innocent lost control of the army he had assembled.

By the winter of 1202/03 Innocent had a new problem—namely, that the excommunicated crusaders might be lured into the political quagmire of Byzantium. In laying the specific circumstances by which the army might receive absolution for their crimes—forgiveness that could only come through the papal legates, not through Frankish bishops—Innocent instructed his reader that they were to "fully guard against similar actions in the future: neither invading nor violating the lands of Christians in any manner unless, perchance, they wickedly impede your journey or another just or necessary cause should, perhaps, arise."[22] Innocent had known for several months that the exiled Byzantine prince, Alexius IV, had requested the assistance of the crusaders.[23] Although Innocent did not initially mention Constantinople or the Greeks specifically, he did so a few months later.[24]

While we need not assess every letter to and from the crusade's leadership, it is clear that Innocent strove to maintain supervision of the army even after he had excommunicated it. He repeatedly warned the crusaders that they should not attack the Byzantines, who were fellow Christians and that they were not to involve themselves in Byzantine political intrigues that would surely disrupt the mission to the Holy Land.[25] When Boniface of Montferrat informed Innocent that the crusaders had gone to Constantinople, that they had installed Alexius IV on the throne, and that they had done both things in order to bring the schismatic Greeks under papal authority, Innocent keenly brushed aside these pietistic justifications and threatened to renew his excommunication against the crusaders.[26] Innocent expressed similar doubts regarding crusader motivation in a pair of critical letters sent to the Frankish bishops accompanying the crusaders.[27]

Of course, when the unthinkable happened and the crusaders seized Constantinople for themselves a few months later, Innocent pivoted and strove to manage the Latin Empire as a new and critical component of the European network in the eastern Mediterranean. Indeed, Innocent and his administrators sought to control nearly every aspect of the Latin Empire: he made episcopal appointments to Byzantine bishoprics, he issued instructions about the subjection of Greek Christians to his authority, he demanded the right to approve or reject political appointments, he redefined the terms of the crusaders' division of spoils, he instituted a tithe on crusader land, and he censored the expropriation of Byzantine religious treasure that did not go through papal channels. To be sure, the crusader leaders resisted Innocent at almost every turn, but there is little denying that the pope viewed the accrual of the Latin Empire of Byzantium as part of a larger colonial project in the eastern Mediterranean that he believed to fall under this own—and not the crusaders'—supervision.

The De-Christianization of Greek Christians

The Schism of 1054 did not have the ecclesiastical ramifications that some might assume. A Latin Christian could still receive the sacraments in a Byzantine Church, and vice versa.[28] Practically speaking, the only significant change was that the bishop of Rome no longer commemorated the patriarch of Constantinople in liturgical services, and similarly, the patriarch of Constantinople no longer recognized the bishop of Rome. The schism did not halt the flow of Greek and Latin Christians between respective territorial bases, nor did it prevent formal negotiations between the papacy and the Byzantines on any number of matters. For example, despite the schism, the papacy and the Byzantine court had worked together throughout the first century of the crusading movement—admittedly with moments of great frustration and even open conflict. Moreover, diplomacy and cultural exchange certainly continued during Innocent's early years as pope.[29] As we noted in the introduction, it was the subjugation, settlement, and exploitation of Greek Christians by the Latins during the Fourth Crusade that caused the permanent rift between Greek and Latin Christians. And, as we will see, Innocent's de-Christianization of Greek Christians in the wake of 1204 both reflects and helped to unlock the epistemic shift that made the colonial subjugation of Greek Christians possible.

To be sure, Innocent began his pontificate believing that the Greeks were prideful and had, through arrogance, failed to show proper respect to papal authority. There is some evidence that Innocent understood the Greek position on papal authority to be an error of doctrinal proportions—in other words, it was more than a failure to adhere to administrative tradition; it was an actual error of belief.[30] Nevertheless, a careful examination of the surviving sources in the years prior to 1204 reveals that there was nothing in Innocent's correspondence to suggest that he believed that the Greeks were guilty of additional errors, no explicit claim that the Greeks were guilty of dogmatic heresy regarding the Trinity, the natures of Christ, or the Eucharist. For Innocent, all problems with Greek teaching were a consequence of their failure to recognize his authority—whatever dogmatic errors the Greeks might possess, they stemmed from a failure to respect papal leadership. That view would change dramatically in the years after 1204.

Insubordinate Christians

A clear purview into Innocent's thinking about Greek Christians at the time of his election can be ascertained from his letter to John X Camaterus, patriarch of Constantinople, dated to November of 1199. Innocent issued the epistle as part of a larger batch of letters sent to the Byzantine capital. A corresponding letter to the emperor announces optimistic plans for the upcoming crusade and proposes a new synod to resolve, once and for all, the schism between Rome and Constantinople.[31] Innocent's letter to the patriarch is more programmatic and direct. In fact, it is little more than an extended defense of the medieval justification of Roman primacy.[32]

By the twelfth century, the papacy had developed a series of stock arguments to justify its spiritual authority in the Church. Those arguments were largely predicated on a deliberate interpretation of the means by which the apostle Peter was understood to preside over the other apostles and the compounding belief that St. Peter had founded the Church of Rome, despite the fact that the Scriptures never connect him to the ancient city.[33] Not surprisingly, Innocent's letter rehearses each of the biblical references to Peter that had become essential to the Petrine-Roman narrative. It is only near the conclusion of the letter that Innocent transitions to his ultimate point—that the Greeks in general and Patriarch John, in particular, could no longer ignore the magisterium of the Apostolic See.[34]

To drive his point home, Innocent responds to a set of questions/ objections to Roman primacy that John had previously advanced.[35] For example, he tries to explain why the Roman Church should be called the "mother" of all churches, even though the historic Church originated in Jerusalem.[36] More importantly, he advances the argument that the Greek refusal to accept papal authority was an error of "dogma" [*dogmata*] because "the member should return to the head and mother, taking into consideration the reverence and obedience" that is due.[37] He further acknowledges that there are additional issues that need resolution—a "disparity of rites and differences of dogma."[38] But Innocent does not name or examine what those issues are.[39] While we can surmise that Innocent here refers to the Greek use of leavened bread and their refusal to accept the *filioque*, he chooses against an elaboration of the ritualistic and dogmatic issues at hand if, for no other reason, than because those issues could be easily resolved if the Greeks would simply acknowledge papal authority. In sum, from Innocent's perspective in November of 1199, the entirety of the Greek schism boils down to their unwillingness to acknowledge his authority.

We find an even more irenic view of Greek Christians in the letters that Innocent sent to the crusaders in the months between their destruction of Zara and their siege of Constantinople. In June of 1203, when the crusaders had already set off for Constantinople but before Innocent was aware of what was happening, he offered his first explicit warning that they should avoid any entanglement in Byzantine affairs. Innocent warns that they should never again attack fellow Christians.[40] Nor should they conspire to embroil themselves in Constantinopolitan politics on the false premise that they were doing so to avenge Greek obstinacy vis-à-vis their unwillingness to accept papal authority. "For this reason, we warn, and exhort more attentively, and enjoin Your Nobility . . . that you not deceive yourselves or allow yourselves to be deceived by others so that under the guise of piety you do those things (may it not be so!) that redound to the destruction of your souls."[41] A little later he explicitly warns, at pain of excommunication, that they should not violate the lands of any Christians, including the Greeks.

By February of 1204, Innocent had learned that the crusaders had not only gone to Constantinople but had also enabled a violent transfer of power from Alexius III to his nephew Alexius IV. Innocent received the news from Alexius IV, who had written announcing his enthronement and promising to do his best to unite the Churches.[42] Innocent received a more detailed report from the crusader aristocracy at roughly the same time.[43] Innocent responded to the latter with specific instructions for how they might move the patriarch of Constantinople and the Greek Church to demonstrate subservience to the Apostolic See.[44] At no point does Innocent suggest that the Greeks are not Christians or that there are any doctrinal issues, apart from the question of papal authority, that separate Greeks and Latins. In fact, much of the letter accuses the crusaders of using the possibility of Christian unity as camouflage for their wickedness. If the Greeks fail to accept papal authority, Innocent warns, the crusaders will have shown themselves to have sinned grievously by employing violence against fellow Christians.[45]

Writing in the same dispatch of letters to the French bishops who had accompanied the crusaders, Innocent again questions the army's true intentions.[46] He exhorts the bishops by presenting his own view as theirs: "You ardently desire that the Greek Church come back to Rome and that the member return to the head and the daughter to the mother, that there be one flock and one shepherd, and that there be no distinction whatsoever between Latins and Greeks but that they be made one in both the Catholic faith and ecclesiastical unity."[47] What is interesting about a statement such is this is that it reveals a sort of existential fissure. On the one hand, it presents a view of true Christian unity in which there is no hierarchy between Greeks and Latins because both are equal. As such, there is no construction of cultural or religious orientalism. On the other hand, the statement is aspirational; the reality of the situation confounds its desire. Greek and Latin are not united. And it is precisely because they are not united that the Greeks must be brought to unity through submission to the papal magisterium. In other words, the very instruction for how to obtain unity belies the possibility of actual unity.

Despite this breakdown in internal logic, the letter is also revealing in that it affirms once again Innocent's view that the primary thing separating Greeks from Latins is the recognition of papal authority. As elsewhere in the period prior to the sack of Constantinople, Innocent makes no reference to *filioque*, or azymes, or any other dogmatic problem. Rather, in one of the most precise and revealing elements of his correspondence from this period, Innocent declares that the only thing needed to end the schism is a written recognition of papal authority from the patriarch of Constantinople.

In short, whether writing to the Greeks or about them, Innocent's position prior to the siege of Constantinople was that they were obstinate and difficult, but they were Christians nonetheless. At no time in these letters does Innocent refer to the Greeks as heretics or even schismatics. They are fellow Christians and they are to be treated as allies in the fight against the Saracens. Anyone who might suggest that the crusaders should employ violence against the Greeks, whether the pernicious Byzantine prince or the Venetian doge, does so at the risk of excommunication because such a person places personal greed before the cause of the Holy Land.

One likely explanation for the whitewashing of Greek error in Innocent's early correspondence is the pontiff's pragmatism. For a century, the papacy had sought the assistance of the Byzantine court for their plans in the eastern Mediterranean. The relationship was fraught for a number of reasons (political, religious, cultural, and economic), but Innocent understood that the campaign to liberate Jerusalem would only benefit from a stronger relationship with the Byzantine court, and the schism within the Church only complicated matters. In the early years of Innocent's pontificate, Greek theological error—apart from the issue of papal authority—was not something that animated his thought or his rhetorical strategies.[48] But when events moved in ways that he could neither predict nor control, his view of the Greeks and their Christian Otherness began to shift.

Greek Perfidy and the Sack of Constantinople

When Baldwin of Flanders wrote to Pope Innocent III in May of 1204 to announce that the crusaders had taken Constantinople for themselves, he had a great deal of help in crafting a theological justification for the crusaders' actions.[49] The long letter offers a detailed accounting of events leading up the "miraculous" conquest. But the letter also underscores the colonial opportunity of the victory and orientalist assumptions of the victors. Throughout, Baldwin offers a number of reasons designed to explain crusader action. Among other things, he proposes that the crusaders had simply followed papal instructions to guarantee that the Greek Church would accept papal authority; when the new emperor Alexius IV revealed his deception in this regard, the crusaders acted accordingly. Baldwin also claims that when the negotiations between Alexius IV and the crusaders began to break down, the Greek clergy stirred the people against them, saying that they "should be wiped from the face of the earth."[50] Thus, the crusader siege of Constantinople was an act of self-defense.

Additional justifications follow but perhaps the most significant are those that attempt to establish that the Greeks had perverted the Christian tradition.[51] Baldwin repeatedly links the Greek rejection of papal authority to their moral depravity and to God's punishment against them. But he expands his list of Greek theological errors to include improper iconography, the development of false rituals, the use of lay monks to grant absolution, and the (especially scandalous) practice of second baptisms.[52] The incompatibility of Greek and Latin worship is made explicit, Baldwin asserts, because the Greeks would not give a single church to the Latins for their use.[53]

Baldwin's letter contains another important justification that Innocent would, himself, eventually appropriate, which is that the capture of Constantinople should be likened to the liberation of Jerusalem.

> Residents of the Holy Land, clerics and soldiers, were on hand. In comparison to everyone else, their joy was incalculable and unrestrained, and they were more thankful in declaring manifest homage to God, just as if the Holy City had been restored to Christian worship, because the royal city, which for so long now has vigorously stood in opposition to and been and adversary of both, has dedicated itself to the Roman Church and the land of Jerusalem—to the perpetual confusion of the enemies of the Holy Cross.[54]

In this context, Baldwin also goes to great length to detail the ways in which Greeks make pacts with infidels, which further obstructs the cause of true religion and the crusaders' mission to Jerusalem.

In many ways, Baldwin presents the Greeks in a middle space between the Christian and the oriental Saracen, between the righteous and the infidel. It is because they are only partial Christians that the Greeks have failed in every way to assist the army of the Lord.[55] But the conquest of Constantinople offers a new opportunity, not only for the mission to Jerusalem, but also for the conversion of the Greeks to true religion. To this end, Baldwin proposes that Innocent send "ecclesiastical men of whatever religious order or rite to light a fire [among the Greeks] by means of public preaching and potent sermons" so as to establish a true and canonical Church in the Latin Empire.[56]

Baldwin concludes the lengthy letter with an urgent request that Innocent dispatch settlers, of both sexes, to the new Latin Empire. Advertising the economic opportunity for potential colonists, Baldwin notes that "[Greece] is a land made stable by grain, wine, and oil. It is rich in produce, lovely in its forests, waters, and pasture lands, quite spacious for settlement, and temperate in climate (of which there is no equal in the world)."[57] But Baldwin is also careful to frame this request and the continued support of the Latin Empire within the broader evangelical mission of the crusades. To that end, he asks that the pope expand the Apostolic indulgence to include settlers because the defense of the Latin Empire is ultimately a defense of the crusader colonial network and its mission in the Holy Land.

The Ambivalence of 1204/1205

An analysis of Innocent's correspondence during the first year of the Latin Empire of Byzantium reveals a startling transformation—albeit an ambivalent one—of his perception and presentation of Greek Christians. Even though the unexpected capture of Constantinople offered a great opportunity for the cause of Christian unity on papal terms, some of Innocent's letters began to critique a broader set of Greek theological errors both as a means to explain God's punishment of the Byzantines and as a means to authorize new crusader violence against them. What is noteworthy, however, is that Innocent did not always employ this newfound flare for anti-Greek rhetoric. The pontiff also expressed sympathy for the Greeks as Christian victims of crusader violence. On more than one occasion, he suggested that Greek resistance to ecclesiastical unity was understandable, given the terrible treatment they received from Latin soldiers. That ambivalence notwithstanding, as we will see, Innocent's adoption of centuries-old critiques of Greek theological error ultimately foreshadowed his willingness to authorize a subsequent crusade against Greek Christians on the basis that they were not truly Christian.

Innocent's first recorded response to the news of the capture of Constantinople was one of joy, thanksgiving, and opportunity.[58] Like Baldwin, he attributes the unexpected victory to divine intervention. Like Baldwin, he believes that the Greeks have been punished for their misdeeds. And, like Baldwin, he expects a swift reconciliation between Greek and Latin Christians, made possible by Greek submission to the "Mother Church." But whereas Baldwin had expanded the ring of Greek theological error, Innocent's first response reflects the view that the divide between Greeks and

Latins rests entirely in terms of disobedience to the papal throne. From Innocent's point of view, God humbled the haughty Greeks through his chosen instrument—the crusaders.[59] Not only would this bring healing to the schism, a renewed and absolved crusader army would march successfully from the Latin Empire of Byzantium on to Jerusalem.

The next letter surviving in Innocent's correspondence, catalogued as 7.154, was likely first preached as a sermon in Rome, prior to its repackaging as a letter to the East. It was directed to the clergy accompanying the crusaders and presents an exuberant Innocent, who is now trying to figure out the best way to take control of the Greek Church. The sermon/letter borrows directly from Joachim of Fiore's commentary on Revelation and, thus, tries to tie the capture of Constantinople to the eventual reconquest of Jerusalem.[60] Innocent describes the capture of Constantinople as an act of God, who humbles the proud, renders obedient the disobedient, and makes Catholic the schismatic. Innocent argues that the Greek failure to affirm the *filioque* (a Trinitarian error), is akin to the Jewish error of not recognizing Christ's divinity.[61] And, as such, the pontiff suggests that both Greek error and their downfall were predicted in Revelation.

For our purposes, what is most significant about this letter is that it is the first time that Innocent treated Greek theological dissent as anything other than a failure to recognize his institutional authority. Although hopeful that the capture of Constantinople—an event of divine intervention—would hasten Greek correction, Innocent moves dramatically into the mold of a dogmatic apologist. The consequence of this move is made explicit in the final paragraph of the letter, where Innocent exhorts the Latin clerics of Constantinople of the need to instruct the crusader army that Greeks are Trinitarian deviants and, thus, need to be successfully subjugated in obedience to the Roman Church.[62]

Innocent dispatched his initial response (7.153 to Baldwin and 7.154 to the crusader clergy) in November of 1204. In January of 1205, he started a new round of missives to the East. The first of these letters, 7.203, to the crusade clergy, very much picks up where his previous letter had left off. Innocent continues to view the unexpected events of April 1204 through the lens of Joachim of Fiore's apocalyptic reading of Revelation. He proposes a specific plan for new leadership in the Church of Constantinople, despite the fact that the Greek patriarch was, at that time, still alive.[63] And he continues to develop the line of thinking—first introduced by Baldwin—that the submission of the Greeks to the true Church will enable a united Christendom to convert the heathens and/or destroy the infidels.[64] But this letter also reveals a remarkable return to Innocent's earlier restraint regarding the error of Greek Christians—he makes no mention of *filioque* or other theological deviations. Instead, Innocent presents the problem solely in the fact that the Greeks have drifted away from obedience to the Roman Church.[65]

By May of 1205, Innocent's enunciation of Greek error shifted once more. Writing to Baldwin, Innocent offers his most exhaustive list of Greek theological sacrilege to date (including *filioque*, superstition, and using the wrong form of bread in the Eucharist). But what is interesting about this particular set of accusations is that the list of errors is framed entirely as a consequence of disobedience to Roman authority.[66] The Greeks have lost "the first principles of the beginning of God's words, because [they] have sinned against Him who teaches every truth."[67] For this reason, God brought about their destruction. For his part, Innocent has appointed a cardinal delegate to take over the task of bringing the schismatic Greeks back into the full Christian fold. What Innocent wants Baldwin to know is that his very survival as emperor depends upon the submission of the Greeks to the true Church.[68] Innocent's letter to the crusade clergy a few weeks earlier had made no mention of Greek errors, apart from disobedience, but it stated in equally strong terms the necessity of bringing the Greek Church to heel.[69]

Innocent had taken Baldwin's request for assistance seriously. In the same month that he wrote to Baldwin of the importance of suppressing the Greek Church, the pontiff also wrote to Latin bishops throughout the West, imploring them to send assistance to the newly established Latin Empire.[70] Indeed, Innocent fully embraces Baldwin's request for a fresh round of soldier-settlers, men and women, lay and clerical, who would sustain a permanent colony of Latin Christendom in the midst of the Greeks. This letter offers an extremely caustic and polemical critique of Greek theological error. According to Innocent, God has punished the Greeks for their Trinitarian heresy, their insubordination, and their sin. It was now incumbent upon the Latin bishops of the West to encourage the good men and women of their dioceses to join the cause of the righteous.[71] It is, perhaps, indicative of the mindset of the anonymous author of the *Deeds of Pope Innocent* that this letter was one of few from this period included in the papal biography.[72]

It would appear that Innocent did not know the full scale of the crusaders' savage behavior in Constantinople until July of 1205. Writing to
his new cardinal legate, Peter Capuano, the pontiff lets loose on a series of
stinging criticisms.[73] The most pertinent of these accusations is Innocent's
prediction that the Greeks will never accept Latin supremacy of their
Church because they have been treated so badly by the crusaders.[74] "[The
crusaders] committed acts of lewdness, adultery, and fornication in the sight
of all, and they exposed both matrons and virgins, even those dedicated to
God, to the filth of the lowborn."[75] What is particularly illuminating about
the letter is that Innocent was not instructing Peter to suppress or correct any
particular heresy among the Greeks. Rather, he is bemoaning the fact that
events have developed in such a way that it is increasingly unlikely that
the Greeks will ever accept his authority.

But perhaps nothing puts Innocent's ambivalence about the status of
the Greeks on display more fully than the letter he wrote to Boniface of
Montferrat, recently elevated to lord of Thessalonika and Crete, in the late
summer of 1205.[76] On the one hand, Innocent argues that the cause of the
Holy Land will be secured by establishing a permanent Latin stronghold
in the heart of Byzantium and, for that reason, he encourages Boniface to
expand his domain among the Greeks. On the other hand, Innocent
criticizes the former leader of the crusade for misdirecting his attention (and
that of the crusader army) from the true purposes of his mission—the battle
against the Saracens and the liberation of the Holy Land. He further
criticizes him for acts perpetrated against the local population and the theft
of church resources. Indeed, it is for these reasons that the local population
is now unwilling to accept papal authority. What is most striking about
the letter from Innocent to Boniface is the contradictory presentation of
the Greeks. They are the innocent victims of crusader greed and violence.[77]
But they are also worse than the crusaders and, for this reason, God has
allowed them to be subjected to crusader rule.[78] Whether as victim or
malefactor, Innocent's view of the Greek Christian is inescapably bound
by a broader crusader project of colonial conquest across the eastern
Mediterranean.

Innocent's correspondence in the first year after he learned of the capture
of Constantinople reflects a roller coaster of emotion and ideas played out
in his letters to the Latin Empire. This correspondence reveals the transformation of the pontiff's view of the crusade in general as well as his view

of Greek Christianity. Hope and elation give way to disgust and anxiety. Already by the close of that first year, the establishment of the Latin Empire of Byzantium had begun to frustrate and even upend Innocent's expectations of what a crusader colony in the East should be. As the reality of a Latin kingdom among the Greeks took shape and required unanticipated assistance, the very foundations of crusader ideology vis-à-vis the application of violence against the Christian Other began a profound transformation.

Colonizing Christianity after 1205

The Fourth Crusade, of course, was not the first time that a European colony in the Christian East disrupted the lives and institutions of indigenous Christians. The capture of Jerusalem by soldiers of the First Crusade in 1099 profoundly transformed the experience of local Christians. Some were slaughtered alongside Muslims, some were displaced, and many lost control of their churches, which were overtaken by Latin clergy. To be sure, Palestine and Syria was a land rich in Christian diversity (Chalcedonians, Copts, Assyrians, and Armenians) prior to the arrival of the crusaders and the Latin displacement of clergy, churches, and hierarchies was not always consistent.[79] But it is certainly the case that the Latin Church had some experience of colonizing and subordinating fellow Christians when Innocent learned of the capture of Constantinople in 1204.[80] And a key component of its rhetorical strategy involved the de-Christianization of the local population.

As we have chronicled in the previous sections, Innocent's view of the Greek Christian began a profound transformation with the unexpected capture of Constantinople in 1204. With his letter to the Latin bishops of the West at the end of the summer of 1205, Innocent marked the Greek Christian as an enemy of the faith, effectively reframing the Latin Christian imagination of religious boundaries and the possibilities of violence, settlement, and resource extraction vis-à-vis Byzantine territory.[81] As Nikolaos Chrissis has argued, whatever hostility the West might have had for the Byzantines vis-à-vis their efforts in the eastern Mediterranean during the twelfth century, the papal endorsement of a new crusade targeting the Byzantines on the basis of their heresy was the defining shift that both enabled violence against Eastern Christians and altered Western Christian thinking about its own boundaries and identity.[82] In this section, we will identify and analyze a few examples of the ways in which the experience of colonial rule (and its resistance) intensified Latin Christians' negative attitudes toward Greek Christians.

Historians seeking to understand Innocent's views and activity in the years after 1205 are hobbled by the fact that many parts of his *Register* from those years are no longer extant. We do know that he appointed Nivelon de Quierzy, bishop of Soissons (1176–1207), to organize the new crusade that was to reinforce Latin troops in Constantinople in August of 1205. Philip of Namur (brother of Latin emperors Baldwin and Henry) was charged with the military leadership of the expedition.[83] We also know that Innocent maintained a diplomatic correspondence with Theodore I Laskaris (claimant to the Byzantine throne from the Greek successor state of Nicaea), despite papal plans to reinforce the Latin state.[84]

What is intriguing about Innocent's exchange with Theodore is that it continues to reflect a deep-seated ambivalence. On the one hand, Innocent argues that the Greeks deserved the harsh treatment they have received because the schism had been their fault and because they had failed to assist in the crusading effort despite their proximity and ample resources to do so. On the other hand, he claims (rather defensively) that the crusaders had taken Constantinople without papal sanction and that he had rebuked he crusaders many times for their poor treatment of the Greek population.[85]

One arena in which we see the changing nature of Innocent's attitude lies in his decision to drop all efforts toward a council between East and West. Whereas prior to 1204 Innocent had made repeated requests to resolve the schism via a gathering of bishops, after 1204 he made no further serious overtures in that direction. When Baldwin proposed to Innocent in the summer of 1204 that a new council might be called to resolve the schism once and for all, Innocent simply ignored the suggestion, preferring instead to ask Greek bishops, one by one, whether or not they would accept the papal magisterium. For Innocent, it would seem, union in a post-1204 world could be achieved through imposition, and did not require a formal discussion of dogma. Indeed, since the Latins had forced the Greeks into submission, there was no need for a council to affirm the rightful hierarchical structure of the Church.

But what is so interesting about this approach is that Innocent's policy suffers from repeated self-contradiction. He determines that he does not need a council because he has effectively achieved union through the imposition of his magisterium upon the clerics of the Latin Empire. But the reality is that the Greeks do not respect the Latins and they do not accept his authority, even when it is imposed upon them. What is equally intriguing is that Innocent and his successors continued to pursue diplomatic opportunities for union with those members of the Greek Church (and their political leaders) who were not inside the Latin Empire. But papal policy for those Greek Christians living within the boundaries of the Latin Empire was never pursued diplomatically—there the policy remained one of coercion.

For the remainder of his pontificate, Innocent continued to see the subjugation of Greek Christians primarily through the prism of his broader objectives for Jerusalem and the Holy Land.[86] But for his successor, Pope Honorius, crusading in Frankish Greece was driven more explicitly by a desire to suppress the schismatic Greeks who were "enemies of God." Like Innocent, Honorius engaged in a two-fold approach to the Greek resistance outside of the Latin Empire. For example, when Theodore Doukas, the leader of the Greek successor state in Epiros, captured the Latin emperor Peter of Courtenay and Cardinal Legate John Colonna in 1217, Honorius both sought a diplomatic solution with Theodore and made plans to call a crusade against him.[87] When Theodore unexpectedly released the cardinal in 1218, Honorius responded appreciatively and took the incredible step of placing Theodore's renegade kingdom under papal protection.[88] By 1222, as Theodore was laying siege to the Latin Kingdom of Thessalonika, Honorius pivoted once more and issued a call for a full-blown crusade to reinforce the Latin colony of northern Greece.[89] In the span of just a few years, Honorius's presentation of Theodore Doukas had whipsawed from "papal son" to "enemy of the faith."

Perhaps what is most significant about Honorius's promotion of crusading in Frankish Greece in both 1217 and 1222–23 is that he offered no practical or even rhetorical connection between those military efforts and the Holy Land. The Greeks had become a target of Christian violence in their own right. Theodore Doukas is a "son of Belial"[90] and the Greeks are "enemies of God"—*inimici Dei*.[91] As Chrissis argues, the most significant transformation in the papal rhetoric in this period is the presentation of the Greeks as theological deviants who were legitimate crusading targets. While efforts in the Holy Land do not disappear from papal discussion of crusading in Frankish Greece, they were now subservient to the notion that Latin Christendom must fight its newest enemy—the heretical Greeks.[92]

The most extensive crusading effort against Greek Christians during the Latin Empire lay between the years 1235–39, under the pontificate of Pope Gregory IX.[93] It was Gregory who first instituted the Inquisition as a means to punish those guilty of heresy and we might observe a parallel in efforts to enforce theological conformity between the Inquisition and the crusade called against Greek Christians. Gregory's initiative in Frankish Greece focused on a pair of military objectives.[94] The first and primary goal was to reinforce Latin Constantinople. A second but related effort was designed to thwart the capabilities John II Asan, the Bulgarian ruler, who was now aligned with the Empire of Nicaea and presented the Latin Empire with a prolonged two-front war.

Just prior to his summoning of a crusade against the Greeks, however, Gregory had pursued a significant ecclesiastical negotiation with the Empire of Nicaea from 1232–34. While that effort ultimately failed, it is noteworthy because it reveals a hardening of polemical positions that take as their starting point the historical events surrounding the siege, pillage, and occupation of Constantinople. As Chrissis documents, the Greeks of Nicaea ultimately resisted reunion with the papacy in 1234 because they had not yet forgiven the papacy for the events of 1204. The papal delegation, in turn, rejected any responsibility for the events of 1204 because, they claimed, the crusaders acted on their own, without papal sanction. But more importantly, from the papal perspective, union with the Greeks would not occur until such a time as they were willing to acknowledge and repudiate their various heresies.[95]

The rhetorical framing of Gregory IX's call for a crusade against Greek Christians follows but stiffens previous lines of argumentation. Gregory maintains the connection between the Holy Land and Latin Empire but he shifts the calculus connecting them. Whereas Innocent had seen a robust Latin Empire as an asset to broader goals in the Near East, Gregory inverts the connection and argues that the collapse of the Latin Empire of Constantinople would deal a serious blow to any and all efforts for Jerusalem. This recalibration of the connection between the Latin Empire and the crusading mandate against Islam is further evinced by Pope Gregory's polemical charge that the Greeks "hate the Latins more than the pagans do."[96]

In December of 1236, Gregory issued a new papal bull, *Ad subveniendum imperio*, which took matters against the Greeks a considerable step further. *Ad subveniendum imperio*, for the first time, explicitly frames military support for Latin Constantinople as an effort to preserve the true faith of Christians living in East.[97] Indeed, Gregory writes that if the Latin Empire was to fall, "the Lord's field would be taken over by the thorns and thistles of various heresies, and there would be fear of great peril for all the Latins residing in the Eastern parts."[98] The Greeks are a threat to the Latin community not only because they will seize land and property or because they will thwart the crusaders objectives in the Holy Land. The Greeks are a threat to the Latin Empire of Constantinople because, if unchecked by military force, they will spread their heresies among Latin settlers in Greece.

One of the interesting elements in the background of Pope Gregory's crusade against the Greeks is the figure of Frederick II Hohenstaufen, who had a long history of hostility with the papacy. Frederick showed little support for the Latin Empire and repeatedly forged alliances with Greek resistance groups in Epiros and Nicaea.[99] In 1238, in the midst of Gregory's effort to recruit a crusade against the Greeks, Frederick marked a new alliance with John Vatatzes, emperor of Nicaea, which culminated in the marriage between John and Frederick's daughter, Constance/Anna, in the early 1240s.

In some ways, the marriage reveals just how little effect the increase in papal polemic was having on political leaders, such as Frederick, who brokered political alliances as they saw fit.[100] But perhaps we should look at this from another angle. In other words, it may be the case that it is precisely because Greek and Latin aristocrats were engaging in political and sacramental alliances as they saw fit—with complete indifference to papal pronouncements—that figures like Pope Gregory felt the need to escalate the rhetoric against the Greeks in order to build the support that the crusading effort desperately needed. On this particular score, it is worth noting that Gregory's successor, Pope Innocent IV, arranged for the First Council of Lyon (1245) to issue an official condemnation of the German emperor Frederick II Hohenstaufen, in part, because he had married his daughter to a heretic.[101] And it is worth noting that the Latin patriarch of Constantinople, Nicholas, was present at this council. But, as Chrissis observes, it is also significant that the same council made no effort to renew calls for crusade in defense of the Latin Empire indicating a continued ambivalence in the West about the status of Greek Christians and the practicality/necessity of future crusades against them.[102]

In the decades after the capture of Constantinople in 1204, the bishops of Rome sought military and financial support from various regions of Latin Christendom with the goal of supporting a Latin Empire of Byzantium. Although the bishops of Rome never excused the brutality of the initial event and sought to stem the flow of Greek treasure (religious and otherwise) into the hands of Western aristocrats, they became increasingly determined to not only support but orchestrate a permanent Latin colonial project in the heart of Byzantium. To recruit the soldiers and financing necessary, they increasingly portrayed the Greeks as enemies of the true faith who posed as great a threat to the faithful as the infidels. And, in the process, they identified the Greeks and the Byzantine successor states of Epiros and Nicaea as targets in their own right for new crusades.[103]

Viewed from the perspective of the surviving papal correspondence, the Latin Empire of Byzantium was turning into a failing endeavor. As far as the popes knew, the Greeks almost universally despised their Latin overlords and at nearly every turn became even more obstinate in their rejection of the true faith. Perhaps worse still, Latin colonists in the East were losing ground on nearly every front. The capture of Constantinople, which had initially offered so much promise to the expansion and success of the crusader network, was turning into a nightmare. As the years passed, the possibility that the Latin Empire would lead to the capture of Jerusalem grew less likely. Instead, the Latin Empire required an endless stream of resources, soldiers, and rhetorical justifications for its very survival. In all of these ways, we see an uncanny foreshadowing of later European colonial networks to the global South that would ultimately collapse as they became financially and rhetorically unsustainable.

Interrogating Innocent's Ambivalence

As this chapter has shown, there was a profound shift in the way that the bishops of Rome described Greek Christians and the possibility of employing the crusades as instruments against them as a consequence of the Latin capture of Constantinople in 1204. Prior to 1204, Pope Innocent III had repeatedly referred to the Greeks as fellow Christians—albeit disobedient ones—just as he had repeatedly warned the crusaders (on pain of excommunication) that they should do nothing to intervene in Byzantine political affairs nor should they do any harm to the Greeks themselves. But when the crusaders unexpectedly took Constantinople in May of 1204, Innocent saw an opportunity to end the schism on his own terms and he appropriated Baldwin's optimistic expectation that a successful Latin Empire of Byzantium would prove an asset to the broader crusading objectives in the Near East. When both expectations began to disappoint, Innocent recalibrated the very purpose of the crusades so as to redirect Christian violence toward the wayward Greeks who were no longer simply disobedient but had become the enemies of God.

But more than show the ways that capture, pillage, and settlement of Constantinople transformed Innocent's view of the Greek Christian, this chapter has also brought forward many of the ways in which crusade discourse in the age of the Latin Empire contained discrete ambivalences and ideological fissures. Indeed, with a theoretical apparatus provided by colonial and postcolonial critique, we are able to assess Latin ambivalence toward Greek Christians not merely as theological or historical inconsistency but as the consequence of an unsustainable epistemic horizon that, in the process of enunciating one's dominant position, is undone by the very recognition of rejection.[104] As Homi Bhabha observes, colonial discourse is always bifurcated, split between the reality of the present world and the product of desire.[105]

Bhabha is one of the most celebrated scholars in contemporary postcolonial studies, in large part, because he is responsible for advancing reflection on some its most important theoretical categories, including hybridity, mimicry, and ambivalence.[106] In psychoanalysis, ambivalence is a technical category, which means both desire for a thing and its opposite. Bhabha draws on the psychoanalytical framework but broadens the theoretical import of the term to disrupt the notion that there is any simple relationship between the colonizer and colonized. He describes the failure of the colonizer to impose his/her culture on the colonized as one of ambivalence. Thus, for Bhabha, there can be no discourse of colonial mimicry or imitation that does not entail some level of mockery (resistance). What is more, for Bhabha, even the discourse of the colonizer encodes ambivalence, asserting its ideology but always encumbered by the possibility that the fantasy will not be.

I conclude this chapter on Innocent's "ambivalence" by proposing that we find colonial ambivalence functioning on several levels in the papal correspondence from the era of the Fourth Crusade. Most obviously, it exists in explicit statements that offer counter or contradictory statements about Greek Christians and their status vis-à-vis the Roman Church. In the lead-up to 1204 and shortly thereafter, Innocent repeatedly defined the Greeks as Christian, albeit disobedient Christians who failed to acknowledge the magisterium of Roman authority. The explicit nature of Innocent's ambivalence regarding the status of Greek Christianity is most acute in letters where he simultaneously laments the violence inflicted upon the Greeks but also asserts that God intervened to punish them through the crusaders because of their various crimes.

A more profound and existential ambivalence exists within Innocent's affirmation of papal authority as the normative Christian hierarchic structure. Innocent's repeated acknowledgment that the Greeks do not accept papal rule exposes the inherent contradiction within the discourse of papal sovereignty. Indeed, each papal recognition of Greek disobedience reveals a gap in the very premise of papal authority, whether the premise is constituted on the Petrine myth or some other foundation. The assertion of papal sovereignty is "put on trial" by its every iteration and, thus, its dissonance is exposed. If the bishop of Rome is truly and authentically the source of all hierarchic power and Christian teaching that its advocates claim it to be, then any acknowledgment from the bishop of Rome that there are "Christians" who do not accept such a principle undercuts all value in the claim of papal authority as a first principle. In Bhabha's terms, Innocent's assertion of papal authority encodes its own inevitable undoing; its very iteration establishes an ambivalent situation that disrupts its claim to monolithic power.

As discourse, the Roman claim of papal sovereignty in the Church bears at one and the same time a striking ambivalence—both possibility and dispossibility. Thus, papal discourse vis-à-vis Greek Christians in this period implicitly dictates either that Greeks are not Christians (because they fail to acknowledge papal authority, which is a measurement of authenticity imposed by the discourse); or the recognition that papal authority is not a meaningful measurement or requirement of Christianity (because the discourse admits that no Greek acknowledges papal authority). Either way, the assertion cannot withstand its own logical weight.

Innocent's correspondence further reflects ambivalence with respect to the ways that the advocacy of a Latin Empire of Byzantium reveals a fissure in the papacy's ideology of the crusades, which had until that point been predicated on the application of violence against Saracens for the sake of liberating the Holy Land. When Innocent and his successors authorized the seizure, settlement, and extraction of resources from Christian Byzantium, they employed crusade discourse to justify the colonization of fellow Christians. Aware that such a diversion of resources and intent might compromise goals in the Latin Holy Land, Innocent and the crusade leaders developed rhetorical arguments that promised that the Latin Empire of Byzantium would be a boon to the broader crusader objectives. But ambivalence and self-doubt exist in every letter that seeks to justify the presence of the Latin Empire on the basis of the benefit it provides to their broader colonial projects. The very formulations of these justifications are set against their opposite assumption, which is that the Fourth Crusade was a failure, that it wrongfully targeted Christians, and that the crusader network in the East was further compromised as a result. At best, the assertion that the Latin Empire would assist the broader objectives was an aspirational one—something that Innocent and his interlocutors hoped for, but something that had not yet been achieved.

The broadening of crusade discourse to include attacks against the Greeks and to authorize the permanent settlement of Latins in Byzantium not only transformed the targets and goals of the crusades as a mechanism of coordinated violence but it also enabled a reimagining of the boundaries of Christian identity and violence in the name of Christianity. Perhaps the most significant long-term consequence of the Fourth Crusade was the ultimate de-Christianization of the Greeks in the Latin Christian imagination. That process was uneven and in its earliest iterations it was deeply ambivalent. With the insight of postcolonial critique, we might say that, to Innocent's eyes, the Greek Christian was similar to the Latin Christian but not quite; his was a slide to the menace of difference but never fully different.[107]

4

DEMETRIOS CHOMATIANOS: COLONIAL RESISTANCE AND THE FEAR OF SACRAMENTAL MISCEGENATION

A mong the many important insights of postcolonial critique is the observation that indigenous populations often produce complicated and overlapping responses of acquiescence, assimilation, and resistance to the colonizer. This multiplicity of responses often leads to intense factionalism—a factionalism that not only outlasts the physical presence of the colonizer, but transforms the very discourse of communal identity. As I have argued elsewhere, several debates within contemporary Orthodox Christian circles reflect the consequences of a long-running Western colonialism and these debates are among the most divisive aspects of modern Orthodox Christianity.[1]

Whereas previous chapters analyzed texts produced by those who supported the crusades, this chapter offers a close reading of a pair of texts produced by a Greek author who saw himself as an ecclesiastical leader and judicial authority for Greek Christians living either within the Greek successor state of Epiros or under Latin occupation of Thrace, Thessaly, and the Peloponnese. Specifically, this chapter examines a pair of canonical rulings by Demetrios Chomatianos, archbishop of Ohrid from 1216–36, that were the first to address the possibility of Greek/Latin sacramental comingling after the events of 1204. Playing on the insights of postcolonial theorist Robert Young, the chapter argues that these rulings by Chomatianos reflect an effort to preserve an authentic Orthodox communal identity against the taint of "sacramental miscegenation" that could be caused by either the recognition of or support for Latin rule in the East.[2] Indeed, one of the most important features of these rulings is that they are not about Latins per se. Rather, they were about the way in which an observant Christian should respond to the political reality of Latin occupation and the possibility of resistance to the Latins within the realm of Christian sacramental rites. What is clear from these texts is that Chomatianos believes that the difference between authentic and inauthentic membership in the Church could be understood by how one responded to the presence of Latin Christians in the East.

Political and Biographical Overview

The medieval city of Ohrid (located in the modern-day FYROM [Former Yugoslav Republic of Macedonia], near both the Albanian and Greek borders) is first attested in Byzantine sources in the eleventh century as hosting one of the four palaces of the Bulgarian *basileis*.[3] As part of the Bulgarian kingdom, Ohrid belonged to the Bulgarian Church, which claimed ecclesiastical autocephaly (i.e., self-governing independence)—a claim that was intermittently accepted or denied by the Church of Constantinople during the Middle Ages. During the twelfth century, there was an effort by some Bulgarians to associate the city with the ancient birthplace of Justinian, Justiniana-Prima, a city that the emperor had granted ecclesiastical independence.[4] The question of Bulgarian ecclesiological independence was often viewed in the context of a broader political question about the relationship between the Bulgarian kingdom and the Byzantine empire—a relationship that had included a number of violent conflicts between them.

Questions of Bulgarian autocephaly notwithstanding, the Church of Ohrid had deep (often subservient) connections to the Byzantine Church from the eleventh century onward. For example, Theophylact of Ohrid, the most prominent churchman of the see prior to Chomatianos, was a native of Euboea and a student of Michael Psellos. Theophylact had remained very much engaged with Byzantine political and religious affairs after his election to the Bulgarian see.[5] By the early thirteenth century, Ohrid was uniquely positioned at the crossroads between a newly emergent independent Byzantine successor state centered in Epiros[6] (encompassing modern-day western Greece and Albania), the Bulgarian kingdom, and the Frankish Kingdom of Thessalonika. Theodore Doukas, the second ruler of an independent Epiros, captured Ohrid in 1216. During Theodore's reign, Ohrid became the primary ecclesiastical home for the Greek state of Epiros, likely because it was removed from the immediate threat of the Franks, who controlled the historic center of Epirote ecclesiastical life, the see of Naupaktos. It would be this association to Epiros and the proximity to the Bulgarians and the Franks that would thrust the archbishop of Ohrid into the center of thirteenth-century geo-ecclesial politics.

Prior his election, Demetrios Chomatianos served as *apokrisiaros* (ecclesial ambassador) from the archbishop of Ohrid to the ecumenical patriarchate in Constantinople. He also served as *chartophylax* (one of the highest-ranking ecclesiastical administrators) of the archdiocese of Ohrid.[7] Theodore Doukas appointed Chomatianos archbishop of Ohrid shortly after he seized the city from the Bulgarians in 1216. When Doukas captured Thessalonika in 1224, it was Chomatianos who crowned him "emperor." As scholars of Byzantium well know, the coronation was controversial because it was perceived by the Greek aristocratic class of the "empire" of Nicaea to be an affront to their claim to the Byzantine throne and because it implied that Chomatianos was asserting for himself one of the most exclusive privileges of the patriarch of Constantinople (i.e., the right to crown an emperor).[8]

Following his election as archbishop, Chomatianos not only became the leading spiritual authority in the state of Epiros but he also emerged as the de facto spiritual authority for many Greek Christians living under the Latin occupation.[9] Although technically not authorized to adjudicate canonical matters within the territories that constituted the Latin Empire of Byzantium, Chomatianos was known and respected by Orthodox churchmen and noblemen of Greece alike, and they frequently journeyed to his ecclesiastical court in Ohrid in hopes of legal redress or a theological opinion. Because the source material from Chomatianos's ecclesiastical court is so extensive and because so many Greek Christians sought extrajurisdictional legal redress from Chomatianos, his rulings offer unparalleled insight into the ways in which the theological, political, and cultural assumptions of elite members of the Greek Christian community were simultaneously threatened and hardened by the crusader occupation of Byzantine territory during the early thirteenth century. For our purposes, what is uniquely significant about Chomatianos's canonical rulings is that they are the oldest surviving accounts to engage questions of the potential for sacramental comingling with Latins in the wake of the Fourth Crusade.

Byzantine Views of Greek/Latin Sacramental
Comingling Prior to 1204

Despite the enormous amount of scholarly attention that has been devoted to the so-called Great Schism of 1054 and its place in the estrangement of Eastern and Western Christians, it is unlikely that the mutual anathemas of 1054 did much of anything to suspend sacramental unity between ordinary Christians of the East and West.[10] Indeed, although some suggested that Latins should be denied the sacraments, we have no Byzantine sources that say that Latins were refused the sacraments in Byzantium between 1054 and 1204, nor do we have any evidence that Greeks were refused the sacraments in the West in the same period.[11] As noted in the previous chapter, in practical terms, the most significant thing that occurred with the Schism of 1054 was that the pope of Rome and patriarch of Constantinople no longer commemorated one another during their respective Eucharistic services and they no longer maintained permanent representatives at each other's ecclesial courts.

It was not until the late twelfth century that some Byzantine canonists first proposed that the sacraments should not be extended to Latin Christians unless those Christians were willing to denounce certain Latin errors (especially the *filioque* and papism).[12] Theodore Balsamon, serving as a theological advisor to the ecumenical patriarchate, famously responded to a series of questions from the Chalcedonian patriarch of Alexandria, Mark III, recommending that the latter should not offer the Eucharist to Latin prisoners captured in battle because of the historic breach between the bishop of Rome and the Eastern patriarchs.[13] According to Balsamon, if and when a Latin soldier was willing to renounce unspecified Latin dogmas and customs by way of a verbal confession, then he could be admitted to the sacraments.[14] We are left to assume that the errors the soldiers were supposed to renounce were somehow related to the authority of the pope.[15]

Balsamon was also the first Byzantine canonist to identify "Latin errors" as an impediment to Greek/Latin marriage, holding that Latins who wished to marry Byzantine women were compelled to "renounce their separation from the [authentic] Church."[16] Alas, Balsamon did not explain what he actually meant by that. Like other canonists of the period, Balsamon had a great deal to say about heretics and marriage but very little to say, explicitly, about Latins and marriage.[17] Based upon these two brief recommendations, we might conclude that Balsamon believed the Latins to inhabit a middle-space between Orthodoxy and heresy. They are in error—to be sure—but their error is not so great that their reentry to the Church requires a sacramental solution (such as baptism or chrismation).[18]

Balsamon is an intriguing figure. He was well educated and held a number of high-ranking ecclesiastical positions in Constantinople (including *nomophylax* and *chartophylax*). Probably in the year 1185, Balsamon was elected patriarch of Antioch but was never able to take possession of his see on account of the fact that the crusaders had long-since established their own kingdom in Antioch.[19] It is difficult to know how this appointment in exile impacted the small portion of his canonical interpretations that related to interaction between Greek and Latin Christians. But it is worth noting that most modern assessments of Balsamon have been harsh, seeing his denial of the Eucharist to Latin soldiers as an example of intolerance and bitterness.[20]

Patrick Viscuso, intriguingly, has proposed that we consider the exchange between Constantinople and Alexandria concerning the Eucharist and Latin soldiers from the perspective of Mark III's interests rather than Balsamon's. In other words, rather than focus on Balsamon's answer and its assumed bigotry, Viscuso suggests, we should consider the likelihood that Patriarch Mark came to Constantinople to seek support for a plan to stymie the rampant comingling that was likely occurring between the various Christian communities in Egypt.[21]

Whatever we might make of Balsamon's view of sacramental comingling with Latin Christians, his opinions were read and recycled by later Byzantine canonists, including Demetrios Chomatianos. And it is precisely because Balsamon had provided a precedent for deeming the Latin Christian as beyond the sacramental community that Chomatianos, under the pressure of Latin conquest, was able to turn the very question of inside/outside communal identity upon Greek Christians who took opposing views of how to respond to the trauma of 1204.

Ponemata 54

Ponemata 54 is a post facto transcript of a canonical question put to Chomatianos's ecclesiastical court concerning the fragmentation of communion between monks on Mt. Athos that occurred in the wake of the Fourth Crusade. According to the text, an Athonite monk named

Gregorios Oikodomopoulos traveled to Ohrid to seek counsel concerning whether or not an unspecified group of "Greek" monks of Athos should maintain communion with the monks of the Iviron Monastery on Mt. Athos. According to Chomatianos, the monastery of Iviron was composed of monks speaking two languages—presumably Greek and Georgian—and they had lived together harmoniously according to the precepts of the foundation of the monastery, being separated "by language alone."[22] But harmony between the two groups was thrown into disarray by the events of the Fourth Crusade. Shortly after the fall of Constantinople, a group of "Italian" priests came to Mt. Athos and demanded that Eucharistic cele-brations commemorate the name of the bishop of Rome. Those monks and monasteries that did not consent to this were "subjected to tortures, to all manner of evils, and to the loss of property."[23] The Iberian monks (it is unclear if this means only those actually from Georgia or simply from the monastery Iviron) not only conceded to the request for the commemoration of the pope but some traveled to the Latin cardinal in Thessalonika where "they gave themselves wholly over to the will of the pope and followed the Latin customs, and immediately made plain the sign of communion, namely, the placing of their heads in the hands [of the Italians], and they thus confused and blurred lines of their conduct with the Greek monks."[24] What the monk Gregorios asks Chomatianos to settle is the question of whether or not it is appropriate for him and other Greek monks of Mt. Athos to suspend communion with the monks of Iviron who "approached the cardinal and through him the pope."[25]

Chomatianos's initial overview of the case does not provide a full ac-count of the multicultural setting on Mt. Athos or the peculiar situation of the Iviron monastery. Founded by Georgian monks in the tenth century, Iviron was by the early thirteenth century perhaps the most multicultural of any of the monastic settlements on Mt. Athos, and included not only Greeks and Georgians but also several Latin-speaking monks from the West. But Iviron was not the only monastery on Mt. Athos with Latin monks prior to 1204; Benedictines, primarily from Amalfi, had been present on Mt. Athos as early as the tenth century.[26] It is impossible to know if Chomatianos deliberately or innocently fails to acknowledge the Latin presence on Mt. Athos and at Iviron. But the fact that Latin monks were present on the Holy Mountain further confirms that the Schism of 1054 had little practical bearing on sacramental intercommunion be-tween Greek and Latin Christians. Indeed, a multicultural and multilinguistic religious life seems to have continued uninterrupted on Mt. Athos after 1054. But that coexistence was upended by arrival of Latin clerics in 1204 who demanded recognition of the pope.

What is clear from Chomatianos's reconstruction of events is that the Greek monks of Mt. Athos who refused to commemorate the pope (and ostensibly suffered for that refusal) did not know what to do with respect to those monks at Iviron and elsewhere who were willing to commemorate the pope. Some held that they could no longer share the Eucharist with the monks of Iviron, while others held that it was acceptable to remain in communion with them.[27] But what further complicated the situation was the theoretical expansion of the ring of contamination. In other words, because some monasteries on Mt. Athos were divided as to whether or not they should maintain communion with Iviron, a further question arose as to whether or not those who resisted communion with Iviron must also refuse communion with those Greek monks who were willing to maintain communion with Iviron. What the petitioner, in fact, wants Chomatianos to answer is whether or not he must not only sever communion with Iviron but whether or not he must sever communion with every Greek monk who does not sever communion with the monks of Iviron. Put simply, the petitioner wants to know where exactly he should understand the border to be between purity and contamination vis-à-vis Western Christians.

Chomatianos declares that, even though the Italians share a common confession of the Trinity and the rite of baptism, they hold other teachings that are alien and, as a consequence, it is in keeping with a long-standing tradition of the Eastern patriarchal thrones to refuse the authority of the Roman bishop.[28] Explaining his rationale, he observes that "it follows, then, that whoever communes with them [the Italians] in both doctrine and teaching (which we, for our part, have rejected), shall in no matter have communion with us or be one of us, but instead is reckoned as a foreigner [ἀλλότριος]."[29]

The suggestion that those who fail to denounce Latin customs will themselves be regarded as "foreigners" is fascinating in its own right—a rearrangement of the theological community in terms of proximity, familiarity, and distance. But theologically, Chomatianos defends his ostracizing of the unnamed Greek monks on a rather strained reading of Galatians 2.9 (wherein Paul recounts that James, Cephas, and John "extended the right hand of friendship" to him once they determined that grace had been given to him). Chomatianos's use of the passage is problematic because he equates the grace God bestowed upon St. Paul with the "orthodoxy" that individual monks choose to embrace. In other words, Chomatianos asserts that anyone who "offers the right hand of friendship" to another person ultimately consents to everything that other person believes or practices. Therefore, a Christian cannot offer "friendship" to—cannot be in communion with—anyone whose confession of faith or practice of faith is deemed imperfect.[30]

In Chomatianos's continuation of his ruling he likens those monks of Mt. Athos who refused the demands of the Latins to the martyrs, and castigates the monks of Iviron for their imitation of Judas.[31] Indeed, he concludes the ruling by noting:

> We also proclaim, then, that it is not permitted for the Greeks to commune in anything with the Iberian monks, and whoever is of like mind with those who have adopted the customs and rites of the Italians (which have been rejected by our holy Church) is at no time and in no way to be joined with in prayers, or in any other sacraments, or to be put forward for leadership, or to participate in any other kinds of such things (which would have been common up until recently by means of these exemplary precepts that had been in practice through lengthy custom), unless those who have thus transgressed should repent (for this is offered by the philanthropic custom of the Church), and having been well purified of these defilements by fasting, tears, and supplications to God, and having utterly cast out from their hearts the things by which they were defiled, should walk again according to the customs and teachings of our holy Church.[32]

In short, Chomatianos declares that the Greek monks of Athos cannot commune with the monks of Iviron or with anyone else who is willing to commune with them because of their acceptance of Latin teaching and custom. This was an unprecedented expansion of the ring of theological contamination vis-à-vis Latin Christianity.[33]

When Chomatianos characterizes the Italians as "similar but different," he does more than repeat centuries-old condemnations of theological error—he eliminates the ecclesiastical diversity that had existed on Mt. Athos for generations despite different sacramental customs and theological traditions. Neither the Schism of 1054 nor the aggression of Western crusaders during the twelfth century had been sufficient to rock the cultural, liturgical, or even theological diversity that was active on Mt. Athos prior to 1204. But the demands of papal recognition and the seizure of ecclesiastical land and treasure that accompanied the Fourth Crusade challenged the continuation of that monastic diversity. Chomatianos unequivocally calls for an end to the theological and sacramental hybridity that had allowed Latin traditions to continue on Athos. In short, Chomatianos rules that Greek monks (and everyone else) must guard against the dilution of their Orthodoxy, a dilution that presents itself according to a Greek/Latin binary and in which there is no middle space.

Ponemata 22

Ponemata 22 is a much longer and more complicated case about marriage and divorce in the wake of the Fourth Crusade, wherein Chomatianos rules that an arranged marriage between a supporter and an opponent of Latin rule in the Peloponnese was not contracted in good faith and is, thus, canonically dissolved. More important than this particular case, however, is the practical implication of Chomatianos's ruling that marriages between Greeks and Latin-sympathizing Greeks are not permissible because they cannot be entered in good faith. In effect, Chomatianos rejects the possibility of marriages between Greeks and Latins.

After a lengthy preamble, wherein Chomatianos explains that God authorizes pious rulers such as Justinian and Theodore Doukas (the ruler of Epiros) to regulate marriage and divorce for the good of the commonwealth, he provides a lengthy overview of the case in hand.[34] The petitioner in this case, John Chamaretos, was a Peloponnesian aristocrat who was one of the few Greek noblemen consistently opposed to Frankish rule. Chamaretos entered into a marriage alliance with the unnamed daughter of another Peloponnesian landowner, George Daimonoioannes.[35] According to Chomatianos's summary, the most important aspect of the marriage contract was the stipulation that Daimonoioannes would join Chamaretos in his resistance to Latin rule.[36] But shortly after the marriage, not only did Daimonoioannes fail to adhere to his pledge, but the daughter/bride attempted to poison her husband, illegally transferred property from her husband to her father, and sent secret messages about her husband's military plans.[37] After a second round of pledges and broken oaths, Daimonoioannes captured his son-in-law, but the latter escaped and fled to the "Roman Empire [Ρωμανίαν]," which for Chomatianos means the territory held in western Greece by Theodore Doukas, the ruler of Epiros.[38]

Chomatianos's summary narrative continues with Chamaretos's petitioning Doukas for both an annulment of his marriage and a new bride chosen by the emperor himself. In order that he not overstep his authority, Doukas ultimately refers the case to Chomatianos, asking the latter to render an ecclesiastical confirmation of his own support for annulment.[39]

Chomatianos not only allows for the annulment but also declares that there had never been (nor could there have been) a lawful marriage between the Peloponnesian aristocrats because the contract was not entered in good faith.[40] In part, the ruling is based on the presumption that the unnamed wife was complicit in her father's attempt to kill the husband. But for the precise legal rendering, Chomatianos relies on a sixth-century law that prohibits a bride from transferring property from her new husband's household to that of her parents.[41] While part of the petition does claim that the bride has stolen property from him (sending it to her father), the long narrative and multiple witnesses emphasize the extent to which the woman is guilty of plotting with the Latins against the Byzantine resistance centered in Epiros.[42] In other words, Chomatianos's ruling is based on the bride's planned theft of her husband's goods, but the extensive documentation explaining his verdict emphasizes political concerns that are not canonically or theologically relevant to a case about marriage and divorce.

The final paragraph of the verdict takes the case a step further in that it clears a path for Chamaretos to remarry by abrogating any future legal claim against him that he might enter such a marriage illegally (i.e., having been married previously). What is particularly noteworthy about this further legal action is the final sentence, which affirms the trustworthiness and honor of Chamaretos on the basis of his political support of Theodore Doukas (i.e., the Roman emperor). Chomatianos then juxtaposes Chamaretos's dignity and political fidelity to the dishonor and treasonous character of Daimonoioannes, specifically because the latter is politically aligned with the Latins.[43]

Despite the length of the ruling and the implicit sacramental incompatibility of marriages between Greeks and Latins (or, specifically, between Greeks and Greeks sympathetic to Latins), there is nothing in Chomatianos's judgment of a theological nature.[44] There is no examination of the theological expectations of a lawful marriage. There is no examination of Latin theological error. There is no explanation about how or why Greeks sympathetic to Latin rule are sacramentally polluted by their political sympathies. The only concrete assertion that Chomatianos offers is that individuals sympathetic to Latin rule, such as Daimonoioannes, cannot be trusted. Indeed, trust and honor in this case align both theoretically and materially with political support for the successor state of Epiros in the war against the crusaders.

A Postcolonial Reading

To be sure, Christians had always refused to distribute the sacraments to non-Christians or to those deemed heretical. Moreover, since at least the fifth century, Christian leaders had attempted to bar their followers from marrying heretics.[45] But the situation reflected in *Ponemata* 54 and 22 is different from the late-ancient prohibitions not so much because Chomatianos is asserting sacramental limitations against Latin Christians (which did have some precedent in Theodore Balsamon), but because he is applying the same sacramental prohibitions against fellow Orthodox Christians who fail to acknowledge the danger posed by Latin Christians. I would like to propose that one of the most fruitful ways for interpreting such an innovative development is to situate it within the context of the crusader colonization of the Christian East and to understand the profound, deteriorating, and transformative effects that experience had on religious self-understanding among some Greek Christians.

Drawing on the insights of postcolonial critics like Robert Young, we see the extent to which Chomatianos's efforts to safeguard the integrity of Orthodox purity reflect many of the same anxieties that Western cultures experienced with the encounter of other races and the need to explain difference within a totalizing discourse that simultaneously reinforced a collective identity and authorized collective action against outsiders.[46] In both cases, the protagonist sought to explain why a perceived enemy was "similar but different" from his audience. And in both cases, it was argued, there was an urgent need to construct a community identity that devalued any "similarity" and emphasized the "difference" of the foreign threat.

As Young compellingly traces in *Colonial Desire*, the encounter with alien races (i.e., African, Asian, and American) and the production of children of "mixed race" that resulted from early-modern colonial expansion prompted Europeans to produce theories of racial differentiation that simultaneously explained its origins and warned of the potential danger that continued miscegenation posed to European power.[47] Some postulated that non-Europeans were separate species—even though Europeans and non-Europeans might be able to procreate, it was argued, such intermingling would ultimately lead to sterility and/or genetic denigration. Others suggested that non-Europeans were the descendants of Ham (son of Noah), forever cursed by God. No matter how "scientific" these studies were, they were all grossly distorted by cultural subjectivity by assuming the superiority of European bloodlines. And, equally important, they warned of the cataclysmic threat posed to European purity by continued miscegenation.

Indeed, one of Young's most important insights is that racial theory only functions when it is proposed against the possibility of intermixture—a hybridizing of race.[48] The central thesis of his study, therefore, is that there has always been an intrinsic link between sexuality and racism and between sexuality and colonial exploitation. But a further analogue of Young's investigation is the insight that the authors of these racial theories were largely motivated by a concern that members of their own community failed to see the danger of mixed race.

For each of these reasons, I would like to propose that Young can help us to illuminate both the context for and the implications of Chomatianos's statements about "orthodox" or "Greek" identity in the context of the colonial encounter of the Fourth Crusade. Replacing the racial framework of Young's European/African or European/Asian binary with Chomatianos's Greek/Latin and orthodox/heterodox offers several fruitful possibilities for reconsidering the Orthodox/Catholic dialectic that took its first mature form during the thirteenth century in the context of the Fourth Crusade.[49]

For example, in *Ponemata* 54, Chomatianos situates the Latins within a narrative framework of "similar but different." They are similar because they believe in the Trinity and understand the theological significance of baptism; they are different because they have adopted additional dogmas that place them in error. Because they are set apart, because they are insufficiently the same, the Orthodox can have no communion with them—in fact the Orthodox can have no communion with *anyone* who has communion with them. Chomatianos seeks to erase the middle space; he seeks to eradicate the interstitial reality of liturgical comingling that is occurring between Greeks and Latins on Athos and elsewhere.[50] The multicultural experiment at Iviron may have been acceptable in the past— the monks there and elsewhere may have once been deemed sufficiently

"similar." But in the wake of 1204 and the demands of universal acceptance of papal authority, the monks of Iviron were no longer similar, they
were "different;" they were foreign; they were ἀλλότριος.

Chomatianos's extension of this sacramental proscription into the realm
of marriage, which we see in *Ponemata* 22, offers an even stronger parallel
to Young's thesis that the fear of miscegenation, the fear of mixed-race, is
an intrinsically sexually motivated anxiety. Just as the reality of racial
integration in the colonial endeavor led Western European intellectuals to
invent theories of racial differentiation for the purpose of excluding the
mixing of the races, so too Chomatianos's ruling can be interpreted as a
prohibition against a miscegenation that is at once both sacramental and
material precisely because so many Greek landowners in the Peloponnese
and in Thrace seemed to have been so indifferent to viewing Greek/Latin
marriage as problematic. In other words, it is precisely because Greek
aristocrats were marrying Latins or because Greeks were willing to support
Latin political power that Chomatianos seeks to erect a barrier to preserve
the purity of a conceptual orthodox community.

Indeed, perhaps what is most significant about *Ponemata* 22 is that the
situation it describes (marriage between one Greek aristocratic family that
did and another that did not support the Latin presence) could hardly have
been exceptional. The historical record demonstrates that a large percentage
of the land-owning Greek aristocracy (especially in the Peloponnese)
accepted Latin rule and only rarely joined in the military effort to restore
Byzantine control to the region.[51] Greek chroniclers from the period, in
fact, recount multiple aristocratic marriage alliances between various
crusader and Greek factions, showing no concern that the arrangement of
a Greek/Latin marriage might be somehow unacceptable on canonical
grounds.[52] So, if marriages among the Greek aristocratic classes in this
period are not only blending Greek and Latin families but even more
frequently combining Greek families of mixed or changing affiliation vis-
à-vis Latin rule, it is hard to imagine Chomatianos's ruling as anything
other than an effort to assert an ecclesiastical boundary that will help to
distinguish "us" from "them."[53] And, on this score, it is not inconsequential
that the ruler of Epiros had personally petitioned the archbishop to rule in
this way.[54]

In other words, it is precisely because the political borders in this period
were so porous, so ambiguous, and so fraught with uncertainty that
Chomatianos's ruling came to be understood as both a theological and a

cultural judgment against Greek/Latin marriage, when, in fact, the text never actually forbids such a marriage on theological grounds.[55] And it is for this reason—and all of the possible anxieties that it reflects—that our analysis of the religious identity construction in this period benefits from analogous historical episodes when the dynamics of colonial conflict prompted new grammars of cultural integrity and purity, like the colonial-era category of the "hybrid" child.

Scholars of Byzantium have been increasingly intrigued by the so-called *gasmoules*—persons of "mixed race"—who emerged in the wake of the Fourth Crusade and what their position in the later stages of Byzantine society might mean for larger trends in identity sensibility in the Middle Ages.[56] While there remains a great deal of disagreement among scholars concerning this group, it is clear that they were a significant and identifiable community from the thirteenth to the fifteenth centuries, despite the fact that there were explicit prohibitions against "mixed marriages" from both Greek and Venetian authorities.[57]

For the guardians of ethnic or religious boundaries, hybridity is problematic not only because it blurs genealogical or racial purity but, more importantly, because it blurs the markers for cultural, social, and/or religious cohesion. As such, we can understand the concern about hybrid children to be as much about the fear of the dissolving of assumed social structures as it is about the miscegenation of blood lines. But we can also understand the hybrid child to pose a threat to those, like Chomatianos, who overlay theological significance to the boundaries between social groups. For intellectuals like Chomatianos, the blending of Frankish and Greek society that is occurring among the Greek aristocratic class is doing more than disrupting established political and cultural structure—it is threatening the very integrity of the faith community. Thus, Chomatianos seeks to erase the middle space, he seeks to eradicate the interstitial reality of liturgical comingling that is occurring between Greeks and Latins throughout the Christian East—even on Mt. Athos.

One final observation regarding the way that I have employed Robert Young's categories for analyzing Chomatianos is to recognize that I have inverted postcolonial critique as it is typically employed. In his *Colonial Desire*, Young examines the way that European societies (i.e., the hegemonic force) sought to develop an epistemic framework to prevent the dilution of their own race as they spread their influence across the globe. But Chomatianos's efforts were designed to preserve the authenticity/purity of his victimized community. Chomatianos's community was not the colonizer; it was the colonized. We might not go so far as to call it subaltern, but it was certainly on the receiving end of crusader aggression. And yet it was this victimized community that produced new religious and cultural resources to respond to the various crises presented by a transformed political reality. What does it mean for Young's insights about race and hybridity if we can make such a fruitful, "inverted" comparison between the intellectual transformations that occur for the victims of colonization? And, more importantly, what does such a comparison mean for our understanding of Christianity and its Others?

While I am not suggesting that the Byzantine experience during the later Middle Ages was akin to that of the global South, scholars of Eastern Christianity need to reconsider both the way that we think about the relationship between Christianity and hegemony and the way that we think about the colonization "of" Christianity. If we can accept the premise that the crusades offer the first examples of European colonialism, then we need to think more seriously about the fact that a wide variety of Christians were among the first victims of colonialism. Indeed, such realizations have the potential to transform our very understanding of history of Eastern Christianity (Armenian, Coptic, Syrian, Byzantine, etc.) and the way that we analyze the various dynamics within each of those communities in the present day. Materially, this colonialism may have ended centuries ago. Nevertheless, its consequences not only continue to dominate the epistemic horizon of Eastern Christians but its significance has been almost completely unacknowledged by scholars.

It simply will not do to think of Christianity in Russia, the Balkans or, especially, the Middle East in the same way that we think about Christianity in Europe or America.[58] Just as Christians in the global South must negotiate so many competing and conflicted concerns, so too Eastern Christians, wherever they live, must confront what it means to be both "Oriental" and "Christian" in a world that is perceived by them to be increasingly neither.

Sharpening Community Division

In a recent book on the later Byzantine period, Gill Page details the ways in which the Frankish occupation of Byzantium upended many of the dominant themes of earlier sources of identity construction.[59] In the present context, perhaps one of her more intriguing insights is that there was a real difference in the way that "Orthodoxy" functioned for Greek writers, depending upon the extent to which they were living under Frankish occupation. In effect, those "cultural" or "ethnic" Romans who lived under foreign rule (particularly in the Frankish Peloponnese in the thirteenth and fourteenth centuries) were the most likely to employ "Orthodoxy" as one of the primary markers of cultural Roman (i.e., Byzantine) identity.[60]

Chomatianos, who is not examined by Page, would seem to offer a critical nuance to these observations in the sense that he is writing from a politically hybrid space (he oversees a Bulgaria archdiocese but he is in league with the Roman/Greek ruler of Epiros who is a claimant in exile to the Byzantine throne) and he is adjudicating cases well outside of his geographic authority (both on Athos and in the Peloponnese). Perhaps most importantly, *Ponemata* 54 and 22 show Chomatianos to be particularly concerned with establishing which Greek Christians are and which Greek Christians are not suitably "Orthodox" on the basis of how they respond to Latin settlers in the East. Will Greek Christians distance themselves from those other Greeks who are willing to commemorate the Pope? Will Greek Christians enter into marriage contracts with those who support Latin rule?

What we find in Chomatianos is an effort to sharpen community identity in the wake of the crusader occupation of Byzantium by ostracizing members of the Greek community who were either explicitly in league with the Franks or who did not sufficiently see the threat posed by them. Chomatianos's efforts were both unprecedented and largely ignored. But with the ascendency of the Ottomans in the centuries that followed, the cultural barriers between Orthodox and Catholics that were erected within the colonial framework of the crusades began to take hold on the imagination of Eastern Christians such that they would provide a powerful epistemic horizon for those religious thinkers in the nineteenth and twentieth century who would, for the first time since the crusades, attempt to imagine an Orthodox Christian identity that was free from contamination by the West.[61]

5

GEORGE AKROPOLITES
AND THE COUNTEREXAMPLE(S)

T he previous chapter began with the recognition that one of the most important insights of postcolonial critique concerns the way that a colonial encounter can fracture an indigenous community along a variety of fault-lines. Often, this occurs because members of the community pursue disparate responses to the colonizer—those who acquiesce, those who resist at all cost, and the many permutations in between. Indeed, postcolonial critique emerged largely as an effort to assess this fracturing and to combat the residual effects of colonialism (in all of its political, economic, and cultural manifestations) that continue to overshadow a society long after the colonizer has left.

With the same considerations in mind, this chapter turns to a very different kind of Greek response to the experience of 1204 and the legacy of the Latin Empire of Byzantium. The *History* of George Akropolites, likely written in the 1270s after the restoration of Greek power to Constantinople, is different in genre, different in political orientation, and different in religious preoccupation.[1] Indeed, although Akropolites has very few positive things to say about the Latins (or the Bulgarians or the Epirotes for that matter), his *History* never identifies religious difference with the Latins as a cause for genuine concern. And it is not that he was ill-informed or disinterested in religion. Akropolites was very much involved in Church affairs and a patron of the monastic life. But quite unlike Chomatianos and those who would become known as the "anti-unionists," Akropolites viewed religious unity with Western Christians as a key component of a broader strategy to ensure the survival of the Byzantine state.

Following a biographical overview, this chapter is divided into two parts, each of which explores an important counterexample to themes that we have examined throughout this book. The first part evaluates Akropolites in light of what he says (or does not say) with respect to Latin Christianity and the efforts of the crusaders to force Greek Christians to accept religious unity on Western terms. Given the previous analysis of Chomatianos with respect to the potential for sacramental contamination, it is especially pertinent to see just how frequently Akropolites identifies marriage with Latins as an effective diplomatic tool employed by the aristocratic houses of the Palaiologan dynasty. Significantly, Akropolites, like his patron Michael VIII Palaiologos, never appears to suggest that such marriages are theologically or canonically problematic. In effect, Akropolites's *History* provides a direct counterexample to Chomatianos's view that Latin Christianity poses a threat to Orthodox purity.

The second part of this chapter takes up the methodological question first identified in the introduction, regarding the challenge of applying a postcolonial analysis to a colonized society that continues to think of itself as superior to its colonizer. Specifically, the second half of this chapter asks the rhetorical question of how one gives a postcolonial reading to a text that does not easily yield to one. As we will see, Akropolites's *History* adheres to a well-worn Roman historiographical tradition that, among other things, presumes a cultural and political superiority against all adversaries. As a result, Akropolites presents the Latin occupation of Constantinople as just another of the many political challenges that befell an empire that had lasted more than a millennium. He certainly does not present the Latin occupation of Byzantium in terms of the existential and epistemic rupture that most modern historians of Eastern Christianity believe it to be. Nor does he present the Byzantines as any kind of backward or inferior society that needs the rejuvenation provided by its colonial masters. In these ways, Akropolites appears to offer an important counterexample to some of the very assumptions that underlie the framework of this book—that the Fourth Crusade so shattered the political, economic, and religious structures of the Byzantine world that that society never recovered from its subjugation to Latin Christianity. But as we will see, the loss of Constantinople and the continued presence of Latins in the East were not just routine political upheavals in the long epoch of Roman history. The crusaders are, at every level, inescapable for Akropolites. While he may have claimed that the Palaiologan empire of Nicaea was simply business as usual for an empire that stretched back more than a thousand years, neither Akropolites nor his account of Nicaean history could ignore the tremendous significance of 1204. Indeed, for Akropolites and all of his contemporaries, the "Latin" empire had opened an inescapable rupture in the narrative of Byzantine political and religious life.

George Akropolites as Teacher, Diplomat, and Historian

George Akropolites was born and died in Constantinople (1217–82) but he spent the majority of his life in the "empire" of Nicaea, where he served first as a teacher and later as a prominent civic official.[2] George's family seems to have been of some importance in Constantinople in the generations before his birth and it is probable that his father was in the employ of the Latin authorities after the siege of 1204.[3] George's initial education was in Constantinople and may have been conducted in Latin. Around the age of seventeen, his family sent him to Nicaea so that he might receive his advanced education in a form and fashion that was more customary for a member of the Byzantine aristocracy.[4] In Nicaea, George was brought up in the imperial court and likely received his instruction alongside the imperial children and under the direction of the famous scholar Nikephoras Blemmydes.[5]

Following his own education, Akropolites moved into the ranks of the imperial scholars, where he served as one of the private tutors for the future Nicaean emperor, Theodore II. The relationship between the Theodore and Akropolites is documented in a collection of thirty-nine letters preserved by Akropolites and offered to the emperor as a gift.[6] Even before Theodore assumed the throne, his father, Emperor John III, entrusted Akropolites with a series of diplomatic responsibilities. George drafted imperial correspondence and took part in the peace negotiations with Michael II of Epiros in 1252.[7] When Theodore became emperor in 1254, he gave an expanded role to his former teacher. Akropolites accompanied the emperor on campaign and eventually made the transition from diplomat to commander with his appointment as *praitor* in Macedonia in 1256.[8] But his lack of military experience no doubt contributed to his swift defeat by the Epirotes when war resumed shortly thereafter. Indeed, he lost the majority of the territory under his control and spent two years in an Epirote prison, likely in Arta.[9]

Akropolites returned to Constantinople and to teaching after the capital was taken by Michael VIII Palaiologos in 1261.[10] The new emperor established an academic position for George for the explicit purpose of reestablishing Greek learning. It is possible that Akropolites was the lone instructor of advanced education for several years after the Palaiologan restoration.[11] Ruth Macrides, the most important of Akropolites's modern commentators, argues that George should be credited with enabling the subsequent "Palaiologan Renaissance."[12] Among other things, Akropolites mentored the future patriarch of Constantinople, Gregory II of Cyprus.[13]

While it is certainly true that teaching was George's primary activity after the return to Constantinople, he also maintained a role in civic government and diplomacy.[14] And it is worth noting that he married a relative of the emperor.[15] Given George's civic responsibilities and familial ties, we should never lose sight of the fact that any effort to interpret George's *History* must account for the fact that he was an active participant of the Palaiologan administrative apparatus. This is especially true of Akropolites's diplomatic efforts with Latin Christians, which are never far from the hermeneutical and rhetorical structuring of his chronicle.

In 1274, Akropolites led the Byzantine delegation of imperial representatives to the Second Council of Lyon, which, in principle, reunited the Byzantine Church with the Christian West but did so on Western terms.[16] While there, Akropolites, both personally and on behalf of the emperor, affirmed the primacy of the Roman Church and pledged obedience to it.[17] For the remainder of his rule, Michael VIII Palaiologos strictly enforced the ecclesial union achieved by Akropolites at Lyon and he openly persecuted those Greeks clerics who refused to acknowledge it.[18] But as with so many previous political interventions into the affairs of the Byzantine Church, the tides shifted after Michael's death and public opinion similarly turned against Akropolites at the end of his life. Even George's own son, a monk who inherited a monastery refurbished by George's beneficence, repudiated his father's unionist position and refused to offer prayers on his behalf.[19]

It would be easy to suggest, as both his contemporary detractors and modern polemicists have, that Akropolites's eagerness to bridge the Churches was motivated by political considerations. But we should observe that such an assertion might uncritically associate those who hold an antiunion position with those who care first and foremost about matters of faith, whereas, conversely, it might uncritically assume that those who hold a prounion position prioritize political concerns. In point of fact, there was rarely a political or theological debate in the period between the restoration of Constantinople in 1261 and its fall to the Ottomans in 1453 that did not become entangled with the question of reunion with the Latins. It is no easy matter to separate political and religious motivation or to understand how one concern trumps the other in this period, particularly as they concern Western Christians. In the case of Akropolites, such uncritical assumptions are especially problematic because he was, in fact, a figure well versed in the theological debates of his day and had even authored two tracts, *On the Holy Spirit*, that defended the traditional anti-*filioque* Byzantine position.[20] Indeed, it is precisely for this reason that a postcolonial reading of Akropolites's history can yield unanticipated insights—such as the ways in which it offers an important counterpoint to Chomatianos's canonical decrees.

In the *prooimion* to the *History*, Akropolites explicitly situates his work within the long historiographic tradition of previous Roman chroniclers.[21] He notes that whereas other historians start with the beginning of time or with the emergence of a people (the Greeks, the Romans, etc.), Akropolites proposes to begin with a rupture in history—the sack of Constantinople—and to convey the story of the Romans until that rupture was set right—i.e., the restoration of the city by its true ruler, Michael VIII.[22] Indeed, the twin arguments that run throughout the *History* are, first, that Michael VIII is the only legitimate heir to the imperial throne and, second, that the empire of Nicaea was the only legitimate successor state during the period of crusader occupation of Constantinople. Both positions, of course, situate the point of reference in the period after 1261, but they also suggest that the argument needed to be made. In other words, the very formulation of Akropolites's thesis demonstrates that there were still those Greeks in the Byzantine theatre (whether in Epiros, in Frankish Peloponnese, or in Trebizond) who questioned Michael's claim to imperial authority. It was precisely those challenges to the Palaiologan claim to rule in the wake of the crusader displacement of the Byzantine political establishment that Akropolites sets out to answer.

Latins, Latin Difference, and Latin Religious Difference

Given Akropolites's explicit interest in connecting his *History* to the Roman historiographic tradition of political writing, his chronicle does not naturally lend itself to a postcolonial reading. As I noted in the introduction, Byzantium may have been colonized by the crusaders, but one should never describe it—and especially its intellectual elite—as subaltern. In many ways, Akropolites assumes and asserts a cultural arrogance and superiority that one would attribute to a colonizing, rather than a colonized, community. As I will argue, however, there are multiple ways in which the insights of postcolonial critique can help to illuminate aspects of the *History* that we might otherwise fail to observe. To that end, this section will pay particular attention to ways in which Akropolites provides a very different kind of account of Byzantine identity vis-à-vis Latin Christians from Chomatianos and other antiunionists, even if his presentation of the Latins, like theirs, is a negative one. In other words, whereas Chomatianos used opposition to Latin theological and political error as a way to assert the boundaries of the Orthodox community, Akropolites affirms Roman (i.e., Byzantine) identity and superiority, without seeing sacramental unity with the Latins as a threat to that identity. The Latins are "Other" and they are dangerous, but they are sufficiently Christian. According to Akropolites, association with the Latins does not pose a direct threat to Orthodox teaching or community. In fact, he suggests that the Latins are no more a threat to Orthodox community than that other "Western" race, the Epirotes, who similarly promote false claims to the Byzantine throne.[23]

   To be clear, Akropolites is no lover of Latin Christians, especially not the crusaders who have brought devastation to the Byzantine world. In a particularly acute polemical aside, Akropolites observes, "the Latin race, which always nurtures a passionate hatred for us, was even worse disposed because of the recent attack on them by the emperor John."[24] In this particular passage, George chronicles a change in political fortunes for the Nicaean emperor, John III Vatatzes, in 1237, when the Bulgarians, under the leadership of John Asan, revoked their support of the Nicaeans and allied themselves with the crusaders.[25] This new alliance between the Bulgarians and the Latin Empire was, in fact, orchestrated by the diplomatic efforts of Pope Gregory IX.[26] Akropolites offers no acknowledgment of papal involvement. Rather, he focuses on aspersion by association, emphasizing the barbarity of additional allies the Latins recruited to their side: "Then, along with [Asan] they drew to themselves the Scyths, barbarian men, vagrants, and intruders, and made these accomplices in their deeds."[27] Like his predecessors in the Greek and Roman historiographical traditions, Akropolites associates the enemies of legitimate rule with the barbarous and the uncivilized. Both barbarity and incivility are attributes of the Italians and Latins (he uses the words interchangeably) as well as their allies.

Nevertheless, Akropolites only rarely presents Byzantines and Westerners as civilizational opposites through phrases like "the Latins who hate us." The claim appears only once in such sweeping terms and in the specific context of the temporary forfeiture of an important alliance with the Bulgarians.[28] To be sure, the chronicle contains other cultural disparagements, such as the suggestion that "the Latin race does not have great endurance in battle."[29] And, of course, the Latins of Constantinople are consistently presented as the political enemies of the true Romans.[30] But Akropolites was also willing to acknowledge that certain crusade leaders, including the emperor Henry of Constantinople, were capable of nobility and generosity to the indigenous population.

> Henry, even though a Frank by birth, behaved graciously to the Romans who were natives of the city of Constantine, and ranked many of them among his magnates, others among his soldiers, while the common populace he treated as his own people. When he conquered the Roman towns of Lentiana and Poimanenon and found warlike men who displayed acts of a noble soul, he welcomed them as a godsend.[31]

Not only does this passage ascribe virtuous behavior to the Latin emperor of Constantinople, it attests to the fact that Byzantine aristocrats and their soldiers accepted Latin rule and were ultimately willing to wage war in support of it.

Akropolites's most hostile description of Latins is reserved for the Latin churchmen, sent by the pope, who were tasked with bringing the Greek Church to heel in the years after the conquest of Constantinople in 1204. Akropolites specifically maligns Pelagius, the papal legate to Constantinople from 1213–15, who was "a rather wild character and arrogant."[32] As a prounionist at the time he is writing the chronicle, it is not that George believes Pelagius's task to be problematic—indeed, he calls it "reasonable." Rather, it is that Pelagius was so incapable of handling his assignment with sensitivity and competence.[33] Akropolites observes: "Monks were confined, priests were bound, and every church was closed. In this situation, one could do one of two things: either acknowledge the pope as the first bishop and commemorate him in holy services, or death was the penalty for the person who did not do this."[34]

According to the *History,* Greek aristocrats remaining in the capital at the time went to the emperor Henry and offered to accept his political authority on the condition that he allow them to maintain their own religious traditions, independent of papal authority. Akropolites reports them requesting:

> Although we are of another race and have another bishop we have subjected ourselves to your rule, so that you rule over our bodies, but certainly not our spirits and souls. It is of necessity that we fight for you in war but it is utterly impossible that we should give up our beliefs and practices. Either deliver us from the terrible things which have come upon us or release us as free men to go to our own kind.[35]

Apparently, the Latin emperor granted the request and countermanded Pelagius's orders—Greek churches were reopened and monks and priests were released from prison.

The entire passage is fascinating, both in terms of what it purports to have happened vis-à-vis Henry and his Greek subjects and because of the internal contradictions that it reveals about Akropolites's thinking on the matter. On the one hand, the passage suggests a bifurcated residential identity—Constantinopolitan Greeks can accept Latin political authority but only if they are able to maintain their independence from the Latin Church. This is a rather different situation than what we find in the Peloponnese, where Greek aristocrats shifted their political allegiance back and forth between the Franks and the Byzantine successor state of Epiros but seem to have not been terribly concerned about strict boundaries between Greek and Latin religious rites. Indeed, as we discussed in the previous chapter, Chomatianos's canonical interventions were designed to harden what was otherwise a porous line between Greek and Latin sacramental communities.

On the other hand, what is equally intriguing about this passage of the *History* is that it seems to present a direct counterpoint the political project that Akropolites seeks to advance through the writing of his *History*—namely, that true Romans recognize only the political authority of the Empire of Nicaea. Indeed, Akropolites uses the word "Roman" (*Rhomaikoi*) to describe the citizens of Constantinople who accept Henry's rule.[36] Later, in paragraph 22, Akropolites further acknowledges Greek aristocratic support for the Latin Empire when two of the brothers of the late Nicaean emperor, Theodore I Laskaris, are shown to have fought alongside the Latin

Empire against the Nicaean emperor John III in the Battle of Poimane-non.[37] In other words, Akropolites's *History* records multiple examples of Greek political activity that runs counter to the author's thesis that the only true Romans are those who support the Nicaean/Palaiologan claims.

Perhaps even more surprising in the passage about Henry's deference to indigenous religious independence is Akropolites's emphasis on the commitment of the Constantinopolitan community to their Orthodox identity. Given his own support for union with the Latin Church, it is intriguing that he would provide such a positive gloss on a series of events that invert his personal investments and those of his patron, Michael VIII Palaiologos. Perhaps this unexpected gloss simply reflects his own eventual assessment that Latins adhere to errant teachings (such as the *filioque*), but those teachings are not so problematic that they stand in the way of ec-clesiastical unity.[38] Indeed, it is precisely because passages like those from paragraphs 16, 17, and 22 seem to undermine the political and ideological project developed elsewhere in the text that postcolonial critique provides a means for understanding the internal dissonance of a text designed to narrate the ambivalent sense of identity that is forged by a colonial encounter.

And, of course, the text contains other markers of cultural and political uncertainty that we might expect in a colonial setting. Perhaps the most fascinating is an account of a Byzantine "trial by combat" that seems to reflects a Latin accretion to Nicaean courtly life.[39] That fascinating story is followed by a second Latin-accretion, a trial by "hot irons."[40] Interestingly, it is only the latter, the trial by irons, that Akropolites suggests is both "barbaric" and not part of the authentic Roman tradition.[41]

Like the *Ponemata* of Chomatianos, Akropolites's *History* attests to vari-ous ways in which the Latin Empire uprooted aspects of Byzantine politi-cal and religious life. And while his opinion of the Latins is more positive than Chomatianos, it is not particularly positive. The most obvious dis-tinction between the two authors vis-à-vis the question of the Latins con-cerns the question of sacramental unity—for Chomatianos the Latins are insufficiently Orthodox, and association with them pollutes the Chris-tian body; for Akropolites, the Latins are not so different theologically that the Byzantines should resist sacramental union with Rome, even sub-mission to the Roman pontiff.[42] Because the *History* never speaks about theological questions directly (and it does not cover events after 1261, like the Second Council of Lyon), his discussion of Greek/Latin aristocratic marriage offers valuable evidence of his theological view of the Latin question, at least with respect to the *History*.

For example, in paragraph 15, Akropolites chronicles the way that the Nicaean emperor Theodore I Laskaris successfully arranged marriages for each of his four daughters with various members of the Frankish nobility in the years just after the Latin conquest of Constantinople.[43] Theodore's own second marriage was to an Armenian bride and his third was to the sister of the Latin emperor of Constantinople, Robert.[44] Interestingly, we learn in paragraph 18 that when Robert's own wife died, he and Theodore twice attempted to arrange a marriage with Theodore's third daughter, Eudokia, but this match was deemed uncanonical by the Greek patriarch on the grounds that the two were already of the same "spiritual" family through the marriage of Theodore and Robert's sister.[45]

What is most significant about this latter case is that the intervention of the patriarch to oppose a union between Robert and Eudokia in 1221 indicates that Orthodox officials were perfectly willing to obstruct marriage alliances that were in the diplomatic interests of ruling aristocrats when such marriages were perceived to break canonical restrictions. The fact that none of the other marriage alliances between Nicaeans and Latins chronicled by Akropolites met with ecclesiastical resistance suggests not only that Akropolites viewed these alliances as viable diplomatic opportunities but it also suggests that his view of the possibility of Greek/Latin sacramental union through marriage was likely more commonly held than that of Chomatianos who was inclined to bar Latins from the sacramental community of the Church.[46] To the extent that intermarriage can be understood to represent the most personal and direct comingling between two communities, whether in a colonial setting or any other, Akropolites offers a direct counterexample to those antiunionist Christians, like Chomatianos, who were increasingly determined to identify marriage with Latin Christians as an offense against the community of authentic Christians.

In sum, the *History* of George Akropolites was ostensibly a chronicle of the political fortunes of the rightful inheritors of Byzantine political authority (the Empire of Nicaea) during the period of the Latin occupation of Constantinople. But through his presentation of Latins and Latin Otherness in the *History*, Akropolites was attempting to instruct contemporary and future Greek Christians about the ways that they could and should negotiate the presence of Latins in the East. From his perspective, the

Latins were not going away: They were (and were expected to remain) permanent stakeholders in the Christian East. While Akropolites believed that there were good reasons to be suspicious of Latin political intentions, he did not believe that Latin Christianity posed a threat to Orthodox purity, nor did he believe that Latin religious difference presented sufficient grounds to prevent Greek aristocrats from employing the sacrament of marriage as a diplomatic strategy. In each of these ways, the *History* presents not only different picture of Orthodox Christian identity than Chomatianos, in the wake of 1204, but carefully advocates for the possibility of Orthodox/Catholic unity.

Is There Anything "Postcolonial" about Akropolites's *History*?

In the introduction to this book, I proposed that there is much to gain by reconsidering the history of Orthodox-Catholic difference by treating the Fourth Crusade as a colonial encounter. I observed that it was in the context of the Fourth Crusade, not the Schism of 1054 or any other historical event, that Greek and Latin Christian apologists developed their most hostile caricatures of one another, caricatures that called for and eventually led to full-blown ecclesiastical separation. I proposed that the escalation in polemic was connected to the political, economic, and cultural friction caused by the crusade rather than any new theological argument, insight, or apostasy. Thus far, I have applied the resources of postcolonial critique to the texts under consideration not only because such an analysis illuminates the operative discourses that either authorized the subjugation or the resistance to the Christian Other in the context of a colonial encounter, but also because the texts themselves lend themselves to postcolonial analysis.[47] Thus far, I have not yet fully engaged with the implications of the fact that the subjugated Byzantines were not a typical colonized people—they certainly were not "subaltern" according to the categories of postcolonial critique. To that end, this section considers how George Akropolites's *History* might disrupt some of the very assumptions about colonialism, decolonialism, and postcolonialism with which this book has operated from the outset.

Akropolites's chronicle emerged in the kind of political situation that we might rightly call "postcolonial." Not only was he writing from Constantinople after the crusaders had abandoned the city but his text was purposefully constructed to assert one claim of indigenous political authority over and against another in the sudden absence of the colonizer. But, despite these important contextual elements, the text does not explicitly read as postcolonial. At no point does it describe the Byzantines as any kind of backward or marginalized community, seeking cultural meaning or relevance vis-à-vis a colonial master. And at no point does the text explicitly reveal any kind of cultural, intellectual, or political inferiority vis-à-vis the Latins that must be negotiated in one way or another. Indeed, the rhetorical conceit of the *History* is that it chronicles the unbroken continuity of the Roman/Byzantine political state through its temporary dislocation in Nicaea. To achieve this, Akropolites carefully situates his text within a millennia-long tradition of Roman historiographical writing.[48] In all of these ways, Akropolites reflects a well-entrenched Byzantine model of historical writing that implicitly resists any notion of colonial subjectivity that the Franks may have sought to impose upon them.[49]

What, then, might this mean in terms of seeing the Fourth Crusade as a colonial encounter? Does Akropolites's continuation of the Roman historiographical tradition or his attitude of cultural superiority vis-à-vis the Latins mean that his text will yield misleading insights when put to a postcolonial reading? And, given that George's text is just one of a myriad of Greek texts from the period that employ the discourse of Byzantine political and cultural superiority, might this mean that the effort to interpret the Fourth Crusade through the lens of postcolonial critique is inherently compromised because of the existence of these counterexamples?

Without disavowing the inherent tension that these questions pose, I would like to suggest that there are several reasons that the shadow of Latin colonization is not as far removed from Akropolites's concern as it might otherwise appear. To begin with, there is little doubt that the narrative is designed to authenticate the Nicaean succession of Byzantine political authority. And while the text explicitly acknowledges (and refutes) the counterclaim made by the (pseudo-) Romans of Epiros, it also implicitly accounts for the fact that the Latins had their own legitimate claim to rule Constantinople, Thrace, and the Peloponnese.[50] Akropolites refers to the Latin emperors Henry and Robert as "emperor"[51] and he acknowledges (without censure) that members of the Byzantine aristocracy fight for the Latin Empire against the Nicaeans.[52] Indeed, the chronicle may emphasize the Nicaean/Palaiologan claim of legitimacy over and against that of the Epirotes, but that dispute only existed because of political disruption caused by Latin colonization and the subsequent inability of the Byzantines to coalesce behind a united political resistance. Put another way, the entire narrative emerges in the context of and seeks to respond to the legacy of the Latin Empire of Constantinople.

What is more, as we examined in the previous section, Akropolites's discussion of Latins and Latin difference evinces the profound ways in which elite Greek authors could hold negative attitudes toward the Latins in general but propose very different policy prescriptions for how to deal with them, especially when it came to matters of religion. Akropolites affirms that the cause of Latin/Greek ecclesiastical unity (even submission to the Roman bishop) is a "reasonable" undertaking.[53] He also depicts Nicaean/Latin aristocratic alliances through marriage as one of the most important diplomatic options available to the Laskarid and Palaiologan dynasties—a position that clearly puts him at odds with Byzantine anti-unionists like Demetrios Chomatianos. As *Ponemata* 54 of Chomatianos helps us to understand, there were important Greek intellectual figures who believed that ecclesiological tolerance of Latin difference, as advocated by individuals like Akropolites, was grounds for breaking sacramental unity within communities of Greek Christians. As such, we should not see Akropolites pro-unity policy as one of ecclesiastical indifference nor as a prioritization of politics over theology but rather we should see it as an explicit ecclesiological position that was advanced in a highly contentious context regarding the borders of the Greek sacramental community vis-à-vis Latin Christians. In this way, Akropolites's *History* offers clear testimony to the internal religious dislocation that occurred as a consequence of the Latin occupation of Byzantium.

Even though he never explicitly acknowledged it, Akropolites's *History* marks a transitional moment in Byzantine historiography because of the way in which it accounts for the Western Other in the Byzantine debates about political legitimacy and religious boundaries. In recent years, scholars of Byzantium have been increasingly occupied by questions of identity. Anthony Kaldellis, especially, has forced the field to reconsider many aspects of Byzantine society that had been unchallenged for decades. Was Byzantium an empire or a city-state? Was Christianity a central aspect of Byzantine identity? (Kaldellis is skeptical.) What was the relationship between Byzantium and ancient Hellenism? And so forth.[54] While scholars like Kaldellis, Cameron, Page, and Stouraitis offer a variety of opinions about these matters, they are in near unanimity that the Latin Empire of Constantinople forever scrambled the way that the Byzantines made sense of their own identity. While most of these scholars have not emphasized Akropolites's role in this shifting identity discourse and while many have focused on other innovative elements in the late-Byzantine discourse of identity—especially the return to Hellenistic themes—there is little doubt that Byzantine authors, like Akropolites, would never again be able to engage in a discourse of political or religious identity that did not account for the shadow of Latin Constantinople.

6

THE CHRONICLE OF MOREA

C hapters 1 and 2 examined the ways in which Frankish authors employed Orientalizing and colonial discourse to authorize the attack, looting, and settlement of Christian Constantinople in ways akin to Western European authors of later centuries. Chapter 3 investigated the context and mechanisms by which the papacy and its correspondents de-Christianized the Byzantines as part of a broader strategy to authorize their religious and political subjugation in the context of Latin Empire of Byzantium. Chapters 4 and 5 took altogether different approaches to our subject by looking at the way that the Fourth Crusade fueled internal divisions among Eastern Christians along the lines of whether and to what extent resistance to Frankish rule in the East translated into an exclusion of Latins (and Latin-sympathizing Greeks) from the authentic Church. Our final chapter approaches the colonization of the Christian East in a different manner by assessing the ways in which the prolonged, often peaceful, cohabitation of Franks and Greeks in the Peloponnese led to subtle transformations in the identity and ideology after generations of mixed population under Frankish rule.

Founded in 1205 by William of Champlitte and his vassal, Geoffrey de Villehardouin, the "Principality of the Morea" was one of three crusader vassal states of the Latin Empire, established in 1204.[1] Geoffrey took control of the principality in 1209 when William returned to France and by 1213 his army, which consisted of both Franks and indigenous Greeks, controlled most of the Peloponnese. The Villehardouin dynasty ruled the Morea relatively unchallenged until 1262, when Geoffrey's younger son, William

II, was forced to forfeit three powerful castles in the southeast to a resurgent Nicaean/Byzantine empire.[2] The truce between William II and the Byzantines soon fell apart and William was forced to seek new Western alliances. That support came in the person of Charles of Anjou, who was able to extract personal suzerainty of the principality from William.[3] From 1278–1307, Charles and then his son, Charles II, retained control of Frankish Morea and administered it through a series of appointed baillis. Members of the Villehardouin family continued to be involved in the government of the Morea but a series of contested successions, which pitted various Frankish rulers against one another, greatly diminished the dynasty's influence. Frankish presence in the region continued until the 1430s.

It was in the context of the bitter succession battles and loss of Villehardouin's dynastic prestige of the early 1300s that the text known as *The Chronicle of Morea* first appeared. More than anything else, the author and the subsequent editors sought to intervene in the political quagmires of their day by offering a nostalgic glimpse of a time gone by, when Frankish governance of the Morea had flourished politically, economically, and culturally under the Villehardouins.[4]

Following an overview of the text (its composition, its content, and its historiographical challenges), this chapter will assess *The Chronicle of Morea* from the vantage point of postcolonial critique.[5] Like Robert de Clari and Gunther of Pairis, the author of *The Chronicle of Morea* provides a series of discursive juxtapositions between the Franks and the Greeks. But whereas the chroniclers of the Fourth Crusade typically offered no distinction among the Greeks themselves, *The Chronicle of Morea* offers a far more nuanced exposition of Greek error, almost always attributing their perdition, dishonesty, and effeminacy to those Greeks who align themselves politically with the emergent neo-Byzantine/Palaiologan court. Thus, in the first part of the chapter, we will explore the ways in which Greek error is presented not so much as an ethnic, cultural, or theological construction as it is a political one. Building on this, the second part of the chapter analyzes the ways in which the *Chronicle*'s effort to advance the superiority of the Franks of the Morea was ultimately undone by the weight of its own self-contradictions. I argue that this was, in large part, the consequence of the rapidly changing nature of Moreot identity and ideology in the period, indicative of the transformation of a newly colonized society. In the final section of the chapter, I employ the postcolonial category of hybridity to identify and examine the traces of the transformation contained within the *Chronicle*. Hybridity offers one of most insightful, if contested, categories of postcolonial critique and it is precisely because the *Chronicle* constructs and celebrates a distinctive Frankish Moreot identity that we can assess the means by which the conditions of Frankish settlement in Greece were transformative for those Franks who came to reside there.

The Text, the Textual Issues, and Its Historiographical Challenges

Following a brief prologue that attempts to offer a justification for the crusades as a whole and the siege of Constantinople in particular, *The Chronicle of Morea* provides a detailed (albeit occasionally inaccurate) historical account of the creation of a Frankish feudal state in the Peloponnese of Greece. The narrative begins by explaining how William of Champlitte and Geoffrey de Villehardouin began to subdue the Peloponnese with a mere hundred knights and five hundred footmen in 1205. By and large, this was achieved by offering generous terms to local aristocrats who retained their positions of privilege in exchange for fealty to their new Frankish lords.[6] The majority of the narrative chronicles the reigns of the Villehardouins: Geoffrey (1209–28), Geoffrey's eldest son, Geoffrey II (1228–46), and Geoffrey's second son, William II (1246–78).[7] It attests to the particular structure of the feudal arrangements that the Franks developed in the Morea (initially including twelve but later thirteen baronies, each with their own fiefs), along with a "Grand Court," and distinctive legal system (known as the Assizes of Romania) that combined elements of Frankish and Byzantine law. And while these aspects of the bureaucratic structure are historically significant, most of the *Chronicle* is devoted to narratives of military exploits, honor among soldiers, and the disavowal of treasonous behavior.

While it is well beyond the scope of this chapter to resolve any of the complicated textual questions that continue to animate scholars of the *Chronicle*, it is necessary to identify the core issues. Eight medieval manuscripts of the *Chronicle* survive in four languages. There are five Greek texts as well as one French, one Italian, and one Aragonese.[8] Western scholars had been aware of the Greek version as early as the seventeenth century but the discovery and publication of the French text in 1845 by J. A. C. Buchon has led to a series of debates about the *Chronicle*, not the least of which concerns the language of its original composition.[9]

It is now generally agreed that the original text no longer exists. In all likelihood, someone closely affiliated with the Villehardouin family composed the missing original in the early years of the fourteenth century.[10] It is also generally agreed that it initially only chronicled the years 1204 to 1292, whereas subsequent editions and emendations not only continued the narrative—the Aragonese text brings its story to 1393—but also recalibrated authorial bias according to the idiosyncratic concerns of each editor. In some cases, the difference in ideological commitment of the individual editors led to considerable shifts in outlook and presentation, particularly with respect to the presentation of Byzantine political actors.[11]

Perhaps the most contested issue among scholars of the *Chronicle* is whether or not the original text was composed in Old French or Greek. Harold Lurier, who produced an English translation based upon the Greek verse version (Ms. Havniensis 57), maintained that the original prototype was likely a French composition with his Greek manuscript being its closest and most reliable replica.[12] Teresa Shawcross offers a less definitive conclusion but believes that the original was probably of Greek composition.[13] Whatever the case, the mere fact that scholars are unable to resolve the question testifies to the fact that Frankish Morea was a mixed society, where Franks and Greeks moved between cultural worlds and where language and custom frequently melded together.

Indeed, *The Chronicle of Morea* is a significant artifact of the Middle Ages precisely because it offers one of the most detailed literary examples of a society that thrived in the context of rapid and radical change of its composition and identity. Rather than celebrate the destruction or subjugation of the Greeks as Robert de Clari and Gunther had, the *Chronicle* typically presents the Greeks of the Morea as welcoming Frankish rule and the Franks as integrating and respecting their new subjects.[14] Such a positive assessment of Frankish/Greek cohabitation is historically plausible, but we should not lose sight of the ideological payoff for presenting cohabitation in such a positive light. In the context of the early fourteenth century, the author and subsequent editors would have been keen to show that the Greeks of the Morea preferred Frankish rule to that of the resurgent Byzantines who were increasingly gaining ground in the Morea.[15]

To be sure, there are some obvious chronological errors with the received text. For example, it repeatedly claims that four castles in the Morea continued to resist Frankish rule beyond the reign of Geoffrey I (in actually it was only one castle, Monemvasia).[16] The text claims that the Latin bishops of the Morea excommunicated Geoffrey II for his excessive taxation of their lands (they actually excommunicated Geoffrey I). And, it claims that the Latin emperor of Constantinople, Robert, negotiated a marriage for his daughter with the royal house of Aragon, when in fact, such an arrangement would have only made sense in the fourteenth century (after the arrival of Aragonese troops), not in the 1220s. For our purposes, such anachronisms and errors of fact are not so important as is the epistemic horizon upon which the chronicler and his subsequent editors sought to etch their epic of a thriving Frankish Morea.

Cultural Superiority

Like Robert and Gunther, the author of *The Chronicle of Morea* repeatedly and in multiple ways asserts the cultural superiority of his protagonists, the Frankish ruling class of the Morea. And like Robert and Gunther this typically reflects the militaristic and moral assumptions of a Frankish chivalric code. But a careful analysis of the *Chronicle* reveals important, if subtle, differences, particularly in regard to the juxtaposition between Franks and Greeks.[17] While it is true that the *Chronicle* often speaks of the Greeks in sweeping terms, juxtaposing their deceit and effeminacy to Frankish honor and manliness, a more careful examination reveals that the author is targeting only those Greeks who align themselves with neo-Byzantine political authority (whether it is the resurgent successor states of Nicaea and Epiros or the restored empire under the Palaiologans) against Frankish rule in the Morea.

The most repeated assertion of Frankish superiority concerns honor in warfare.[18] Whereas enemy Greeks are oath breakers, treasonous, and willing to victimize their own people, the Franks respect their oaths and conquer land honorably. Perhaps the most precise expression of this is couched in a defense of the Frankish right to rule the Morea. In fact, the chronicler dramatizes its essential political claim by presenting the moral authorization of Frankish rule as part of a dialogue between Prince William II and the Byzantine *sevastokrator*, Theodore Doukas of Vlachia.[19] When Theodore suggests that the Morea rightfully belongs "by inheritance" to the Byzantine throne and that the Frankish aristocracy should, thus, return to France, William responds that everything he and his family has accomplished in the Morea was achieved with honor and according to the rules of war: "If I, brother, tried to increase my honor, my wealth, and my glory, you ought to praise me, for the man who bears arms ought to increase his wealth and honor, so long as he does not act unjustly, take from his relatives and disinherit those of his body and the friends of his body."[20] In other words, the Villehardouins have obtained the Morea honorably, even gloriously.[21]

Apropos of what we might consider a colonial outlook, the *Chronicle* repeatedly authorizes the seizure and settlement of the Morea by juxtaposing Frankish honor to Byzantine treachery. Indeed, the *Chronicle* opens with a series of stock accusations against the treasonous and oath-breaking Byzantine rulers, which led to the siege of Constantinople and the dishonorable death of their leaders.[22] Explaining the historical context of the emergence of the Frankish Morea, the chronicler offers a somewhat confused excurses on the development of the Byzantine dynastic succession in exile (Nicaea). He presents Michael VIII Palaiologos's elevation to the throne as a series of treasonous and murderous acts and proposes that the Romans (i.e., the Byzantines) are now slaves all over the world because of their deception.[23] Other examples of Byzantine lawlessness appear throughout the text, including the juxtaposition of their "perjury," "faithlessness," and "inability to keep to an oath" to the honorable way in which Charles of Anjou honors his obligations to his in-law, Prince William II.[24]

Perhaps the longest diatribe against Byzantine treachery is reserved for Michael II Doukas, despot of Epiros, who abandoned William II just before the fateful Battle of Pelagonia, which not only led to William's imprisonment but the eventual forfeiture of three Frankish castles in the Morea. Here, the Havniensis manuscript adds an especially blistering censure: "Who will ever hear of this and ever believe a Roman, either for love or friendship or for any relationship? Never believe a Roman in whatever he may swear to you; when he wants and desires to betray you, then he makes you godfather of his child or his adopted brother, or he makes you an in-law so that he might exterminate you."[25] As damning as this statement is, it is important to note that no matter how critical of the Greeks the original author and his subsequent editors may have been, the accusations of Greek perfidy/treachery are not universally applied to all Greek-speaking Christians. Rather they are directed against those Greek aristocrats who represented a political threat to Frankish rule in the Morea, typically the leaders in Nicaea (Constantinople after 1261), Epiros, and a small handful of Moreot archons who switched their allegiance to the Byzantines.[26]

A second way in which *The Chronicle of Morea* frequently affirms the cultural superiority of the Franks over and against the Byzantines is through a juxtaposition of Frankish courage versus Byzantine cowardice and/or effeminacy. The *Chronicle* consistently presents the Franks as manly men, who prefer to fight face to face or as mounted knights wielding their (phallic) lances. The Byzantines, by deliberate contrast, are said to rely on deception and typically run like women from the battlefield. While much of this juxtaposition relies on well-established tropes like those we examined in Chapter 1,[27] the *Chronicle* does offer a few interesting and original riffs on the well-worn theme.

For example, in one episode purporting to convey a conversation between Byzantine aristocrats after their defeat at the Battle of Prinitsa, one reminds the other that the only way for them to defeat the Franks is to do so with deception and cunning because "one Frank on a horse is worth twenty Romans."[28] He further observes that his colleague should have ordered his archers to aim for the horses, for that is the only way to unseat a Frankish knight. A similar exchange is later put into the mouth of the leader of a band of Turkish mercenaries, who opines that the Romans can never match the Franks with a lance or sword: "Everyone knows it, and it is the truth; in the use of the lance or the sword the Franks are soldiers. But we [i.e., the Turks] were shamed that day because of the Romans and we fled from the battle through no fault of our own."[29] The added insult here is that the chronicler presents Turkish infidels as more courageous and manly than the Byzantines.

In a similar vein, the *Chronicle* repeatedly asserts that Byzantines volley their arrows and then run from the field. What is intriguing about this accusation is that the author simultaneously presents the tactic as shameful and effective. Nowhere is this double meaning more on display than in the description of the fateful Battle of Pelagonia, which weakened the principality more than any other event. According to the chronicler, the *sevastokrator* ordered his archers to fire into the scrum, even though his own mercenaries were in the midst of it.[30] He may have killed his own soldiers, but the decision carries the battle. In some ways, the effectiveness of the tactic seems to compensate for its unmanliness. Indeed, in a later section of the text, Prince William II advises Charles of Anjou that he should employ the deceptive tactics of the Byzantines when he confronts the Germans. In sum, even though the *Chronicle* typically employs courage and manliness as attributes that affirm the cultural superiority of the Franks, which in turn authorizes them to rule the Morea, the text also reveals a latent appreciation for the effectiveness of military tactics that would not otherwise be considered "manly" according to Frankish chivalric traditions.

One additional way in which the chronicler attempts to assert the cultural superiority of the Frankish ruling class in the Morea with respect to military bravery is to remind the reader that while the Franks are able to enlist loyal and honorable knights of both Frankish and Greek origin, the Byzantines must rely on multiple contingents of Turkish, Cuman, Persian, Slavic, and Hungarian mercenaries. It is certainly true that the Byzantines employed a large number of mercenaries, but it is also true—as the *Chronicle* recognizes—that the Franks of the Morea also hired Turkish soldiers. The notion that the Byzantines would have the cash on hand to pay so many mercenaries potentially plays into the preexistent Orientalizing narrative of Byzantium as a wealthy but morally bankrupt society that lacks the conviction and means to fight for itself. For the chronicler, the Franks of the Morea are able to achieve more with less, which reinforces the narrative of Frankish superiority and the right to rule the Peloponnese.[31]

A final aspect of the *Chronicle*'s presentation of Frankish cultural superiority concerns the role of religious difference. One of the most significant features of the *Chronicle* is that it says so little about religious conflict, especially with regard to the Greeks of the Morea.[32] Rather, the chronicler acknowledges that the Greeks who accepted Frankish rule in the Morea were permitted to retain their religious traditions.[33] He also notes that William II not only endowed monasteries for the Franks but also for the Greeks, and at the time of his death, he took measures to insure that they would be protected and independent in perpetuity.[34] We might interpret these episodes not only as an indication that the chronicler and the Villehardouins themselves saw the squabbles between Eastern and Western Christians as having little genuine significance but also that they viewed a minimization of religious difference to be a key component of their plan to govern an integrated Moreot society.

So while it is clear that the *Chronicle* generally minimizes religious difference, it is worth noting that it does, at times, employ religious difference as a way to undermine the credibility of the Villehardouins' Byzantine rivals. For example, as the author establishes the justification for the siege of Constantinople in 1204, he notes that the Byzantines claim to be the only true Christians and routinely disparage the faith of the Franks. In response, the chronicler lists a series of Greek theological errors.[35] It is intriguing, given the chronicler's typical lack of interest in theological difference, that this particular discussion of Byzantine theological error is more extensive than anything offered by Robert de Clari, who devoted his entire text to the siege of Constantinople.[36]

One of the more conspicuous accusations of Byzantine theological error is their supposed willingness to entertain Turks: Byzantine rulers negotiate with Turkish rulers, they employ Turkish soldiers, and they show no concern for being in the presence of Turkish infidels. The issue is identified for the first time in the opening salvo of Byzantine theological error in 1204, but it is also repeated later and with more frequency than any other theological problem.[37] For example, when the Franks and Byzantines are at war with one another during the 1260s, the chronicler takes particular issue with the Byzantines' Turkish mercenaries who, "because they have no respect for religion," burn Latin-rite monasteries and everything else in their wake.[38] Given that the text recognizes that William II also employed Turkish mercenaries to burn villages and slaughter defenseless enemies, the chronicler's attempt to disparage the Byzantines by their association with the Turks is just one of many self-contradictions contained in the text.

Why did the chronicler present the association with the Turks as one of the most problematic of the Byzantine theological errors? In part, no doubt, this line of condemnation simply reflects a recurrent theme of crusader discourse, which authorized Western aggression on the basis of the sacrilege of Muslims. But we might also consider the way that the *Chronicle* uses association with Turks as a part of deliberate strategy to delegitimize the Byzantine political class as a kind of proto-orientalization. By placing the Byzantine ruling class so comfortably among infidels, the chronicler not only presents the political enemies of the Villehardouins as treacherous and effeminate but he also subtly suggests that the Palaiologans, not the Franks, are the foreigners, which therefore negates any claim that they might make to rule the Morea. By emphasizing the foreignness of the Palaiologans, the chronicler not only offers an implicit explanation for why Greek subjects support the Villehardouins, but also seeks to show why the Palaiologans are not legitimate rulers of a neo-Byzantium.

The Fissures in the Master Narrative of a Frankish Morea

Despite the efforts of the original chronicler and his subsequent editors to demonstrate that the Villehardouins were the rightful rulers of the Morea on the basis of their military, political, and cultural superiority, *The Chronicle of Morea* contains a surprisingly large number of internal fissures that appear to belie the very image of strength and superiority that the text seeks to convey. Indeed, the *Chronicle's* repeated affirmations of Frankish nobility (military prowess, chivalric honor, etc.) are undone by many of the narrative episodes it recounts. Incorporating the resources of postcolonial critique not only helps to identify but also to explain some of these incongruences because, rather than viewing these disconnects as an error of composition, it helps us to see these fissures as evidence of a broader rupture of Frankish ideological assumptions that were the consequence of prolonged experience in the East.[39]

Frankish Honor

Perhaps the most surprising of the ideological fissures in the *Chronicle* concerns the very honor, trustworthiness, and adherence to oaths that the Frankish chivalric ruling class value. On this score, the means by which Geoffrey de Villehardouin assumed control of the Morea is particularly surprising. According to the *Chronicle*, when William of Champenois returned to France in 1209, he appointed Geoffrey as his temporary bailli—William's plan was to send a younger relative who would take control of the colonial outpost. According to the text, the Moreot archons (both Frankish and Greek) loved Geoffrey so much that they convince him to take the suzerainty of the land of the Morea for himself.[40] The problem, of course, is that he had both sworn an oath of fealty to William as lord and specifically promised to turn over control of the Morea once William's designate arrived to claim it.[41] To overcome this moral dilemma, the *Chronicle* offers a series of fanciful episodes detailing the way that Geoffrey and his coconspirators employ deception to delay the arrival of William's cousin, Robert. According to the narrative conceit, if Robert failed to arrive and claim his title within one year of Geoffrey's appointment, then the Champenois family's claim to suzerainty would lapse and Geoffrey would gain sole control of the Morea. The narrative reaches its climax in a meeting of Peloponnesian aristocrats and bishops who declare that Robert arrived fifteen days too late, thereby forfeiting his claim of suzerainty to Geoffrey.[42]

What is, perhaps, most striking in this account is the way that the *Chronicle* seeks to present the adjudication of the claim of suzerainty according to the standards of Frankish law and justice. At no point does Geoffrey attempt to establish his rule through force. His victory is handed to him by the decision of a council of vassals and prelates. Indeed, this is just one of several examples where the *Chronicle* asserts the sovereignty of a council of lords in the Morea. And, yet, the entire affair is one that is predicated upon the betrayal of an oath and an effort to disinherit the rightful suzerain. According to the norms of Frankish chivalric behavior— standards repeatedly affirmed throughout the *Chronicle*—Robert's claim to rule the Morea should have been recognized by everyone, especially Geoffrey.

Another dramatic break in the narrative of Villehardouin honor follows soon after the first and concerns the deception and dishonesty employed by Geoffrey II (Geoffrey I's eldest son) to abscond with the daughter of the Latin emperor of Constantinople and to make her his wife despite her father's intentions.[43] According to the *Chronicle*, the Latin emperor Robert had arranged a marriage between his daughter and the king of Aragon.[44] As the young woman travelled from Constantinople to Spain, she stopped at the Peloponnesian castle of Pondikos. Geoffrey, who happened to be in the area, offered the princess hospitality. After a few days' time, Geoffrey's counselors approached him with the idea that he should pursue a marriage with the woman, not only because she was young and beautiful but because it would be of great advantage to the Franks of the Morea for him to be married to the Latin emperor's daughter and to continue his biological line through her.

The episode offers another reminder of the link between sexual conquest and colonial conquest in crusader literature, but the primary narrative purpose of the story is to explain how the Villehardouin family received its honorific title in the Morea vis-à-vis the Latin emperor. Indeed, when the emperor begrudgingly acknowledges the wedding, he grants Geoffrey the title "Prince of the Morea" in exchange for Geoffrey's fealty. It is noteworthy that the chronicler chose to dramatize that political arrangement by having one of his heroes abscond/rape the unnamed daughter of the Latin emperor. And there remains a profound irony embedded in its authorization in that the story is introduced, and the idea of a marriage put forth, in the context of Geoffrey needing to produce a biological heir. But just a few pages later, the *Chronicle* acknowledges that Geoffrey II still did not have an heir by the time of his death in 1246. In other words, the chronicler attempts to justify Geoffrey's unchivalric seizure of an aristocratic woman on the grounds that it was necessary for the line of succession in the Frankish Morea, but he ultimately acknowledges that this proved unsuccessful.

Like the story regarding Geoffrey I's acquisition of authority in the Morea, this episode slights traditional Frankish expectations of political and chivalric honor, in part, so as to advance a model of governance wherein the ultimate sovereignty lies not with the suzerain himself but with his counsel of advisors. Not only is the decision to pursue the woman initiated by Geoffrey's advisors, but the emperor himself seeks the counsel of his own advisors when he first receives the news of his daughter's fate. While it is true that the Frankish feudal structure acknowledged the importance of a lord building consensus among his vassals, it is through these and other dramatized elements of the *Chronicle* that we see how the dynamics of the Frankish Morea (and Latin Constantinople) had subtly shifted political structures to the realities of ruling Christians in former Byzantine lands.

An additional way in which the *Chronicle* contains an inherent break in its presentation of Frankish nobility concerns the ways in which the Byzantines routinely reject the Frankish right to govern the Peloponnese. The issue comes to a dramatic head after the Battle of Pelagonia where an imprisoned William II engages in dialogue with his captor, the *sevastokrator* of Thessalonika, Theodore, concerning Frankish presence in the Morea. Theodore, no doubt reflecting the core position of the Byzantine ruling class, asserts that the Franks have no claim in the Morea because it belongs to the Byzantine royal family as a "dominion of inheritance."[45] Theodore's position is repeated by the Byzantine emperor, Michael VIII Palaiologos, who engages William in a subsequent, but ultimately fruitless, debate.

The charge against Frankish rule in the Morea appears once more in the mouth of the Byzantine grand domesticos after he is captured during the Battle of Makry-Plagi. In this episode, the grand domesticos declares:

[All] men know, and it is the truth, that the land of the Morea is not yours by rightful inheritance; you hold it by despotic force, but it is the patrimony of the *basileus* of the Romans; and with rebellious sinfulness your forefathers came and seized the land of the *basileus* and you hold it. Behold how your murdering and sin brought you into the hands of my holy lord, the *basileus*; and if he had wished, as *basileus*, he had the power to do whatever he wishes to you at that time. But he is very merciful and Christian to all men; with honor he released you from prison, with agreements he released you, and you swore him an oath that you would never attack him and his troops with arms; and he made you a relative by baptism that your friendship might be strengthened.[46]

William, of course, responds to these accusations by asserting that his family obtained the Morea honorably through the rules of war and conquest (i.e., in 1204) and that it rightly passed to him through the dominion of inheritance. What is perhaps most significant about all of this is that the *Chronicle* preserves a Byzantine political invective against Frankish rule in the Morea that turns primarily upon a French chivalric code of honorable conduct—the dominion of feudal inheritance. The inclusion of an argument against Frankish rule, predicated upon Frankish principles, reveals a specter of doubt about Frankish governance in the Morea in the very document that, more than any other, functions as the de facto justification for the very existence of the Frankish Morea.

Perhaps the most unsettling challenge to the honor and respect that the Villehardouins are projected to command of their subjects concerns the treasonous behavior of one of William II's most capable and dependable vassals, the lord of Karytaina, Sir Geoffrey. Sir Geoffrey was William II's nephew and served as a heroic colleague at arms for decades. Like William, he was captured and imprisoned by the Byzantines at the Battle of Pelagonia. But after their release, when war resumes, Sir Geoffrey initially aligns himself with Michael Palaiologos despite his ties of family, vassalage, and cultural ancestry to William. The chronicler dramatizes Sir Geoffrey's spiral of depravity with a lengthy aside about how he absconded with the wife of one of his own knights and traveled with her to southern Italy under the pretext of a religious pilgrimage.[47] Eventually, Sir Geoffrey comes to his senses and returns to William's side, but the episode offers yet another fissure in the master narrative of the honor and nobility by which the Franks govern the Morea.

Military Prowess

The second major way in which the *Chronicle* includes content that appears to conflict with the ideology it advances is that of the Frankish military prowess and valor in war. Typically, the *Chronicle* presents the Franks as being far superior to their opponents in terms of military talent and tactics. For example, they repeatedly carry the field despite being outnumbered. And, as noted, even their enemies acknowledge that no one can match a Frank with the sword or lance, especially when he is mounted on a horse. Despite the frequency of these conceits, which underline the ideological justification for Frankish dominion of the Morea, the *Chronicle* also indicates several ways in which the prolonged exposure to the military and political realities of the East require the Franks to modify their approach to warfare in ways that compromise previous assumptions of what constitutes military honor.

Perhaps the most obvious example concerns the way in which the chronicler condemns and then endorses deception as a military tactic. In order to explain William II's disastrous defeat at the Battle of Pelagonia in 1259, the author employs two strategies to deflect from the possibility that William was outmatched. First, he dramatizes both the scope and the last-minute nature of Michael II of Epiros's defection to the Byzantines. But given that the *Chronicle* celebrates William's courageous and honorable decision to continue the fight, we must conclude that the text's core justification lies elsewhere.[48] Indeed, as we noted in an earlier section, the chronicler emphasizes the extent to which the Byzantines defeated William through the dishonest and unmanly decision to fire arrows at the Frankish horses and that they continued their volley of arrows despite the fact that their own troops were in the midst of a scrum with the Frankish knights.[49] Such an unambiguous condemnation of dishonorable tactics would appear to be at odds with later passages in the *Chronicle* that not only have William encouraging Charles of Anjou to employ deception "like the Turks and Romans," but also have him developing the precise strategy by which an opponent is deceived and then trapped.[50]

A surprising aspect of this apparent inconsistency is that the *Chronicle* makes plain the connection between geography and the concession of principle. Indeed, William tells Charles that this is the way one fights in "Romania" (i.e., the East). And, as an indication of just how slippery that slippery slope had become, Charles responds to William's suggestion by noting "there is not a thing today in the existing world, either slyness or cunning or any cleverness, that I would not commit against my enemy, so long as I defeated him and seized his dominions."[51] In effect, the *Chronicle* acknowledges the concession of military honor to unbridled political ambition and lust for power.

Another dramatic break between the ideology of Frankish military honor and the realities of Moreot warfare concerns the use of mercenaries. One of the ways that the *Chronicle* advances a theory of Frankish superiority is to emphasize that the Villehardouins are able to recruit strong and effective armies from the lands of their domain, men of both Frankish and Greek origins. As noted, this ability to command respect and allegiance of the Moreots is juxtaposed to the Byzantines who must purchase the support of their soldiers. But in a surprising twist, just before the Battle of Makry-Plagi, a battalion of Turkish mercenaries abandons the Byzantine grand domesticos (for lack of payment) and then offers their support to William, who eagerly accepts them.[52] Not only does this turn of events undermine the credibility of the chronicler's accusation that the Byzantines must rely on foreign troops, it also compromises the critique that Byzantines are illegitimate because they associate with Turkish infidels.

The story of the Turkish mercenaries offers an interesting example of the porous cultural, political, and ideological borders that exist in a frontier, colonial society. More than anything, the chronicler employs the episode to slight Byzantine honor—not only do they fail to keep their promises to their soldiers, they are shown to be less courageous than infidels. But the continuation of the story of the Turks reveals further gaps in the master narrative of Frankish military honor. For example, when a community of Moreots rebels against William, the prince orders his Muslim soldiers to slaughter its inhabitants and to burn their fields.[53] This is precisely the kind of behavior that the *Chronicle* had earlier criticized the Byzantines for performing.

Beyond the ideological compromises regarding military honor that the Franks conceded in order to retain control of the Morea, the chronicler also struggles to account for two of the most alarming developments that befell the Villehardouin dynasty during the reign of William II: the concession of the castles of Monemvasia, Mistra, and Grand Maine to Michael Palaiologos and the forfeiture of suzerainty of the Morea to Charles of Anjou. Concerning the former, the *Chronicle* repeatedly celebrates the construction (Mistra and Grand Maine) or conquest (Monemvasia) of these castles, which in many ways represent the zenith of Villehardouin power and courtly culture. Their forfeiture to the *basileus* evinces a rupture in the narrative of the very Villehardouin power that the *Chronicle* was designed to celebrate.[54]

The author devotes considerably more attention to Charles of Anjou and the diplomatic arrangement that would lead to the end of the Villehardouin dynasty. The most dramatized aspects of this story are designed to emphasize that Charles is a king and that the marriage between William's daughter and Charles's son brings great honor to the Villehardouins and the Morea. The arrangement is also set in the context of the superiority of the Frankish "race" and the potential stability that the arrangement will offer for the future of Frankish Morea.[55] But lurking in the shadows of the entire narrative is the unavoidable fact that Frankish fortunes in the Morea are in steep decline primarily because they are no longer able to defend their territory against the resurgent Byzantines.[56] The arrangement with Charles constitutes the end of Villehardouin sovereignty and the beginning of the end of the Frankish Morea.

Colonial Hybridity

The Chronicle of Morea has long been studied as one of the most important documents for the study of the interaction between the crusaders who chose to reside permanently in the East and the local populations who lived under their rule. One of the most important aspects of the *Chronicle* is the way that it—and supposedly the Franks as a whole—accepts Greek/Latin religious difference and makes virtually no effort to impose Latin Christian teaching upon the indigenous population. The *Chronicle* is also celebrated as an example of Frankish courtly and cultural life that was transposed to the Morea. In the final section of this chapter, I will analyze some of the ways in which the interaction between Franks and Greeks and the life of the Franks in Greece evince a cultural and political "hybridity."

When applied to political, economic, religious, or political strata, "hybridity" is generally taken to convey a new transcultural form that arises in a cross-cultural context.[57] In the realm of postcolonial studies, it was first employed as counterevidence to the claim of cultural purity in essentialist theory. For example, postcolonial critics apply the category of hybridity to describe the inability of the colonized to adapt to the cultural or intellectual forms of the colonizer without altering those forms in some way. For scholars like Homi Bhabha, the new altered form, a hybrid form, always carries a trace of colonial resistance. But scholars have further maintained that hybridity exists within colonial discourse itself, within the very master narrative of cultural and political hegemony that the colonial power employs as its self-authorization.[58] As we will see, *The Chronicle of Morea* not only conveys but relies upon hybridity as a way to advance its nostalgic evocation of Villehardouin rule in the Morea.

One of the most obvious ways that we see hybridity in the *Chronicle* is through the appropriation and application of Greek terminology to convey the ideas and ideals of a mixed feudal society. On this score, perhaps nothing is more illuminating than the repeated use of the Greek word "archon" as a substitute for a feudal lord.[59] In most cases, the *Chronicle* applies the term to those Greek aristocrats who entered into feudal alliance with the Franks and, typically, remained loyal to them.[60] But the chronicler also applies the term to Frankish vassals in the Morea[61] and even to the vassals of William Champenois who reside in France.[62] The chronicler appropriates additional Byzantine terms to describe political appointments with the Frankish administration, such as *logothete*, which served in the administration of William II.[63] And the chronicler's appropriation of the Greek term "hamotsoukin" (a Byzantine-style drinking party) to refer to a lengthy festivity that included a jousting tournament offers another example of linguistic hybridity.[64]

Perhaps more significant than the linguistic hybridity that exists in the *Chronicle* are the performative examples, which illuminate the many ways in which the Franks of the Morea—whether consciously or not— appropriated the rituals and gestures of the Byzantine nobility in their governance of the region. As in Robert de Clari's text, the *Chronicle* describes the coronation of the first Latin emperor of Constantinople, an event that shows the crusaders meticulously imitating the rituals of the Byzantine court, including the coronation ceremony, the public confirmation of the emperor, his dress, and his title.[65] But other episodes offer even stronger indicators of a discursive apparatus that reflects genuine hybridity. For example, when Geoffrey II lays on his deathbed and asks his brother (the future William II) to establish a monastery where they might create a family crypt and invest the institution with a sufficient number of monks to pray for the family, he does so with language and ideas that directly reflect Eastern Christian prayer rituals for the dead.[66] Indeed, the dying Geoffrey notes, "and see to it, good brother, that the monastery has psalters and liturgists, and that they have their livings, so that they may commemorate us unto the ages of ages." This is a clear reference to the Orthodox funeral service.[67] Further examples note that the rulers of the Frankish Morea speak Greek and employ the "Roman kiss" when they encounter Byzantine peers.[68]

The *Chronicle* not only attests but actually celebrates the fact that the Frankish Morea is a mixed society, where Franks and Greeks are fully intertwined under the leadership of the Villehardouins. One obvious example of this integration is the composition of the army. From the first decade of the thirteenth century, Greek archons and their subordinates were incorporated into the army and its feudal structure. The princes of the Morea rely on their Greek vassals for advice and courage as often as their Frankish counterparts.[69] Even at the fateful Battle of Pelagonia, Greeks of the Morea are said to have remained loyal to their prince. In fact, in William's prebattle speech, he treats his Greek soldiers as equals and distinguishes Moreot solidarity at arms to the motley crew of mercenaries assembled by their enemies.[70] The chronicler is so well disposed to the cultural mishmash that constitutes the Frankish Morea that he endorses the decision of Turkish mercenaries to convert, marry, and establish permanent households in the Peloponnese.[71]

For all of these positive assessments of Frankish/Greek cohesion, it is also clear that the halcyon days of Greek loyalty to Frankish rulers had passed by the time of the *Chronicle*'s composition. As Shawcross notes, after William II's defeat at the Battle of Pelagonia in 1259, many Greek archons began to develop contacts and allegiances on both sides of the Frankish/ Byzantine frontier.[72] Each manuscript version of the *Chronicle* presents these individuals as traitors, with the Havniensis manuscript offering the most hostile view. But as we have seen, even the loyalty of the Frankish vassals to the Villehardouin dynasty was tested once a resurgent Byzantine power established a foothold in the Morea. And, as Shawcross notes, Peloponnesian identity remained a contested category into the fifteenth century.[73] It is precisely for reasons such as these that the apparatus of postcolonial critique offers such an important set of resources for analyzing a text as complex as the *Chronicle*.

In Chapter 4, we examined the category of hybrid children—and from it the hybrid sacramental family—as a perceived threat to the boundary of an authentic Christian community. *The Chronicle of Morea* discusses several unions between Frank and Greek aristocrats and the children that issue from them. In most cases, the author, like George Akropolites, presents these pairings as a legitimate means to establish lasting diplomatic relationships between various political factions. It also describes the provocative story that Michael Palaiologos and William II sealed their truce in 1262 with the sacramental bond of baptism—William served as godfather for one of Michael's children.[74] Clearly the Frankish Morea was a place where the production of hybrid children and sacramental celebration of the key moments in life (baptism, marriage, and funeral) were sites of intense cultural infusion and transformation.

Throughout this chapter I have maintained that there are a number of interpretive benefits to viewing *The Chronicle of Morea* as colonial discourse. The *Chronicle* advances a narrative of Frankish superiority but also contains a stunning number of internal fissures that appear to undermine the very ideology that it seeks to advance. Those potential inconsistences are made more legible if we situate the *Chronicle* within a colonial context where ideas, ideologies, and identities were constantly shifting. In other words, we should not think of the text as failing to present a cohesive narrative of Frankish superiority so much as we should understand that the text is attempting to address the rapidly changing nature of Moreot society in the early fourteenth century by presenting a vision of colonial harmony under the supervision of the Villehardouins, who had the foresight and conviction of conscience to adapt to the realities of an Eastern Christian world where religious and cultural difference did not preclude peaceful and constructive coexistence. To be sure, such a vision was nostalgic, perhaps even imaginary. It likely did not reflect the full scope of the challenges that the Franks of the Morea experienced. But when we compare the *Chronicle* to other texts that were produced in the context of the Fourth Crusade, we find an author and subsequent editors who were more hopeful about the possibility of coexistence than we find elsewhere, including, of course, many narratives in our own day.

CONCLUSION

I began this book with the explicit recognition that I was undertaking an extended thought experiment. I asked the reader to consider with me how treating the Fourth Crusade as a colonial encounter might alter our interpretation of Orthodox/Catholic hostility, which first took its mature form in that context. For those texts that supported the crusades, I considered a number of questions in this regard: How did these texts authorize the colonization of Byzantium and subsequent engagement in the Greek East? How did they present the Christian Other in the context of such an encounter? How important was religious difference for the authorization of violence, settlement, and resource extraction? How did the vicissitudes of Latin power in Byzantium impact the presentation of Greek Christians and new authorizations for violence against them? How did the prolonged experience of Frankish/Greek interaction alter these views? Similarly, how did the prolonged exposure to Greek Christianity transform notions of Frankish identity in its Christian and broader cultural manifestations?

I also, of course, examined Eastern Christian texts from the same period and similarly interpreted those texts through the lens of a colonial encounter. I examined statements about Latin Christians (as well as statements about other Greek Christians who held favorable views of Latins) in order to understand the ways in which the experience of subjugation at the hands of Western armies not only led to new condemnations of Latin Christian teaching but also introduced sharp fractures within the Greek community. I observed that it was in this context that some Greek

123

Christians first began to exclude other Greek Christians from the sacramental community on the basis of their association with Latin Christians. But I also noted that the effort to impose sacramental restrictions was more aspirational than enforceable and that the desire to impose these restrictions was just one of many Greek responses to Latin Christians in Byzantium.

In addition to setting an interpretive gaze upon the Fourth Crusade from the vantage point of a colonial encounter, this book has proposed at various stages that some of the theoretical insights of the scholarly apparatus known as postcolonial critique illuminate key aspects of our texts. I have argued, for example, that Latin Christian statements about Greek Christianity and Greek Christians functioned largely as a construct of the Western Christian imagination. As such, those statements offer intriguing insights into a Western Christian *mentalité* but little in the way of a reliable accounting of Eastern Christian thought or practice at the time. I also explored the connection between colonialism and sexuality, not only in terms of the ways in which Western authors used examples of sexual domination and homoerotic innuendo to narrate their ascendency over Eastern Christians but also with respect to the ways in which multiple authors were forced to deal with the reality of Frankish/Greek marriage and the production of mixed-race children in the wake of the colonization of Byzantium. As I observed in Chapters 4 and 5, Greek authors offered radically divergent reactions to this situation, indicating the extent to which Frankish settlement in the East produced different (community-dividing) responses among Greek Christians.

In Chapters 3 and 6, especially, I offered extended engagements with some of the more complex insights of postcolonial scholarship in an effort to understand the unique dimensions of the texts under consideration. In Chapter 3, I turned to Homi Bhabha's notion of "ambivalence," which emphasizes an inherent reality/desire split in colonial discourse, to explain the gaps or dissonances in papal correspondence, particularly as they relate to the assertions of papal authority vis-à-vis Greek Christians. In Chapter 6, I engaged the postcolonial concept of hybridity to analyze the ways in which Greek terms, customs, and even religious practices were gradually appropriated by the Frankish aristocracy that ruled the Peloponnese. Hybridity is an especially pertinent analytic framework because it helps us to understand both the slippages and desires that are often encoded within colonial writing, revealing the subtle ways in which the colonizing community is itself transformed by the encounter with the colonized. In both chapters, I argued that these insights help us to make sense of the apparent self-contradictions contained within crusader texts, precisely because those insights illuminate the contested ideological underpinnings of colonial discourse.

And while I hope that all of these observations and arguments will resonate with respect to the individual texts under consideration, I have not yet proffered a sustained argument for why interpreting the Fourth Crusade as a colonial encounter usefully recalibrates our understanding of the rapid escalation of Orthodox/Catholic animus that occurred during the thirteenth century. Indeed, one might respond to the previous chapters by noting that scholars of Byzantium and scholars of Orthodox/Catholic history have long-since identified the Fourth Crusade as a pivotal moment in the history of Orthodox/Catholic disintegration. Why, some might ask, do we need to view the crusades as colonialism per se in order to chart the history of Orthodox/Catholic estrangement? And why do we need the theoretical resources of postcolonial critique to explain something we already know?

To answer these questions, I begin with the historian's first principle: Context matters. The Fourth Crusade was not simply an episode of medieval warfare; it was not simply an event of political opportunism; nor was it simply an example of conquest and plunder. To be sure, it was all of these things; but from the perspective of Christian history it was also much more. And it is precisely this "more" that we need to interrogate if we wish to interpret adequately the texts that were produced to narrate, justify, and/or condemn actions and responses related to the Fourth Crusade.

The siege of Constantinople and the formation of the Latin Empire of Byzantium, which followed from it, completely transformed the way that the papacy and many elite Western churchmen viewed the possibility of Greek/Latin unity. In the wake of 1204, the reconciliation of the Schism of 1054 was no longer a question for councils or theologians; it was no longer a disjointed argument over papal privilege or the legitimacy of the *filioque*. From a Western Christian perspective, the goal of Christian unity was now to be pursued and maintained through the military and political occupation of Byzantium. Thus, by situating the Latin Empire of Byzantium within the context of premodern colonialism, we better understand the transformation of Western Christian approaches to Christian unification in the wake of 1204. For example, when the initial efforts to force union on papal terms proved unsuccessful, neither Innocent III nor his successors made any effort to return to pre-1204 mechanisms for Christian reconciliation. Instead, the Roman Church doubled down on the colonial occupation of Byzantium by calling for more troops and nonmilitary settlers in the East and—critically—by escalating the rhetorical justification for the subjection of Greek Christians to Latin hegemony. It was precisely this colonial context in which we find the first sustained papal accusations that all Greek are heretics.

While there may be multiple examples of Latin Christian texts in the period before 1204 that accused Greek Christians of a variety of political and theological errors, the discourse of Latin/Greek difference underwent a profound (if uneven) transformation in the wake of the 1204. Texts like Robert de Clari's *Conquest of Constantinople* or Gunther's *Hystoria Constantinopolitana* do more than narrate medieval war and pillage—they authorize the conquest, settlement, and resource extraction of Christian Byzantium. Like Western European colonial texts of a later period, these texts encode a variety of "orientalisms" to make their narratives more enticing, justifiable, and fantastic. And like colonial literature of a later era, they employ sexual conquest and sexual innuendo (including the taboo of homoeroticism) to convey the superiority of Latin power and to fantasize about the conquest of the Christian Other.

By situating these texts within a colonial context, we not only gain a fuller understanding of these dimensions of their narrative, but we also gain a fuller appreciation for the internal slippages, dissonances, and ambivalences that these texts contain. Indeed, it is precisely because of their colonial context that we understand that passages that might otherwise appear as internal contradictions are, in fact, efforts to offer ideological consistency in a context where the very ground of cultural identity is shifting.

I would like to propose, however, that the potentially more important (if less recognized) contextual payoff for investigating the Fourth Crusade and Latin Empire as an episode of colonialism concerns the analysis of Greek texts produced in the thirteenth century. It is only when we situate texts like Chomatianos's and Akropolites's within the context of a colonial encounter that we see the profound ways in which these texts not only function as a response to that encounter but evince deep fractures within Greek Christianity as a result of it. Thus, Chomatianos and Akropolites represent alternative elite voices, searching in their own way to narrate what it means to be Byzantine and Christian in the wake of the devastation of the Fourth Crusade. This devastation is not merely an example of medieval warfare, not merely an example of temporary political chaos, but represents a cleavage in the ideological underpinnings of the Byzantine worldview. The Latin occupation of Byzantium was so destabilizing to the Eastern Christian epistemic outlook that it became virtually impossible for Greek Christians in the centuries that followed to narrate Christian identity or teaching in a way that did not account for the Latin Christian.

While historians of Orthodox Christianity have, for generations, chronicled and analyzed the growing hostility between Greek and Latin Christians in the Middle Ages, there has been little effort to situate or analyze Greek anti-Latin polemic as decolonial or postcolonial discourse. But doing so not only helps us to contextualize and understand the erosion of East/West Christian unity, it also enables us to interpret with more clarity the corresponding chasm within Byzantine ecclesiastical literature between prounion/antiunion campaigns. Indeed, by attending to the colonial and decolonial forces at play, we understand that this "ecclesiastical" polemic, in fact, maps directly onto the historical fracturing of the Greek aristocratic community between those who are and those who are not willing to work within the structures of Latin power in the East. It is only then that we come to understand the profound ways in which the militaristic, political, and economic consequences of the Fourth Crusade directly transformed Orthodox theological and cultural discourse. In the wake of 1204, the very definition of what it meant to be an Orthodox Christian—to be a member of the sacramental community—was now increasingly defined in terms of one's attitudes toward Latin Christians living in the East. And, as we have seen, there were multiple ways in which Greek Christians responded to this situation.

Indeed, one of the most important insights of this study has been the fact that there was no monolithic Greek Christian view of Latins, nor a single Latin Christian view of Greeks. As we noted in Chapter 1, Robert de Clari may have been perfectly happy to authorize the seizure and looting of Constantinople on the basis of Greek treachery and effeminacy, but he had virtually nothing negative to say about the content of Greek theological teaching or practice. This, of course, contrasts sharply with Gunther of Pairis, who authorized the looting of religious treasure on the basis of Greek theological error, and the correspondence of Innocent III and his successors who increasingly called for violence against Greeks and the Latin settlement of Byzantium on the basis of Greek heresy.

Clearly, it is not just the Greeks who held radically opposing views of the proximate religious Other—Latin attitudes toward Greeks could be just as mixed. And it is precisely because they are so mixed that we should understand anti-Greek invectives, like those contained in Gunther's and Innocent's writings, as both evincing internal Latin debates and constituting a sharp ideological position in those debates. Indeed, much of the religious polemic in the wake of the Fourth Crusade was directed at internal audiences (Latin to Latin; Greek to Greek) as a means of justifying broader ecclesiological and cultural interactions/restrictions between Greek and Latin Christians.

Perhaps one of the most surprising things that we learn from these texts is that the boundaries between the Greek and Latin sacramental communities were extremely porous in the lead-up to 1204, despite the Schism of 1054: Robert describes Franks visiting churches in Constantinople; Chomatianos affirms that the Athonite communities are international and co-celebratory; and Innocent's correspondence shows considerable engagement with Greek leaders. Of course, we also learn that the boundary between the Greek and Latin sacramental communities began to harden in the wake of 1204. But the efforts to exclude the Greek or Latin from the sacramental community never reflected a universal position and were most often directed polemically against internal, not external, audiences who failed to see the threat posed by the Christian Other.

Let us further recall that the effort to erect a sacramental boundary between Greeks and Latins after 1204 had little to do with theology. There was no new theological insight; there was no new rejection of a prior orthodoxy. There was very little that is theologically innovative about these sources at all. Indeed, neither Gunther nor Chomatianos offers any fresh accusation in their condemnations of the religious Other that had not been articulated by previous polemicists. And while Pope Innocent III's accusations of theological error may have grown more hostile over time, he also appropriates anti-Greek invectives that predate him and that had been routinely employed to assert papal authority against Greek insubordination. In short, the hardening of the religious boundary between Greeks and Latins, between the Orthodox and the Catholics, that occurred in some circles in the wake of the Latin Empire of Byzantium was the result of a colonial encounter rather than the result of new ecclesiastical factionalism.

Like other colonial encounters, the trauma for Greek Christians was not merely one of political or economic loss but, more importantly, lay in the rupture of ideological assumptions. After 1204, elite Greek Christians could no longer define what it meant to be a Christian, or even a loyal Byzantine, without some recourse to a hegemonic Latin Church. Eastern Christian theology had not changed, nor had its Roman counterpart. But the political, economic, and cultural conditions in Byzantium had changed radically and in ways that profoundly reshaped how Eastern Christians understood what it meant to be a Christian. While they may not have responded to this new situation with a single voice, there is no doubt that they were all forced to respond. And the discourse of Orthodox Christian theology has been profoundly transformed ever since.

In other venues, I have begun to explore the ways in which the legacy of the colonial encounter of the Fourth Crusade continues to overshadow contemporary Orthodox discourse.[1] And, for the Christian who cares about the cause of Orthodox/Catholic unity, there is much in the current analysis that might frustrate her or his optimism for the possibility of reconciliation. But I would like to conclude this study with three reasons why I believe that a careful examination of the Greek/Latin encounter of the thirteenth century might actually offer some cause for hope.

First, as we have just reviewed, Greek and Latin Christians were not nearly as divided prior to 1204 as is generally assumed. Indeed, it is clear that antagonism between the Roman and Constantinopolitan sees, even centuries of smoldering polemical accusations, had not prevented sacramental intermingling between Greek and Latin Christians. There are a multitude of examples to suggest that Greeks and Latins intercommuned and married one another despite the Schism of 1054 and this evidence forces us to differentiate between what the consequences of the schism were in the Middle Ages and what many today falsely assume those consequences to have been. Even though the Fourth Crusade played an instrumental role in the ultimate sacramental separation between the Orthodox and Roman Catholic communions, it did not do so immediately and—as we have seen—there were authors and communities who resisted the call for sacramental isolation for centuries. Indeed, as Kallistos Ware's excellent study of Eustratios Argenti has shown, there is evidence of sacramental comingling between Greeks and Latins well into the seventeenth century.[2]

Second, because the rupture between Orthodox and Catholics that resulted from the Fourth Crusade was primarily the result of political, economic, and cultural alienation rather than the result of new theological developments, the possibility for a theological common ground remains a viable possibility. In the eyes of most medieval Christians, there was nothing theologically insurmountable about East/West theological difference. Even in those settings, like the colonization of Byzantium, where political and cultural conflict gave rise to theological polemic and increasing calls for sacramental isolation, both elite and ordinary Christians continued to cross the Greek/Latin boundary to commune, baptize, and marry with one another. My sense is that this occurred precisely because those who were advocating for sacramental isolation failed to develop theological justifications for that isolation that satisfied those who believed otherwise.

Finally, what we found with respect to the extended encounter of Franks and Greeks in the Peloponnese during the thirteenth century is that these two communities of Christians developed an experience of religious cohabitation, appreciation, and appropriation, even if they remained largely independent of one another. Historically, this coexistence occurred because both the Frankish lords and their Greek aristocratic subjects refused to use religious identity as a means of subordination or resistance. And, what is perhaps most unique in this respect was the extent to which the Frankish and Greek rulers in the Peloponnese largely sought to set their own policies with respect to the Christian Other rather than adhere to the recommendations of Rome or Constantinople or elsewhere. While the experiment of a Frankish/Greek Peloponnese may be something of a historical anomaly, it does challenge a number of our assumptions about Orthodox/Catholic difference and the possibilities for fruitful coexistence in the wake of 1204. And, perhaps, the next experience of an authentic Orthodox/Catholic mutual dependence will first occur in a similar setting, where local leaders prioritize the realities and needs of the local community in all of its messiness rather than adhere to a set of boundaries that exist as much in the imagination as in real experience.

ACKNOWLEDGMENTS

The inspiration and initial ruminations that prompted research for this book were forged in the context of a Fordham faculty "theory group," which has been in existence for nearly a decade and which dedicated several years of reflection to the analytical resources of postcolonial critique. The group is organized by the Orthodox Christian Studies Center at Fordham University and funded by the Dean of Fordham College at Rose Hill. I would especially like to thank Robert Davis, Ben Dunning, Samir Haddad, Brad Hinze, Brenna Moore, and Aristotle Papanikolaou for their long-standing friendship and encouragement of this project.

In the spring of 2013, I had the honor of presenting at a conference honoring the retirement of Elizabeth Clark. It was in that setting that I first proposed the possibility of applying the resources of postcolonial critique to the Orthodox Christian experience during the Fourth Crusade. Subsequent invitations offered additional opportunities to develop and test the ideas reflected in *Colonizing Christianity*. I would especially like to thank the organizers of the Duke conference, along with the monastic community at Bosé, the Marco Institute at the University of Tennessee, and the Department of Religious Studies at Fairfield University for their generous hospitality and helpful conversations. The majority of the research and writing for this book occurred during a full-year sabbatical in 2016, which was generously funded by the Carpenter Foundation and a Fordham Faculty Fellowship.

Perhaps most importantly, I would like to acknowledge the scholars who contributed most directly to this project. Anthony Kaldellis and

David Perry read drafts of the entire manuscript and offered essential suggestions for revision. Several others, including Alfred Andrea, Nicholas Paul, Fr. Alexander Rentel, Norman Russell, and Fr. Patrick Viscuso, provided expert assistance in matters well beyond my competence. Christopher Sprecher supplied draft translations of some of the Greek texts examined in Chapter 4. And Fordham doctoral students Alexander Miller and Jack Pappas, who served as my research assistants, probably spent far more time thinking about the Fourth Crusade than they ever expected when they arrived. Any errors or shortcomings that remain in this book, of course, are my own.

I would also like to acknowledge the long-standing support of and fruitful collaboration with Fred Nachbaur and William Cerbone of Fordham University Press. To all of these communities, colleagues, and friends I offer my heartfelt appreciation.

NOTES

Introduction

1. For an excellent overview of the various ways that scholars have typically understood the crusading movement, see Giles Constable, "The Historiography of the Crusades," in *The Crusades from the Perspective of Byzantium and the Muslim World*, ed. Angeliki E. Laiou and Roy Parviz Mottahedeh (Washington, D.C.: Dumbarton Oaks, 2001), 1–22.

2. For a solid introduction to the general chronology and consequences, see Donald E. Queller and Thomas F. Madden, *The Fourth Crusade: The Conquest of Constantinople*, revised 2nd ed. (Philadelphia: University of Pennsylvania, 2000) and Michael J. Angold, *The Fourth Crusade: Event and Context* (London: Routledge, 2003). For an introduction to some of the scholarly debates about the Fourth Crusade, see Thomas F. Madden, ed., *The Fourth Crusade: Event, Aftermath, and Perceptions* (London: Routledge, 2008).

3. Although I will not delve very deeply into the actual causes of the Fourth Crusade, a recent study by Savvas Neocleous offers some useful food for thought. Neocleous, "Financial, Chivalric, or Religious?: The Motives of the Fourth Crusaders Reconsidered," *Journal of Medieval History* 38 (2012): 183–206.

4. Although the soldiers of the First Crusade had captured and held Jerusalem for nearly ninety years, it was recaptured by the Muslims in 1187 and the Third Crusade had failed to restore Jerusalem to permanent crusader control.

5. Not only did the crusaders repeatedly demand payment for their assistance but they quickly observed that Alexius IV did not have the support of the population. Indeed, Alexius was resented for two reasons: In order to pay the debt owed to the crusaders, he overtaxed the Byzantine aristocracy, even forcing them to melt church gold; and the local population blamed him for bringing so many foreign soldiers into their midst.

6. To be sure, some historians have called into question the reliability of the lone eyewitness Greek account, Niketas Choniates. See, for example, Angold, *The Fourth Crusade*. For a summary of the ways in which the events have shaped the modern Orthodox imagination, see Demacopoulos, "Crociate, Memoria e Perdono Nella Costruzione dell'Identità Cristiana," in *Misericordia e Perdono* (Bose, Italy: Comunità Bose, 2017), 337–54.

7. When the Ottomans took Constantinople in 1453, effectively bringing an end to the Roman/Byzantine Empire, Frankish and Italian forces maintained small colonial outposts in the eastern Mediterranean for hundreds of years.

8. The term "indigenous" is something of a loaded category in postcolonial studies because of its potential connection to a self-conscious identity that is forged in contradistinction/awareness of alien power. As we will discuss in great detail, the "Greek" and "Orthodox" identities of the local population were transformed by the Fourth Crusade and not always in consistent ways.

9. Robert J. C. Young, *Postcolonialism: An Historical Introduction* (Oxford: Blackwell Publishing, 2001), 5 and 15–19. "Colonialism functioned as an activity on the periphery, economically driven; from the home government's perspective, it was at times hard to control. Imperialism, on the other hand, operated from the center as a policy of state, driven by the grandiose projects of power." Young, *Postcolonialism*, 16–17.

10. See, also, his short handbook: Robert J. C. Young, *Postcolonialism: A Very Short Introduction* (Oxford: Oxford University Press, 2003).

11. For an overview of these authors and Young's assessment of them, see Robert J. C. Young, *White Mythologies: Writing History and the West* (London: Routledge, 1990).

12. And, in addition to the crusades, there are several other historical examples of colonialism, especially in Asia, including Qing and Japanese colonialism.

13. On this last point, see John Kantakouzenos, *Histories*, ed. L. Schopen and B. Niebuhr, 3 vols. (Bonn, 1828–32), II.476.17–18. Although scholars of Byzantium and the crusades have examined the colonial character of the encounter, they typically do not apply the methodological apparatus of postcolonial critique beyond the observation that much of the scholarship reflects a kind of orientalism.

14. The Western European criticism of the Fourth Crusade was twofold: It had been an attack on fellows Christians; and it was a distraction from the broader goals of the crusading endeavor. For an overview of the various ways in which colonial discourse attempted to respond to European anticolonial voices, see Young, *Postcolonialism*, 71–112.

15. This is not to say that the crusades were the only models (the English experience in Ireland, for example, may have informed the American expeditions), but only that they were among the models. Young, himself, even indicates the

"crusading religious motives" of the Spanish expeditions to Latin America without ever acknowledging the precedent of the crusades. Young, *Postcolonialism*, 21. What is more, some of the basic economic principles that enabled mercantilism and colonialism in the seventeenth century (such international investment banking) were first introduced to European economies and armies in the context of the crusades.

16. Joshua Prawer, *The Crusaders' Kingdom: European Colonialism in the Middle Ages* (London: Phoenix Press, 1972).

17. See, especially, the work of his student, Ronnie Ellenblum, who has situated Prawer's work within a centuries-long historiographical context of how European historians from the eighteenth century onward viewed the crusades and colonialism. Ellenblum, *Crusader Castles and Modern Histories* (Cambridge: Cambridge Univ. Press, 2009). For a well-informed critique of the crusades as colonialism paradigm, see Marcus Bull who argues that the typical knight who went on crusade did so almost entirely because of local concerns rather than as part of a grand endeavor. Bull, *Knightly Piety and the Lay Response to the First Crusade: The Limousin and Gascony c. 970–1130* (Oxford: Oxford University Press, 1993). See also Corliss Slack, "The Quest for Gain: Were the First Crusaders Proto-Colonists?" in *Seven Myths of the Crusades,* edited by Alfred Andrea and Andrew Holt (Indianapolis: Hacket Publishing Company, 2015), 70–90.

18. Averil Cameron, *Byzantine Matters* (Princeton: Princeton University Press, 2014) and Anthony Kaldellis, *Hellenism in Byzantium: The Transformations of Greek Identity and the Reception of the Classical Tradition* (Cambridge: Cambridge University Press, 2007).

19. For a summary explanation, see, Kaldellis, *Hellenism in Byzantium*, 2–9. For a more explicit examination, see Cameron, *Byzantine Matters*, who observes in her first chapter that assessments of the Christian East (particularly Anglophone ones) remain caught in a dialectical trap between derogatory caricature and exotic romanticism. For example, in the most acute examples predating the twentieth century, Edward Gibbon and Adolf von Harnack lampooned the Christian East as barbaric, petrified, irrational, and barren. Harnack, *History of Dogma* vol. 4, trans. Neil Buchanan (Boston: Little, Brown and Company, 1898), 235. Perhaps an extreme twentieth-century example of the continuation of this attitude among Western Byzantinists is Joseph Gill's account of the Council of Florence, wherein he argues that "irrationality" was the primary reason that the population of Constantinople rejected the opportunity to reunite with Rome. Gill, *The Council of Florence* (Cambridge: Cambridge University Press, 1959). The dialectical trap of which Cameron writes is now, in a sense, inescapable—even in seeking to overcome it, one deliberately engages it and therefore remains tied to it. And, to be sure, historians from Eastern Christian communities are no less embroiled in their own dialectical quagmires, which have also been determined, albeit in different

ways, by the legacy of the colonial encounter that began with the crusades. But it is precisely for these reasons that authors like Bhabha, Spivak, Chakrabarty, and Young are such important resources for thinking about how to negotiate the dialectical and historiographical traps that are now an endemic part of writing about the Christian East. Indeed, although their concerns lay in other parts of the globe, we might characterize their projects as being focused, first and foremost, upon the challenge the scholar faces when attempting to navigate the interstitial legacies of colonial discourse.

20. For example, scholars such as Suzanne Conklin Akbari and John V. Tolan have shown that there was pejorative discourse of Islam and the Orient that not only enabled and sustained the crusading enterprise in the Middle Ages but connected to later European intellectual circles examined by scholars such as Edward Said. Akbari, *Idols in the East: European Representations of Islam and the Orient, 1100–1450* (Ithaca, N.Y.: Cornell University Press, 2009) and Tolan, *Saracens: Islam in the Medieval European Imagination* (New York: Columbia University Press, 2002). The use of postcolonial critique has allowed for profound refinements in medieval studies. For example, whereas scholars used to study the ways in which the "Medieval West" thought of or encountered "Islam," which sloppily employed abstract geographic space as an oppositional category to a world religion, postcolonial critique has drawn attention to the problems inherent in such formulations and further demonstrated the extent to which Islam was always an object "created by Western representational machinery and offered up to the Western gaze." Sharon Kinoshita, *Medieval Boundaries: Rethinking Difference in Old French Literature* (Philadelphia: University of Pennsylvania Press, 2006), 5. Scholars, like David Nirenberg have also appropriated the insights of postcolonial critique to analyze the shifting dimensions of discourse about minorities, especially religious minorities within the confines of Western Europe. Nirenberg, *Communities of Violence: Persecution of Minorities in the Middle Ages* (Princeton: Princeton University Press, 1996). See also Robert I. Moore, *The Formation of a Persecuting Society: Authority and Deviance in Western Europe 950–1250* (Oxford: Wiley-Blackwell, reprinted, 2007).

21. To be sure, Latin and Greek polemic was not invented in the thirteenth century. Accusations of heresy, of Greek effeminacy, and of Latin greed were wellworn by the time the crusaders seized Constantinople and each of our authors who disparaged the Christian Other worked within a discursive framework that was already well in place.

22. In other words, the Orient exists for the West and is constructed by and in relation to the West. Edward Said, *Orientalism* (reprinted New York: Vintage Books, 1994). Said's position has been critiqued by a seemingly infinite number of scholars, including subsequent postcolonial critics. For a balanced account of

what is at stake in Said's categories and his potential misuse of discourse analysis, see Young's examination in *White Mythologies*, 158–80.

23. See, for example, his commentary on Flaubert. Said, *Orientalism*, 186–91.

24. Charis Messis, "Lectures sexuées de l'altérité: Les Latins et identité romaine menacée pendant les derniers siècles de Byzance," *Jahrbuch der Österreichischen Byzantinistik* 61 (2011): 150–71.

25. The path-breaking essay in this respect was that of Gayatri Spivak, "Can the Subaltern Speak?" in *Marxism and the Interpretation of Culture*, ed. Cary Nelson and Lawrence Grossberg (Urbana: University of Illinois Press, 1988), 271–313.

26. Most notably, it was an effort by historians of the Indian subcontinent to tell the history of a colonial society from the perspective of the colonized, i.e., subaltern, population, rather than from the perspective of the colonizers. For an overview of the subaltern studies group, see Young, *Postcolonialism*, 352–59.

27. Although it has been challenged by some theorists, questions surrounding the status and possibilities for the subaltern typically assume a discourse of modernization and advancement that largely take Western European standards for granted.

28. I would especially like to thank Anthony Kaldellis who reminded me of this episode and encouraged me to consider more fully the structural problems of a subaltern Byzantium.

29. In addition to Kaldellis, see Gill Page, *Being Byzantine: Greek Identity before the Ottomans, 1200–1420* (Cambridge: Cambridge University Press, 2008) and, more recently, Yannis Stouraitis, "Reinventing Roman Ethnicity in High and Late Medieval Byzantium," *Medieval Worlds* 5 (2017): 70–94.

1. Robert de Clari

1. Throughout, I rely on the 1936 McNeal translation: Robert of Clari, *The Conquest of Constantinople*, trans. Edgar Holmes McNeal (New York: Columbia University Press, reprinted 2005). All page references reflect pages in the translation.

2. On the changing role of "eyewitness" accounts in medieval French chronicles, see Cristian Bratu, "*Je, aucteur de ce livre*: Authorial Persona and Authority in French Medieval Histories and Chronicles," in *Authorities in the Middle Ages: Influence, Legitimacy and Power in Medieval Society*, ed. Sini Kangas, Mia Korpiola, and Tuija Ainonen (Berlin: De Gruyter, 2013): 183–204. For a brief account of its structuring in Robert's text, see Gérard Jaquin, "Robert de Clari, témoin et contour," *Et c'est la Fin pour quoi sommes ensemble: Hommage à Jean Dufournet: littérature, histoire et langue du Moyen Age*, ed. Jean-Claude Aubailly, 2 vols. (Paris: Champion, 1993), vol. 2, 747–57.

3. Geoffrey received a fiefdom in Greece for his efforts and his family continued as Latin colonists of the Peloponnese for generations.

4. On the lack or paucity of extant descriptions of Constantinopolitan monuments, whether crusader or Byzantine, see Ruth J. Macrides, "Constantinople: The Crusader's Gaze," in *Travel in the Byzantine World: Papers from the Thirty-Fourth Spring Symposium of Byzantine Studies, Birmingham, April 2000*, ed. Ruth J. Macrides (Aldershot, U.K.: Ashgate, 2002), 193–212.

5. The only explicit reference to the author and composition of the text appears in the final paragraph. For a summary of the scholarly discussion regarding the time of Robert's return, see Philippe Lauer, ed. *Robert de Clari, la Conquête de Constantinople* (Paris: Champion, 1924), vii f. See also Edgar Holmes McNeal's introduction to Robert, *Conquest*, 4.

6. On the former, see, for example, Suzanne Fleischman, who observes that Robert's account reflects a "child-like wonder" of the splendors of the Orient. Fleischman, "On the Representation of History and Fiction in the Middle Ages," *History and Theory* 22, no. 3 (1983): 278–310, at 297.

7. Kinoshita observes, "In a society built upon received cultural models, the sack of Constantinople and the wonders encountered there eluded conventional structures of understanding. It is the singularity of this experience that must have moved Villehardouin and Clari to compose their chronicles. As the crusade leaders, victims of their own 'innumeracy,' fall prey to the calculations of the merchant princes of Venice; as Frankish soldiers gape in wonder at the Christian city they have conquered; as feudal loyalties clash with class interests in the division of spoils, Clari's text struggles to preserve but ultimately abandons traditional notions of lineage, Christian piety, and feudal honor." Kinoshita, *Medieval Boundaries*, 139.

8. Kinoshita, *Medieval Boundaries*, 140.

9. Kinoshita submits that the emergence of French prose at this precise point in history constituted a response to the perceived threat of the "truth value" of verse, reflective of the shifting fortunes of the feudal nobility. For Kinoshita, this is because twelfth-century verse articulated the feudal nobility's efforts to resist the cultural hegemony of the Church and its leadership. The emergence of prose at the beginning of the thirteenth century coincided with the creation of the Latin Empire in Constantinople, which drew young aristocrats to the East, thereby making possible the subordination of nobility to the monarchy. This combination greatly diminished the fortunes of the feudal aristocracy. Kinoshita, *Medieval Boundaries*, 11 and 135–38.

10. Indeed, as Kinoshita observes, religion was never the only (and often not the dominant) criterion for the determination of difference. Unfortunately, she does not apply her observations about vernacular and the religious with respect to Orthodox/Catholic difference (for her it is a matter of Christian/Muslim tolerance). Kinoshita, *Medieval Boundaries*, 6.

11. For an account of "otherness" in the contemporary chroniclers of the Fourth Crusade, including Robert de Clari, see Mihaela Voicu, "Le Regard réciproque ou l'(im)possible connaissance de l'autre: à propos de la quatrième croisade," *Revue des sciences religieuses* 80 (2006): 511–32. References are denominated by paragraph, rather than page.

12. Voicu examines the same juxtaposition. Voicu, "Le Regard," paragraph 23–24.

13. See, for example, Odo of Deuil, *De Profectione Ludovici VII in Orientem (The Journey of Louis VII to the East)*, trans. Virginia Gingerick Berry (New York: Columbia University Press, 1948), 42–43 and especially 56–57.

14. Robert, *Conquest*, 48. As I do not read Old French, all references and page citations refer to McNeal's 1936 published translation (reprinted in 2005). Upon restoring Latin soldiers to his garrison, Manuel is said to declare: "Now I command that no one of you be so bold or so hardy as ever to speak again about my largesse or about my loving the French. For I do love them and put my trust in them more than I do in you, and I shall give them more than I have ever given before."

15. Robert, *Conquest*, 60–61.

16. Robert, *Conquest*, 68.

17. Robert, *Conquest*, 72.

18. Robert, *Conquest*, 85–86.

19. Robert, *Conquest*, 85–100.

20. Robert, *Conquest*, 100.

21. Ruth Mazo Karras, *From Boys to Men: Formations of Masculinity in Late Medieval Europe* (Philadelphia: University of Pennsylvania Press, 2002).

22. William Burgwinkle, *Sodomy, Masculinity and Law in Medieval Literature: France and England, 1050–1230* (Cambridge: Cambridge University Press, 2004).

23. Robert, *Conquest*, 87–88.

24. Robert, *Conquest*, 125.

25. For Geoffrey de Villehardouin, the victory of the Cumans is attributable to crusader tactical error.

26. The premier examination of the shifting meaning of terms and the sense of Byzantine identification with the ancient Greeks is Anthony Kaldellis, *Hellenism in Byzantium: The Transformations of Greek Identity and the Reception of the Classical Tradition* (Cambridge: Cambridge University Press, 2007). See also Gill Page, *Being Byzantine: Greek Identity before the Ottomans, 1200–1420* (Cambridge: Cambridge University Press, 2008).

27. It is also conceivable, if unlikely, that crusade-era authors like Robert de Clari might employ the term "Greek" in order to imply rampant homosexuality among the Byzantines. As we will subsequently see, Robert does believe that the Greeks are sexually deviant but he never explicitly accuses them of homosexual behavior, despite the repeated insinuations of effeminacy.

28. See, for example, the way that the expression *lei de Rome* functions in a text like the law book of James of Ibelin (a thirteenth-century jurist in the crusader kingdom of Cyprus), where it clearly serves as a stand-in for the Latin canon law tradition. Text and translation available at http://www.crusaderstates.org/the-book -of-james-of-ibelin.html. My thanks to Dr. Nicholas Paul, who helped me understand the meaning of the expression in Old French and who directed me to James's text.

29. The passage appears during his narration of the first of the political backstories to the crusade, the account of the lone good emperor, Manuel II. Robert, *Conquest*, 48.

30. Robert, *Conquest*, 94.

31. Robert, *Conquest*, 94.

32. Robert, *Conquest*, 122.

33. See Teresa Shawcross, "Re-inventing the Homeland in the Historiography of Frankish Greece: The Fourth Crusade and the Legend of the Trojan War," *Byzantine and Modern Greek Studies* 27 (2003): 120–52.

34. Voicu, "Le Regard," paragraph 26, covers some of the same material with corresponding echoes in Geoffrey de Villehardouin. For an overview of Latin views of Byzantine treachery prior to the Fourth Crusade, see Bunna Ebels-Hoving, "Byzantium in Latin Eyes before 1204: Some Remarks on the Thesis of the 'Growing Animosity,'" in *The Latin Empire*, ed. K. Ciggaar and V. D. van Aalst (Kaastal Hernen: A. A. Bredius Foundation, 1990), 21–31.

35. For example, Alexius IV attempts to set fire to the Venetian fleet under the cloak of night and Murzuphlus attempts to ambush crusaders who have left the camp looking to secure provisions. Robert, *Capture*, 84 and 88–89 respectively.

36. The one possible exception is Isaac Angelos, who follows the reign of Andronicus. But Isaac's reign is a short one, being the victim of a coup orchestrated by his brother, Alexius III. Robert, *Conquest*, 57. On the rise of Isaac and the death of Andronicus, see Edgar McNeal, "The Story of Isaac and Andronicus," *Speculum* 9 (1934): 324–29, which explores the legendary qualities of Robert's story in comparison to those of other contemporary accounts, including Niketas Choniates.

37. Robert, *Conquest*, 50.

38. Robert, *Conquest*, 50.

39. Robert, *Conquest*, 61.

40. Robert, *Conquest*, 76–77.

41. Robert, *Conquest*, 85.

42. Kinoshita identifies a string of twelfth-century texts that had established a literary/political trope of Byzantine duplicity including Odo of Deuil's *De Profectione Ludovici VII in Orientem*, which attributes the failure of the Second Crusade entirely to Byzantine duplicity, and Chrétien de Troyes's *Cligès*, which

describes the Byzantines as politically chaotic, full of rivalry, and fraternal disputes. Kinoshita, *Medieval Boundaries*, 153.

43. Jean Dufournet, *Les Écrivains de la IVe croisade. Villehardouin et Clari*, 2 vol. (Paris: Presses Universitaires de la Sorbonne, 1973) vol. 2, 295.

44. Nevertheless, Kinoshita argues that the text contains certain historical gaps and silences that gesture toward the fragility of the very ideals that, in good faith or bad, will be called upon to justify the string of events that will lead to the crusader capture of Constantinople. Kinoshita, *Medieval Boundaries*, 145–52.

45. Robert, *Conquest*, 49–51.

46. Robert, *Conquest*, 94.

47. Robert, *Conquest*, 75.

48. Robert, *Conquest*, 118.

49. Technically, it was Boris's niece, daughter of John the Vlach. Robert has the details wrong.

50. Robert, *Conquest*, 118–19.

51. To be sure, Western medieval literature has examples (both Christian and pre-Christian) that delight in describing the luxurious clothing of their elites. Thus, Robert's attention to her dress is not, in and of itself, a feature of the text's colonial gaze.

52. Kinoshita, *Medieval Boundaries*, 172.

53. For a popular account of her life, see Paolo Cesaretti, *L'impero perduto: Vita di Anna di Bisanzio, una sovrana tra Oriente e Occidente* (Milan: Mondadori, 2006).

54. Robert, *Conquest*, 79.

55. For Kinoshita's analysis, which goes in a different direction, comparing the hybridity of her children to the Arthurian legends, see *Medieval Boundaries*, 157–58.

56. In addition to Kinoshita's *Medieval Boundaries*, see also Suzanne Conklin Akbari, *Idols in the East: European Representations of Islam and the Orient, 1100–1450*.

57. Robert, *Conquest*, 45.

58. Robert, *Conquest*, 48.

59. Robert, *Conquest*, 101.

60. Robert, *Conquest*, 103.

61. Robert, *Conquest*, 106.

62. Robert, *Conquest*, 108.

63. On this score the account of one particular miracle-working icon is worth review. Shortly after the usurper Murzuphlus took control of the empire, he and his troops were set to square off against a much smaller contingent of French knights on the plain to the west of the city. Murzuphlus had in his possession a miracle-working icon, which was used as a military talisman and is said to have

conveyed automatic victory to any general to carried it onto the field of battle. But as the battle approached, Murzuphlus, true to character, fled from the conflict and, in the process, dropped the miracle-working icon, which was then recovered by the crusaders. In Robert's telling, the transition from Byzantine to French possession of the icon was divinely sanctioned, but not because of Greek theological error. Rather, it was sanctioned because Murzuphlus lacked the qualities of authentic leadership (manliness, courage, and respect for hereditary governance).

64. Robert, *Conquest*, 110.

65. To be sure, Robert is not the only author to report of a popular opinion that the statue of Athena beckons armies from the West. In his own account of siege of Constantinople, the Byzantine chronicler, Niketas Choniates suggests that this interpretation of Athena's gesture was also common among the drunken vulgar masses of the city. For an English translation, see Choniates, *O City of Byzantium: Annals of Niketas Choniates,* trans. Harry Magoulias (Detroit: Wayne St. University Press, 1984), 305–6. For an analysis of the way that Choniates employs ancient statues in his history as a way to convey coded political messages against the Latins, see Paroma Chatterjee, "Sculpted Eloquence and Nicetas Choniates's *De Signis,*" *Word and Image: A Journal of Verbal/Visual Inquiry* 27 (2011): 396–406.

66. Robert, *Conquest*, 110.

67. Robert, *Conquest*, 78–80.

68. Kinoshita, *Medieval Boundaries*, 160.

69. He is, in fact, visiting Constantinople as a sacred pilgrimage.

70. Kinoshita, *Medieval Boundaries*, 162.

71. Herodotus, *Histories* 4.

72. Kinoshita, *Medieval Boundaries*, 162.

73. Concerning the story of St. Demetrios, see Robert, *Conquest*, 127.

74. Robert, *Conquest*, 94.

75. Robert, *Conquest*, 94.

76. Note, for example, that when Murzuphlus is apprehended by French knights some months after the capture of the city, he is traveling like a dandy in a caravan of expensively dressed women, rather than fighting like a man and being taken on the field of battle. Robert, *Conquest*, 123–24.

77. Kinoshita, *Medieval Boundaries*, 164–66 and 169.

78. Describing the elaborate dressing of the new emperor that is performed by the barons, Robert remarks, "There they divested him of his outer garments and took off his *chausses* [his full-length stockings] and put on him *chausses* of vermilion samite and shoes all covered with rich stones. Then they put on him a very rich coat all fastened with gold buttons in front and behind from the shoulders clear to the girdle." Robert, *Conquest*, 115–16. See Voicu, "Le Regard," paragraph 41.

79. An alternative reading of this passage might see the coronation service in a positive light—a showcasing of Baldwin's incredible success through the display of jewels and silks. A positive reading of this passage, however, would need to account for the fact that Robert is unequivocally critical of the crusade leaders, especially with respect to their greed. Interestingly, there were Byzantine authors, like Niketas Choniates, who believed that aristocratic bedecking in jewelry was a sign of his culture's own decadence and weakness. Choniates, *O City of Byzantium*.

80. Robert appropriates local legends in his telling of Byzantine politics and, of course, describes the various marriages designed to smooth the transition. On the marriages, see McNeal, "The Story of Isaac and Andronicus."

2. Gunther of Pairis's *Hystoria Constantinopolitana*

1. Patrick Geary coined the phrase *furta sacra* to describe a subgenre in Latin literature focused on "holy thefts." See Patrick Geary, *Furta Sacra: Thefts of Relics in the Central Middle Ages* (Princeton: Princeton University Press, 1978). More recently, Geary has explained the relic "economy" of the Central Middle Ages: Geary, "Sacred Commodities: The Circulation of Medieval Relics," *The Social Life of Things: Commodities in Cultural Perspective* (Cambridge: Cambridge University Press, 2013). Importantly, David Perry has demonstrated how the genre of the *furta sacra* functioned in the context of the Fourth Crusade. David Perry, *Sacred Plunder: Venice and the Aftermath of the Fourth Crusade* (University Park: Penn State University Press, 2015).

2. A critical edition of the text is provided by Peter Orth, ed., *Hystoria Constantinopolitana/Gunther von Pairis* (Hildesheim: Weidermann, 1994)—hereafter, *HC*. An English version and introduction is provided in Gunther of Pairis, *The Capture of Constantinople: The "Hystoria Constantinopolitana" of Gunther of Pairis*, trans. Alfred Andrea (Philadelphia: University of Pennsylvania Press, 1997). Unless otherwise noted, all translations employed are those of Andrea.

Geoffrey de Villehardouin and Robert de Clari are, technically, more accurately labeled as chronicles of the Fourth Crusade since they were both eyewitnesses to the events that they describe—Gunther records the story as told to him by Martin. Both Geoffrey and Robert see the actions of the Fourth Crusade as unavoidable even if they were not predictable because duty and honor required the occupation of the duplicitous Greeks. For a quick summary of the scholarly debate concerning its reliability of historical details in each account, see Andrea, introduction to Gunther, *The Capture of Constantinople*, 56–59.

3. The complete list of relics is contained in Chapter 24.

4. For a thorough background of Gunther, including an examination of his other writings, see Andrea's extensive introduction to Gunther, *The Capture of*

Constantinople, 1–63. For a detailed effort to assess the historical reliability of the account, see Swietek, "Gunther of Pairis and the *Historia Constantinopolitana,*" *Speculum* 53 (1978): 49–79.

5. Perry, *Sacred Plunder,* 105.

6. Perry, *Sacred Plunder,* 105. See also Andrea's introduction to *The Capture of Constantinople,* 5.

7. Gunther, *HC,* 1.

8. Chapter 10 notes that Martin arrives in Constantinople on the fore-feast of St. Martin of Tours.

9. However, unlike Urban who mentioned Charlemagne, Martin assuages the soldiers' fear by invoking the courage of their predecessors, the Frankish crusaders who succeeded in conquering Jerusalem. Moreover, Martin offers absolution of all sins for anyone who "takes up the cross." Gunther, *HC,* 3.

10. Gunther, *HC,* 8–9 and 9–10 respectively.

11. For a summary of this scholarship, such as it existed in the 1970s, see Swietek, "Gunther of Pairis and the *Historia Constantinopolitana.*"

12. Given that those arguments were largely predicated on the historically flawed assertion that the Holy Land had until recently been a Christian land, it is important to acknowledge that the typical rhetorical thrust of crusade preaching was incongruent with the conceptual categories that we normally associate with colonial expansion, which were predominately an economic enlargement into new, non-Christian territories.

13. A well-known contemporary Latin critic of the Fourth Crusade was Burchard of Ursberg. See his *Chronicon,* MGH, SS, 23: 369. With time, even Innocent III became very critical of the looting of religious treasure (albeit largely because he wanted it to be controlled from Rome). See Perry, *Sacred Plunder,* 46–74 (69–74 covers nonpapal criticism).

14. The contention that the crusaders are greatly outnumbered appears repeatedly in Chapters 14–18. The claim that only one crusader died in the siege appears in Chapter 18.

15. Gunther, *HC,* 22. Gunther makes two mistakes here: He confuses the Obelisk of Theodosius with the Column of Theodosius (his previous chapter had detailed how Morciflo had been assassinated by being thrown from the top of the column), and he misreads the marble reliefs at the base of the Obelisk; for a more detailed explanation, see my note 56.

16. Gunther, *HC,* 10–15.

17. Gunther, *HC,* 14; *The Capture of Constantinople,* 97.

18. Gunther, *HC,* 18; *The Capture of Constantinople,* 106–7.

19. Gunter, *HC,* 12–14.

20. Gunther, *HC,* 14; *The Capture of Constantinople,* 97. Referring to the short-lived ruler Alexius IV, Gunther acknowledges that the crusaders feared that the

young emperor had either been murdered or had, "like a Greek by nature, been corrupted by them" (*vel tamquam Grecus genere ab eis corruptus*).

21. Note especially his description of the way that the crusade leaders determine who among them will become the emperor of Byzantium. The process is honorable, rational, and nonviolent. This, of course, lies in sharp contradistinction to the murderous activity of the Greek nobility. Gunther, *HC*, 20.

22. The details of the political situation in Constantinople at the time of the siege are well known to Byzantinists and scholars of the crusades. The nonspecialist might consult any of a number of standard accounts, including Donald Quellar and Thomas Madden, *The Fourth Crusade: The Conquest of Constantinople*, revised 2nd ed. (Philadelphia: University of Pennsylvania Press, 2000). For Gunther's description of the assault as an act of political honor, see *HC*, 13–14 especially.

23. Gunther, *HC*, 11; *The Capture of Constantinople*, 91.

24. Gunther, *HC*, 17; *The Capture of Constantinople*, 104–5.

25. Gunther, *HC*, 20. The closing lines of the poem that ends Chapter 19 similarly affirms that righteousness of crusaders authorizes them to rule the Greeks forever. Gunther contrasts this to the Greek victory over Troy, which did not lead to permanent settlement.

26. Gunther, *HC*, 16; *The Capture of Constantinople*, 101–3.

27. Dipesh Chakrabarty, *Provincializing Europe: Postcolonial Thought and Historical Difference* (Princeton: Princeton University Press, 2000), especially 6–11. Edward Said, *Orientalism* (reprinted New York: Vintage Books, 1994).

28. Johnson, "Orientalism's Attempted Resuscitation of Eastern Christianity."

29. For an account of the layers of "myth" in both the initial construction of the "noble savage" by Rousseau and the endearing myth that preoccupied scholarly discussion through the nineteenth century, see Ter Ellingson, *The Myth of the Noble Savage* (Berkeley, Calif.: University of California Press, 2001).

30. For an excellent examination of the role of sexual longing in colonial constructions of racial identity, see Robert J. C. Young, *Colonial Desire: Hybridity in Theory, Culture, and Race* (London: Routledge, 1995), especially 90–117.

31. The monastery was founded by the emperor John II Komnenos (who ruled from 1118–43). He, his wife, Irene, and emperor-son, Manuel I, were all buried in the complex along with several other members of the imperial family. The monastery had extensive land holdings for its support. During the Latin occupation of 1204–61, the monastery was in the possession of the Venetians.

32. The entire story of the looting of the monastery occurs in Gunther, *HC*, 19; *The Capture of Constantinople*, 109–13.

33. I have slightly altered Andrea's English translation of the Latin, not because it is wrong but because a reasonable alternative like what I am proposing opens additional possibilities for considering a sexualized dimension: *Invenit ibi senem*

quondam venusta facie barba prolixa et cana sacerdotem utique, sed nostris sacerdotibus ipso corporis habitu valde dissimilem. Gunther, *HC,* 19.

34. By "exotic" I mean that this character, like the very topography of the Orient, evokes a sense of mythic wonder that is conceptualized by foreignness but overlaid with a latent sexuality.

35. On the role of "beards" in the Orientalizing imagination of Latin authors in this period, see Charis Messis, "Lectures sexuées de l'altérité: Les Latins et identité romaine menacée pendant les derniers siècles de Byzance," *Jahrbuch der Österreichischen Byzantinistik* 61 (2011): 150–71.

36. Again, I have tweaked Andrea's translation of the Latin: *"Age," iniquit, "perfide senex, ostende michi, quas pociores servas reliquias, vel scias te statim mortis supplicio puniendum."* Gunther, *HC,* 19.

37. Previous scholarship assumed that this meant Old French. Andrea proposes that it is a dialect of proto-northern Italian. Gunther, *The Capture of Constantinople,* 172–73n240.

38. Gunther, *HC,* 19; *The Capture of Constantinople,* 111.

39. Gunther, *HC,* 19; *The Capture of Constantinople,* 111.

40. Gunther, *The Capture of Constantinople,* 173n241.

41. Gunther, *The Capture of Constantinople,* 173n241.

42. Gunther, *HC,* 19; *The Capture of Constantinople,* 111.

43. "On seeing it, the abbot hurriedly and lustily [*cupide*] thrust in both hands and as he was girded for action both he and his chaplain filled their folds of their habits with sacred sacrilege." Gunther, *HC,* 19; *The Capture of Constantinople,* 111.

44. *iam ei satis familiariter adherebat.* Gunther, *HC,* 19; *The Capture of Constantinople,* 112. I have slightly modified Andrea's translation, proposing "intimate" for *familiariter.*

45. Gunther, *HC,* 19; *The Capture of Constantinople,* 112.

46. Megan Moore, *Exchanges in Exoticism: Cross-Cultural Marriage and the Making of the Mediterranean in Old French Romance* (Toronto: University of Toronto Press, 2014), 51f.

47. See Messis, "Lectures sexuées de l'altérité." The other target of Latin sexualized assault on Greek masculinity was the use of eunuchs in the Byzantine imperial service—the irony, of course, being that the Latin monks who were typically responsible for these critiques looked like eunuchs because they, too, did not have facial hair and did not fulfill a sexual function. I would like to thank Anthony Kaldellis who first drew my attention to this fascinating article.

48. Mark Jordan, *The Invention of Sodomy in Christian Theology* (Chicago: University of Chicago Press, 1997), especially 6–7.

49. Jordan, *The Invention of Sodomy*—see, especially, Chapter 1, "The Passions of St. Pelagius," 10–28.

50. Recent scholarship has had much to say about the exotic character of Constantinople in the imagination of both the crusaders who journeyed to the East as well as Western European locals who wrote in Latin or the vernacular. I am particularly indebted to Teresa Shawcross, who delivered a masterful paper at Fordham University's *French of Outremer* conference in April 2014. See also Moore, *Exchanges in Exoticism*, especially 22–24.

51. Gunther, *HC*, 16. There is no contemporaneous evidence to suggest that Sylvester and Constantine ever met, let alone that Sylvester played any role in Constantine's conversion to Christianity or his decision to move the empire to the East. For more on the growth the origins of the Sylvester/Constantine myth, see Kristina Sessa, "Exceptionality and Invention: Sylvester and the Making of the Roman Papacy," *Studia Patristica* 46: 77–94.

52. Gunther, *HC*, 19; *The Capture of Constantinople*, 112.

53. Gunther, *HC*, 19; *The Capture of Constantinople*, 113.

54. Not only did the conquest of Troy provide a well-known ancient model of siege and plunder, the myth of Rome's Trojan origins remained popular in Western literary circles in the Middle Ages. See Teresa Shawcross, "Re-inventing the Homeland in the Historiography of Frankish Greece: The Fourth Crusade and the Legend of the Trojan War," *Byzantine and Modern Greek Studies* 27 (2003): 120–52.

55. Gunther, *HC*, 19.

56. Gunther refers to it simply as a tower with a pyramid, but he confuses the Obelisk (produced in Egypt during the reign of Tuthmosis III [1490–36 BCE] and brought to Constantinople by Theodosius I in 390 CE) with the Column of Theodosius (erected to celebrate Theodosius's victory over the Goths). He further mistakes the artistic reliefs on the base of the object, which were produced by Theodosian craftsmen and depict the erecting of the object in Constantinople; Gunther believes they foretell the capture of the city with men scaling the city's walls.

57. For more on the role of the erotic in Greek and Latin polemics in the era of the Fourth Crusade, see Messis, "Lectures sexuées de l'altérité."

58. Although he travels to Acre with a great deal of trepidation, he is received there by members of his own group, "the Germans especially," which brings both relief and joy. According to Gunther, it is Martin who brings news to the leaders of Acre concerning the political developments in Constantinople (i.e., the establishment of Western European feudal structures). Gunther, *HC*, 22; *The Capture of Constantinople*, 118–22.

59. Gunther, *HC*, 22. I have slightly altered Andrea's translation.

60. Gunther, *HC*, 22; *The Capture of Constantinople*, 119.

61. Gunther, *HC*, 22; *The Capture of Constantinople*, 119.

62. While a pairing of Martin and Werner would be a coupling of two Europeans, the unacceptability of explicit homosexual affection within Gunther's circle

makes the possibility of this encounter all the more discursively similar to other forms of taboo sexual pairings as described by Young in *Colonial Desire*.

63. Among Werner's promises to Martin are the command of existing monasteries, the construction of a new one, and "wealth in gold and silver in a quantity that he could never imagine."

64. To be sure, the language of male friendship in the Middle Ages was often more affectionate in its details than is customary today and the encounter is not "colonial" in any specific way, apart from its exotic setting.

65. For example, it not only testifies to a kind moral justification for the extraction of material resources from distant lands, it also functions within a kind of positivist historiographical tradition in which Western Christianity is a more developed form of correct faith, as well as through a prejudicial comparison to Western Christianity that Eastern Christianity is deemed inadequate and justifiably annexed.

66. As noted, it does advocate for the long-term occupation of the Holy Land (*HC,* 3) on the grounds that it had "originally" been Christian and was only recently surrendered to infidels.

3. Innocent's Ambivalence

1. Since the fourth century, there had been efforts to maintain and systematize papal letter collections. While Innocent III's clerks were serious about their task, the collection is not without its problems, especially with regard to the dating of letters and inconsistent tabulation of letters received. These letters are catalogued according to papal year beginning with the date of Innocent's election in 1198. Where possible, I will employ the English translations of letters provided by Alfred Andrea, ed. and trans., *Contemporary Sources for the Fourth Crusade* (Leiden: Brill, 2000). Andrea relies on the critical editions produced by Othmar Hagenedar, et al., *Die Register Innocenz' III* (Graz-Cologne, Rome, Vienna, 1964-f).

2. Among the reasons that the *Gesta* provides access to letters otherwise unknown is that the records of Innocent's *Register* are missing all documents from the third and fourth years of his pontificate. According to James Powell, the anonymous author of the *Gesta* is Cardinal Petrus Beneventanus. James Powell, "Innocent III and Petrus Beneventanus: Reconstructing a Career at the Papal Curia," in *Pope Innocent III and This World*, ed. John C. Moore (Aldershot, U.K.: Ashgate, 1999), 51–62. Powell's translation of the *Gesta* is based upon consultation of four sources, including a 1981 Bryn Mawr dissertation by David Gress Wright. A critical edition of the text does not exist. For consultation of the Latin, see PL 214. For an English translation and discussion of the textual issues, see James Powell, trans., *The Deeds of Innocent III by an Anonymous Author* (Washington, D.C.: The Catholic University of America Press, 2004), esp. xvi.

3. It is worth noting that the use of crusades directly targeting Greek Christians in the post-1204 period coincided with an expansion of the crusading concept, which targeted other Christian splinter groups in Western Europe, such as the Albigensian and the Baltic crusades. See, for example, Nikolaos Chrissis, "New Frontiers: Frankish Greece and the Development of Crusading in the Early Thirteenth Century," in *Contact and Conflict in Frankish Greece and the Aegean, 1204–1453*, ed. N. Chrissis and Mike Carr (Burlington: Ashgate, 2014), 17–42, esp. 27–31.

4. Even after Innocent warmed to the possibilities that the conquest of Constantinople might provide, he continued to rail against the crusaders who treated their fellow Christians with malice and oppression.

5. Philip II Augustus of France, Frederick Barbarossa of Germany, and Henry II of England all participated in the crusade. When Henry died in 1189 his son, Richard the Lionheart, succeeded him and managed to contract a peace settlement with Saladin that allowed unarmed Christian pilgrims to visit Jerusalem.

6. Innocent, *Register*, 1.336; Andrea, *Contemporary Sources*, 10–19.

7. See Andrea, *Contemporary Sources*, 9.

8. Innocent, *Register*, 8.70; Powell, *Deeds of Pope Innocent*, 172.

9. Innocent, *Register*, 1.336; Andrea, *Contemporary Sources*, 15.

10. There are six surviving accounts of Urban's speech at Clermont. All but that of Fulcher of Chartres are derivative of the so-called *Gesta Francorum*. See *Gesta Francorum et aliorum Hierosolimitanorum*, ed. and trans. Rosalind Hill (Oxford: Clarendon, 1967).

11. Innocent, *Register*, 1.336; Andrea, *Contemporary Sources*, 11.

12. Innocent even takes the remarkable step of conjuring a Saracen statement of incredulous mockery in order to shame his reader's sense of chivalric honor. Innocent, *Register*, 1.336; Andrea, *Contemporary Sources*, 11–13.

13. Innocent, *Register*, 1.336; Andrea, *Contemporary Sources*, 16.

14. Innocent, *Register*, 1.336; Andrea, *Contemporary Sources*, 16.

15. Innocent, *Register*, 1.398 and 2.258; Andrea, *Contemporary Sources*, 19–20 and 26–32.

16. Innocent, *Register*, 1.336; Andrea, *Contemporary Sources*, 15.

17. Innocent, *Register*, 1.33; Andrea, *Contemporary Sources*, 15.

18. Innocent, *Register*, 6.48 and, especially, 8.127; Andrea, *Contemporary Sources*, 51–52 and, especially, 163–68.

19. The *Gesta* suggests that Innocent wrote to the rulers of Venice, Pisa, and Genoa, attempting to get them to put aside their squabbles for the greater good of the Christian effort in the Levant. *Gesta*, 46; Powell, *The Deeds of Innocent III*, 61–62.

20. As merchants, the Venetians had historically been at the center of cross-civilizational trade and they had continued to trade with Islamic communities

despite the crusades. Innocent, *Register,* 1.536; Andrea, *Contemporary Sources* 23–24.

21. For example, Innocent, *Register,* 5.160–61; Andrea, *Contemporary Sources* 41–43 and 46–48.

22. Innocent, *Register,* 5.161; Andrea, *Contemporary Sources,* 48.

23. This is revealed by Innocent's letter to Emperor Alexius III, who had been seeking pledges from the pope that he would thwart any effort made by Alexius IV. Innocent, *Register,* 5.121.

24. Andrea believes that *Epistle* 5.161 was specifically concerned about the Greeks, even if Innocent's message was implied. He bases this on corroborating evidence from Gunther and by a comparison to Innocent's subsequent letter (6.48) to his legate Peter Capuano. See Andrea, *Contemporary Sources,* 48n194.

25. "Therefore not one of you should rashly flatter himself that he is allowed to occupy or prey upon the land of the Greeks because it might be too little obedient to the Apostolic See. . . . Moreover, we want you to keep in mind the terms of our prohibition: Under threat of excommunication we have forbidden you to attempt to invade or violate the lands of Christians unless they wickedly impede your journey." Innocent, *Register,* 6.101; Andrea, *Contemporary Sources,* 61–64.

26. Boniface's letter is catalogued as Innocent, *Register,* 6.210; Andrea, *Contemporary Sources,* 80–85. Innocent's response is *Register,* 6.229; Andrea, *Contemporary Sources,* 88–90.

27. Innocent, *Register,* 6.230 and 6.231; Andrea, *Contemporary Sources,* 91–92 and 93–94.

28. For evidence, one need look no further than the accounts examined in Chapters 1 and 2, where Latin Christians are said to visit the holy places of Constantinople prior to the sack of the city.

29. From the spring of 1198 until the summer of 1202, there were eight embassies and twelve letters that passed between the curia and the Constantinopolitan court. See Andrea, *Contemporary Sources,* 33 and, especially the detailed bibliography in the notes. This exchange reveals, on the one hand, Emperor Alexius III's efforts to construct an alliance against Philip of Swabia (who was sheltering the emperor's nephew, the future Alexius IV), and on the other, Innocent's desire to enlist Byzantine support for the upcoming crusade as well as his effort to end the schism on his own terms, which would require the patriarch of Constantinople to recognize papal authority. See, for example, *Gesta,* 60; Powell, *Deeds,* 80, sent to Emperor Alexius III, where Innocent proposes a council to settle, once and for all, that the issue of Roman primacy is not a matter of conciliar decree but is the divine head of the Church. Also contained in Innocent, *Register,* 2.202.

30. See, for example, Innocent, *Register,* 2.202.

31. Innocent, *Register,* 2.202.

32. Innocent's position was firm but his tone was cordial. He occasionally flatters the patriarch and looks forward to their joint work to reunite the Church. Even though Innocent believes that John "should willingly, kindly, and devotedly obey" the Roman Church, he agrees that "on account of many ecclesiastical necessities" that there should be a general council to resolve the issues at hand.

33. For a historical summary and literary analysis of the means by which the fifth-century papacy had first put that rhetorical argument together, see George Demacopoulos, *The Invention of Peter* (Philadelphia: University of Pennsylvania Press, 2013).

34. Innocent, Register, 2.200; Powell, *Deeds*, 86.

35. The letter with John's queries does not survive.

36. She is called the mother "not by age but by dignity."

37. Here, as elsewhere, Powell translates *dogmata* as doctrines rather than dogma. While it is true that Innocent does not adhere to a clear theological distinction between dogma and doctrine that later systematic theologians would employ, I believe it is important to note Innocent's terminology.

38. *et ideo nec pro disparitate rituum nec dogmatum diversitate differre debueris quin nobis.* Innocent, *Register,* 2.200; Powell, *Deeds,* 88.

39. Innocent, *Register,* 2.200; Powell, *Deeds,* 88.

40. "Therefore, not one of you should rashly flatter himself that he is allowed to occupy or prey upon the land of the Greeks because it might be too little obedient to the Apostolic See and because the emperor of Constantinople usurped the empire by deposing and also blinding his brother. Truly, however much so this same emperor and the people committed to his jurisdiction did wrong in this and other matters, it is still not your business to judge their crimes. It was not for this, in order to avenge this injury, that you assumed the emblem of the Cross, but rather to avenge the dishonor done the Crucified One, to whose service you have specially appointed yourselves." Innocent, *Register,* 6.101; Andrea, *Contemporary Sources,* 62–63.

41. Innocent, *Register,* 6.101; Andrea, *Contemporary Sources,* 63.

42. Catalogued as Innocent, *Register,* 6.209; Andrea, *Contemporary Sources,* 77–79.

43. Catalogued as Innocent, *Register,* 6.210; Andrea, *Contemporary Sources,* 80–85.

44. Innocent, *Register,* 6.229; Andrea, *Contemporary Sources,* 88–90.

45. "You will appear to have added a second transgression to the first that you rushed into at Zara, while the weapons that you were believed to have taken up against the enemies of the Cross you turned once again to the ruin of Christians, unless perhaps, to reduce guilt and punishment, you will have taken pains to complete what you had begun regarding the Greek Church out of the zeal that

you have for your mother, the Roman Church, toward which they have been unfaithful." Innocent, *Register,* 6.229; Andrea, *Contemporary Sources,* 89.

46. Innocent sent a second letter (*Register,* 6.231) to the bishops at the same time, which strikes a more critical tone. According to Andrea, Innocent sent two letters assuming that the first would be shown to the emperor Alexius IV as a means to encourage his submission to the Roman Church and that the second was for crusader eyes only. As Andrea notes, the pope was angry and suspicious. The crusaders had soiled themselves and the pope was eager for them to abandon the quagmire of Byzantine politics and get on with the business of fighting in the Holy Land. Andrea, *Contemporary Sources,* 92–93,

47. Innocent, *Register,* 6.230; Andrea, *Contemporary Sources,* 91.

48. As noted, the issue of papal authority was a "dogmatic" issue for Innocent, as it had been for any number of papal apologists in the Middle Ages. Nevertheless, it is significant that other dogmatic issues did not draw his attention prior to 1204.

49. Catalogued as Innocent, *Register,* 7.152; Andrea, *Contemporary Sources,* 100–12.

50. Innocent, *Register,* 7.152; Andrea, *Contemporary Sources,* 102.

51. Perhaps to deflect against the behavior of his own soldiers, Baldwin accuses the Greek aristocracy of "slaughter, conflagration, and rapine."

52. Catalogued as Innocent, *Register,* 7.152; Andrea, *Contemporary Sources,* 109. The accusation that the Greeks required a second baptism first emerged in the context of the Schism of 1054. Most likely, Latin clerics have confused the Greek rite of chrismation with a second baptism—there is absolutely no evidence in the Greek sources that they required a second baptism for Latin converts to Orthodoxy at this time. See Tia Kolbaba, "On the Closing of Greek Churches and the Rebaptism of Latins: Greek Perfidy or Latin Slander?" *Byzantine and Modern Greek Studies* 29 (2005): 39–51. See also her "1054 Revisited: Response to Ryder," *Byzantine and Modern Greek Studies* 35 (2011): 38–44.

53. Catalogued as Innocent, *Register,* 7.152; Andrea, *Contemporary Sources,* 108. This accusation should not be confused with the notion that Greek clerics refused to grant the sacraments to the Latins. That is not at issue. At issue is whether or not the Greeks would forfeit one of their churches to the crusaders.

54. Catalogued as Innocent, *Register,* 7.152; Andrea, *Contemporary Sources,* 108.

55. The same Greeks could barely stand "to hear the name of the prince of the apostles and which conceded not one Greek church to him who received from the Lord himself dominion over all churches." Catalogued as Innocent, *Register,* 7.152; Andrea, *Contemporary Sources,* 108.

56. Catalogued as Innocent, *Register,* 7.152; Andrea, *Contemporary Sources,* 110.

57. Catalogued as Innocent, *Register,* 7.152; Andrea, *Contemporary Sources,* 109.

58. Innocent, *Register,* 7.153; Andrea, *Contemporary Sources,* 113–15.

59. In recognition of their role in the humiliation of the Greek Church, Innocent placed the crusaders, their families, and their territory under the protection of the Holy See.

60. See Andrea, *Contemporary Sources*, 116.

61. Innocent, *Register*, 7.154; Andrea, *Contemporary Sources*, 120–21.

62. "Faithfully expound lessons to the army, so that the feeling of devotion that the Christian army has toward its mother, the Roman Church, might be inflamed; and take care to instruct our most beloved son in Christ, Baldwin, illustrious emperor of Constantinople, and the greater and lesser members of that army to strive to stabilize the kingdom of the Greeks in obedience to the Apostolic See, through whose agency the kingdom, doubtlessly, can be held onto, and without which dominion over it can by no means be held onto by them." Innocent, *Register*, 7.154; Andrea, *Contemporary Sources*, 126.

63. Much of the letter is an effort to dance around the embarrassment of having to accept the Venetians' choice for patriarch of Constantinople, Thomas Morosini. Innocent, *Register*, 7.203; Andrea, *Contemporary Sources*, esp. 137–38.

64. Innocent, *Register*, 7.203; Andrea, *Contemporary Sources*, 132–39.

65. Innocent, *Register*, 7.203; Andrea, *Contemporary Sources*, 132–39.

66. So, on the one hand, Innocent retained the framework of his earlier position—the schism is a consequence of disobedience to Rome. But, on the other hand, events have led to him to speak more critically about the extent and scope of Greek error.

67. Innocent, *Register*, 8.56; Andrea, *Contemporary Sources*, 155.

68. Innocent, *Register*, 8.56; Andrea, *Contemporary Sources*, 155–56.

69. Innocent, *Register*, 8.57; Andrea, *Contemporary Sources*, 158–59.

70. Innocent, *Register*, 8.70; Powell, *Deeds of Pope Innocent*, 170–72.

71. Innocent, *Register*, 8.70; Powell, *Deeds of Pope Innocent*, 170–72.

72. What is especially striking about the inclusion of this letter in the *Deeds* is the fact that it is succeeded by a letter that presents a completely different perspective—namely, that Innocent cannot but sympathize with the Greeks who have been so mistreated by the crusaders.

73. Innocent, *Register*, 8.127; Andrea, *Contemporary Sources*, 163–68.

74. Indeed, Innocent runs through a long list of crusader crimes against the Greeks, including murder, theft, rape, and fire.

75. Innocent, *Register*, 8.127; Andrea, *Contemporary Sources*, 166.

76. Innocent, *Register*, 8.134; Andrea, *Contemporary Sources*, 171–76.

77. "All of you, having no jurisdiction or power over the Greeks, appear to have rashly turned away from the purity of your vow when you took up arms not against Saracens, but Christians, not aiming to recover Jerusalem but to occupy Constantinople, preferring earthly wealth to celestial treasures. And, more seriously, it is reputed far and wide that some showed no mercy for reasons of

religion, age, or sex but committed acts of fornication, adultery, and lewdness in the sight of all, and they exposed not only married women and widows but even matrons and virgins dedicated to God to the filth of the lowborn." Innocent, *Register,* 8.134; Andrea, *Contemporary Sources,* 173.

78. Innocent, *Register,* 8.134; Andrea, *Contemporary Sources,* 174–75.

79. The most extensive study of the experience of indigenous Christians during the twelfth century is Christopher MacEvitt, *Rough Tolerance: The Crusades and the Christian World of the East* (Philadelphia: University of Pennsylvania Press, 2007).

80. Of course, the most important differences between the two historical examples (i.e., 1099 and 1204) was the vastly different levels of contact between Rome and the Christians of Jerusalem (which was virtually nonexistent) and between Rome and Constantinople (which had been continuous) at the time of the encounter. Whereas the Christians of Holy Land were largely unknown to Europeans prior to the crusades, the Christians of Byzantium had been in continuous political, economic, and religious contact.

81. Innocent, *Register,* 8.70. For a clear summary of the transformation of Frankish Greece from an accident to a new crusading frontier, see Chrissis, "New Frontiers," esp. 35–39.

82. This is the thrust his careful study; see Nikolaos Chrissis, *Crusading in Frankish Greece: A Study of Byzantine-Western Relations and Attitudes 1204–1282* (Turnhout: Brepols, 2012) and put especially well on xxxvi.

83. Innocent, *Register,* 9.45 (to Philip) and 9.195–98 (to Nivelon). See Chrissis, *Crusading,* 24–31. See also Jean Longon, *Compagnons de Villehardouin: recherches sur les croisés de la quatrième croisade* (Genève: Droz, 1978), 115–16, 199–200, 173–74.

84. Innocent, *Register,* 11.44. See Chrissis, *Crusades,* 34.

85. Innocent, *Register,* 11.44.

86. For example, by 1210, Innocent had come to believe that if the Greeks were able to recapture the Latin Empire, the other Latin colonies in the East would be put in serious jeopardy, not only because the Greeks had never really assisted in the first place but, more importantly, because they had now come to hate the Latins fiercely as a result of their mistreatment. Among other evidence, see the letter to the Latin patriarch, Thomas Morosini, dated December 1210 and contained in PL 216.353–54. See also Chrissis, *Crusading,* 24n101.

87. Peter had been crowned emperor in Rome. As he traveled to Constantinople, he chose to pass through Epiros, hoping to make a show of strength. But he was defeated and captured by Theodore (the Latin sources suggest that this was the result of treachery). *Bullarium hellenicum: Pope Honorius III's Letters to Frankish Greece and Constantinople (1216–1227),* ed. William Duba and Christopher Schabel (Turnhout, Belgium: Brepols, 2015), no. 24. For more on this, see Chrissis, *Crusading,* 64. Concerning Honorius's willingness to employ a crusade against

Theodore in 1217, see *Vetera monumenta historica Hungariam sacram illustrantia*, ed. Augustin Theiner (Roma: Vaticanis, 1859–60), vol. 1, 8, 14. See Chrissis, *Crusading*, 64 and Adalbert Keutner, *Papsttum und Krieg unter dem Pontifikat des Papstes Honorius III* (PhD diss. University of Münster, 1935), 40–41.

88. *Regestra Honorii Papae III*, ed. Presutti, nos. 1023–34 and 1029–31 from January of 1218. See Donald A. Nicol, *The Despotate of Epiros 1267–1479: A Contribution to the History of Greece* (Cambridge: Cambridge University Press, 1984), 51–53 and Chrissis, *Crusading*, 67.

89. *Regestra Honorii Papae III*, ed. Presutti, nos. 4059–60 (=*Bullarium hellenicum,* ed. Schabel and Duba, nos. 135–36), dated June 27, 1222. And, again, in *Regestra Honorii Papae III*, ed. by Presutti, no. 4354 (=*Acta Honorii III et Gregorii IX*, ed. Tàutu, no. 112). See Chrissis, *Crusading*, 69.

90. *Regestra Honorii Papae III*, ed. Presutti, no. 3877 (=*Bullarium hellenicum*, ed. Schabel and Duba, no. 122), dated March 21, 1222.

91. *Bullarium hellenicum*, ed. Schabel and Duba, nos. 212 (May 20, 1224) and 228 (Dec. 5, 1224). Chrissis, *Crusading*, 75.

92. Chrissis, *Crusading*, 74–75.

93. Gregory IX served as bishop of Rome from 1227 to 1241.

94. Scholars continue to debate the link between the breakdown in diplomatic efforts to heal the schism and Gregory's decision to turn the full force of the crusades against the Greeks. It is, of course, possible that the pontiff might have pursued the two policies simultaneously. See Chrissis, *Crusading*, 96–97.

95. See Chrissis, *Crusading*, 96–97.

96. *Les Registres de Grégoire IX*, ed. Lucien Auvray (Paris: Bibl. Écoles fr. d'Athènes et de Rome, 1890–1910), no. 2872 (=*Vetera monumenta historica Hungariam*, ed. Theiner, 1, 140, no. 249). The papal bull, issued to Hungary calling for this crusade, is also known by the title *Ut Israelem veteris*. Chrissis, *Crusading*, 99–102, provides an overview of Gregory's letters in this context as well as the general parameters of papal rhetoric.

97. See Chrissis, *Crusading*, 103–5. See also Chrissis, "A Diversion That Never Was: Thibaut IV of Champagne, Richard of Cornwall and Pope Gregory IX's Crusading Plans for Constantinople 1235–1239," in *Crusades*, vol. 9, ed. Benjamin Kedar, Jonathan Phillips, and Jonathan Riley-Smith (London: Routledge, 2010), 123–45.

98. Gregory IX, *Ad subveniendum imperio* (=*Les Registres de Grégoire IX*, ed. Auvray, no. 3408–09). Translation by Chrissis, *Crusading*, 104.

99. Frederick forged alliances with Theodore Doukas, Manuel of Thessalonika, and Michael of Epiros. See Chrissis, *Crusading*, 88–96.

100. As we will see in Chapter 4, Greek canonists in this period were increasingly proscribing Greek/Latin marriage even though Greek aristocrats were increasingly arranging marriages between their children and Frankish settlers.

101. The text of the excommunication, included in the Acts of the Council, reads: "and securing a bond by friendship and marriage with those who, wickedly making light of the Apostolic See, have separated from the unity of the church, . . . he gave his daughter in marriage to Vatatzes, that enemy of God and of the Church, who together with his counselors and supporters, was solemnly separated from the communion of the faithful by excommunication." The Bull of his excommunication is titled *Ad Apostolice dignitatis* July 17, 1245. Translation in *Decrees of the Ecumenical Councils: Nicaea I to Lateran V*, trans. Norman P. Tanner (Georgetown: Georgetown University Press, 2016), 278–83; here 282.

102. Chrissis, *Crusading*, 147.

103. As Chrissis argues, the survival of the Latin Empire as a Western Christian colony in the East needed a foundation myth—that myth was the notion that a Latin Empire was, in fact, a justifiable crusade in its own right; the crusaders of the Latin Empire did not need to go to the Holy Land, their pilgrimage for the Cross was constituted in the preservation of Latin Constantinople. Chrissis, *Crusading*, 34–35.

104. Here, I draw especially on Homi Bhabha's engagement of the quality of ambivalence in colonial discourse. See, especially, his essay "Signs Taken for Wonders: Questions of Ambivalence and Authority under a Tree outside Delhi, May 1817," in *The Location of Culture* (London: Routledge, 1994), 145–74.

105. Bhabha, *Location of Culture*, 164.

106. For an overview, see David Huddart, *Homi K. Bhabha*. Routledge Critical Thinkers series (New York: Routledge, 2008).

107. For Bhabha, the ambivalence of colonial authority transitions from mimicry—a difference between colonizer and colonized that is "almost but not quite"—to a menace—"a difference that is almost total but not quite." Bhabha, "Of Mimicry and Man: The Ambivalence of Colonial Discourse," in *Location of Culture*, 131.

4. Demetrios Chomatianos: Colonial Resistance and the Fear of Sacramental Miscegenation

1. See Demacopoulos "'Traditional Orthodoxy' as a Postcolonial Movement," *Journal of Religion* 97 (2017): 475–99; and Demacopoulos and Aristotle Papanikolaou, "The Orthodox Naming of the Other: A Postcolonial Approach," in *Orthodox Constructions of the West*, ed. Demacopoulos and Papanikolaou (New York: Fordham University Press, 2013), 1–22.

2. Robert J. C. Young, *Colonial Desire: Hybridity in Theory, Culture, and Race* (London: Routledge, 1995).

3. *Oxford Dictionary of Byzantium*, vol. 3 (New York: Oxford University Press, 1991), 1514–15.

4. On the twelfth-century claim, see Günter Prinzing, "Entstehung und Rezeption der Justiniana-Prima Theorie im Mittelalter," *Byzantinobulgarica* 5

(1978): 269–87. On Justinian's promotion of the church of his birthplace, see Robert Markus, "Carthage-Prima Justiniana-Ravenna: Aspects of Justinian's *Kirchenpolitik*," *Byzantion* 49 (1979): 277–306.

5. See Margaret Mueller, *Theophylact of Ochrid: Reading the Letters of a Byzantine Archbishop* (reprinted—London: Routledge, 2016).

6. When Constantinople fell to the Latins in 1204, Byzantine aristocrats erected three competing successor states in Epiros, Nicaea, and Trebizond. The fact that each of the three had a partial but not uncontested claim as authentic successor to the Byzantine throne meant that the three typically worked against rather than with one another to wrest control away from the Latins.

7. For more on the ecclesiastical ranks of the Byzantine-era Church, see Milton Efthimiou and Matthew Briel, *Titles, Offices & Ranks in the Byzantine Empire and Orthodox Church* (New York: Order of St. Andrew the Apostle, 2016).

8. The combination of these two actions caused a schism between the two leading Byzantine political factions in exile during the Latin occupation. In the end, it would be the faction based in Nicaea, not Epiros, which retook Constantinople in 1261. But the partisan divide between the two dynasties continued until the demise of the empire in the fifteenth century. Scholarly examinations are plentiful, but for the specific dynamics of the rivalry between the two factions in this period and the ways in which the Church's hierarchy became embroiled in the squabble, see Apostolos Karpozilos, *The Ecclesiastical Controversy between the Kingdom of Nicaea and the Principality of Epiros (1217–1233)* (Thessalonika: Kentron Byzantinon Ereunon, 1973).

9. The vast body of letters and canonical rulings that survive from Chomatianos's tenure as archbishop, in fact, offers the largest resource for the social history of the Balkans in the Middle Ages. However, despite the size of his surviving corpus, scholarly assessment of Chomatianos's career and thought is not particularly extensive. Perhaps the most thorough assessment belongs to Günter Prinzing in his introduction to a critical edition of Chomatianos's rulings: *Demetrii Chomateni Ponemata Diaphora*, ed. Prinzing, Corpus Fontium Historiae Byzantinae series, vol. 38 (Berlin: Walter de Gruyter, 2002), 3–62; I am indebted to Christopher Sprecher who prepared preliminary draft translations of key excerpts from Chomatianos's lengthy collection of canonical rulings during the spring of 2017. For other assessments of Chomatianos, see also Ruth J. Macrides, "Bad Historian or Good Lawyer?: Demetrios Chomatenos and Novel 131," *Dumbarton Oaks Papers* 46 (1992): 187–96; and Paul Magdalino, "A Neglected Source for the History of the Peloponnese in the Early Thirteenth Century: Demetrios Chomatianos, Archbishop of Bulgaria," *Byzantinische Zeitschrift* 70 (1977): 316–23.

10. The scholarly literature on East/West estrangement is vast. For a solid introduction to the material, see Henry Chadwick, *East and West: The Making of*

a Rift in the Church—From Apostolic Times until the Council of Florence (Oxford: Oxford University Press, 2003). An important albeit more apologetic assessment is Aristeides Papadakis's *The Christian East and the Rise of the Papacy* (Crestwood, N.Y.: St. Vladimir's Seminary Press, 1994). For an older account, see Stephen Runciman, *The Eastern Schism: A Study of the Papacy and the Eastern Churches during the Eleventh and Twelfth Centuries* (Oxford: Oxford University Press, 1955).

11. While no Byzantine sources survive to authenticate this, beginning in the eleventh century there were a number of Latin authors who complained of the Byzantine practice of requiring Latin brides to undergo the rite of baptism a second time before they could marry into the Byzantine royal family. If true, this would suggest that some within the Byzantine Church did not believe Latins were sacramentally sound. Tia Kolbaba has argued, I believe compellingly, that the Latins confused (perhaps intentionally so) the Byzantine rite of chrismation for a second baptism. But why the Byzantines would have required a chrismation, let alone a second baptism, for a Latin prior to a marriage with a Byzantine in the eleventh century is unclear. What is more, even though this complaint was recycled by Western authors for centuries, we have no evidence in the Greek sources that an Eastern council of bishops or an individual patriarch ever suggested that Latins should undergo baptism prior to marriage with Eastern Christians. And while it is plausible that some Greek clerics might have required a chrismation, the evidence that chrismations actually occurred is scarce. Tia Kolbaba, "On the Closing of the Churches and the Rebaptism of Latins: Greek Perfidy or Latin Slander?" *Byzantine and Modern Greek Studies* 29 (2005): 39–51. For a critique of Kolbaba's interpretation, see Judith Ryder, "Changing Perspectives on 1054," *Byzantine and Modern Greek Studies* 35 (2013): 20–37.

12. Certainly, East and West had undergone periods of schism as far back as the fourth century and by the ninth century there were increasing accusations of theological error, even heresy, about teachings such as the *filioque*. For an overview of the long history of the *filioque* debates, see A. Edward Siecienski, *The Filioque: History of a Doctrinal Controversy* (Oxford: Oxford University Press, 2010). For a careful examination of how those debates played out during the ninth century, see Tia Kolbaba, *Inventing Latin Heretics: Byzantines and the Filioque in the Ninth Century* (Kalamazoo: Medieval Institute Publications, 2008).

13. The most thorough engagement of the context of this exchange as well as an analysis of Balsamon's views is that of Patrick Viscuso, trans., *Guide for a Church under Islam: The Sixty-Six Canonical Questions Attributed to Theodoros Balsamon* (Brookline, Mass.: Holy Cross Orthodox Press, 2014).

14. Theodore Balsamon, Σύνταγμα τῶν θείων καὶ ἱερῶν κανόνων, ed. G. A. Rhalles and M. Potles, vol. 4 (Athens, 1852–59), 447–96. The question at issue is number 16. For an English translation, see Viscuso, *Guide for a Church under Islam*, 84–85. Viscuso speculates that readmission to the Church under such an injunction

might take any variety of means including baptism, chrismation, or a simple proclamation of correct faith. Such an interpretation might, however, be reading later debates and practices into a text that only explicitly requires a "promise."

15. For a general and up-to-date survey of Eastern Christian attitudes toward papal authority, see A. Edward Siecienski, *The Papacy and the Orthodox: Sources and History of a Debate* (Oxford: Oxford University Press, 2017).

16. Balsamon, Σύνταγμα, vol. 2, 253–54. In this case, Balsamon was commenting on Canon 14 of the Council of Chalcedon, which forbade lower clergy from marrying heretics. The seventh-century council, which met in Trullo, reaffirmed the Chalcedonian proscription and amplified it by extending it to all Christians and by declaring null and void all marriages between Orthodox and heretics that might have already taken place. Of course, it should be noted that there was no Byzantine rite of marriage as we now know it when these canons were issued. Marriage as a sacramental rite did not develop a liturgical form until the tenth century. See John Meyendorff, "Christian Marriage in Byzantium: The Canonical and Liturgical Tradition," *Dumbarton Oaks Papers* 44 (1990): 99–107. For an excellent overview of Byzantine attitudes toward marriage with those deemed canonically outside of the Church, see Viscuso, "Marriage between Orthodox and Non-Orthodox: A Canonical Study," *Greek Orthodox Theological Review* 40 (1995): 229–46.

17. See Viscuso, "Marriage between Orthodox and Non-Orthodox." Balsamon's discussion of heresy and marriage in Byzantium is mostly concerned with contemporary adherents in the Eastern Church of ancient heresies such as Nestorianism and Monophysitism or with the idiosyncrasies of the Armenian community.

18. Indeed, neither Balsamon's directive regarding the Eucharist nor the one for marriage require Latins to undergo baptism or chrismation for participation in the services of the Church. Instead, both situations appear only to require some form of pledge of orthodox faith that might be oriented toward a repudiation of claims of papal sovereignty.

19. See Viscuso, *Guide for a Church under Islam*, 6–9.

20. See, for example, Michael Angold, *Church and Society in Byzantium under the Comneni: 1081–1261* (Cambridge: Cambridge University Press, 1995), 507–08.

21. Viscuso, *Guide for a Church under Islam*, 31–34. Medieval Egypt was a religiously diverse space with many Christian communities that were not in sacramental communion with the Byzantine Church. The largest of these groups, of course, were Coptic Christians, whose dispute with the Byzantines went back to the Council of Chalcedon in 451. As the leader of one of the smaller Christian communities of Alexandria, Mark's efforts to halt not only sacramental comingling between Christian groups but even "public" comingling—such as the sharing of a meal—would have been unpopular.

22. Chomatianos, *Ponemata* 54.1. The monastery was built under the supervision of two Georgian monks (John the Iberian and Tornike Eristavi) between 980 and 983. The name originates from the ancient Georgian kingdom of Iberia (Iveria).

23. Chomatianos, *Ponemata* 54.1.

24. Chomatianos, *Ponemata* 54.1.

25. Chomatianos, *Ponemata* 54.1.

26. Several tenth- and eleventh-century sources affirm the presence of Benedictine monks (originally from Amalfi) on Athos. See, for example, the life of the Georgian monks who founded Iviron written by George the Hagiorite around the year 1045. Leo Bonsall, "The Benedictine Monastery of St. Mary on Mount Athos," *Eastern Churches Review* 2 (1969): 262–7.

27. It is not surprising that such a question emerged—those monasteries that refused to accept papal sovereignty were subject to the confiscation of goods.

28. Chomatianos, *Ponemata* 54.2. The alien theological teachings are the *filioque* and azymes (using bread in the Eucharistic meal that does not contain yeast). By "refusing the authority of the bishop of Rome," Chomatianos likely means that the Eastern patriarchal sees do not commemorate the name of the bishop of Rome during the liturgy (an ancient practice of recognition for one another's authority). Here, especially, it appears that Chomatianos might be drawing on the work of Balsamon who had emphasized the fact that it was the practice of the four ancient patriarchal sees to reject the commemoration of the pope because of the introduction of alien customs.

29. Chomatianos, *Ponemata* 54.2.

30. Chomatianos, *Ponemata* 54.2. Thus, because the Latin view of the Trinity and papal authority are not consistent with Greek theological practice, a Greek monk cannot be the friend of any monk who prays for the pope, nor can he be a friend of any Greek monk who is a friend of any other monks prays for the pope.

31. Chomatianos, *Ponemata* 54.3.

32. Chomatianos, *Ponemata* 54.4.

33. By unprecedented, I refer to the practical implications of canonical interpretation from an ecclesiastical court—I do not mean to suggest that he was the first Eastern Christian to suggest that the Latins were in error or that the Greeks should avoid them. There is, of course, a very long history of both. See Tia Kolbaba, *Inventing Latin Heretics*.

34. Chomatianos, *Ponemata* 22.1–3. In *Ponemata* 22.3, Chomatianos suggests that in such cases he is obliged to follow the direction established by the emperor (Doukas), who is rightly ordained by God to issue laws regulating marriage. Given that Doukas sides with the claimant in this case, it should hardly be a surprise that Chomatianos will do the same.

35. Chomatianos, *Ponemata* 22.4.

36. Indeed, throughout the text, Chomatianos portrays Chamaretos as the lone true patriot of Greek resistance to the Latins in the Peloponnese, and Daimonoioannes as someone willing to exploit the political instability of the period for personal advantage.

37. Chomatianos, *Ponemata* 22.5.

38. Chomatianos, *Ponemata* 22.5.

39. Chomatianos, *Ponemata* 22.6–10. The testimony of the Greek bishop of Pelegonia (*Ponemata* 22.10) is especially important in the case, not only because of his assumed credibility but because he testifies to the fact that both Daimonoioannes and his daughter attempted to kill Chamaretos.

40. Chomatianos, *Ponemata* 22.11–12.

41. Chomatianos, *Ponemata* 22.11. The law was issued by Justinian and then reinforced in the eleventh century by Alexius Komnenos.

42. Indeed, the very petition to Chomatianos's court comes from the ruler of Epiros, Theodore Doukas.

43. Chomatianos, *Ponemata* 22.12.

44. I should note that there is another canonical ruling attributed to Chomatianos that explicitly proscribes Greek/Latin marriage. In a different genre of canonical opinion, known as *Erotapokriseis* (a short question and answer format), the petitioner of question #210 (#ΣΙ) asks whether a Greek priest can offer a blessing to a couple who was officially married by a Latin priest. The answer is that this cannot happen (a blessing after a marriage) because the initial marriage is invalid. The implicit answer is that the couple have separated themselves from the Orthodox body by having a sacrament performed by a Latin priest and they must first undergo some means of reconciliation before their wedding can be recognized. The authorship for this text is questionable. Although it was included in an edition of medieval Greek canonical sources edited by Pitra and attributed there to Chomatianos, this particular question is not among the authentic *Erotapokriseis* listed by Prinzing. Prinzing does propose that many of the *Erotapokriseis* attributed to Chomatianos might actually belong to John of Kitros. Jean Baptiste Pitra, ed., *Analecta sacra spicilegio Solesmensi parata*, vol. 6 (Paris: A. Jouby et Roger, 1876), col. 713. See Prinzing, *Demetrii Chomateni Ponemata Diaphora*, 55. See also Donald Nicol who used this reference in the Pitra edition to conclude that Chomatianos condemned Orthodox/Catholic marriage to such a degree that officiating priests would be suspended and the Orthodox partner excommunicated. Donald Nicol, "Symbiosis and Integration: Some Greco-Latin Families in Byzantium in the 11th to 13th Century," *Byzantinische Forschungen* 7 (1979): 113–35; here, 120. My thanks to Fr. Alexander Rentel who helped me unpack the many layers of this attribution.

45. Canon 14 of the Fourth Ecumenical Council at Chalcedon forbid the lower clergy from marrying heretics. Canon 72 of the seventh-century council,

which met in Trullo, reaffirmed that proscription and amplified it by extending it to all Christians and by declaring null and void all marriages between Orthodox and heretics that might have already taken place. Given the context, the primary targets of these measures were those whose marriages united Chalcedonian and non-Chalcedonian Christians. To my knowledge, there has never been a study of the implementation or reception of these impediments to Chalcedonian/non-Chalcedonian marriage in the Byzantine era. Centuries later, several middle-Byzantine canonists, such as Balsamon, reaffirmed the general thrust of these canons. See Viscuso, "Marriage between Orthodox and Non-Orthodox."

46. Although not reliant upon Young, Megan Moore demonstrates the ways in which Old French Romance literature frequently relies upon cross-cultural and heterogeneous marriages with Byzantine women to advance the fiction of cultural cohesion for the medieval French nobility. Moore, *Exchanges in Exoticism: Cross-Cultural Marriage and the Making of the Mediterranean in Old French Romance* (Toronto: University of Toronto Press, 2014).

47. Young, *Colonial Desire*, see especially, Chapter 2, "Culture and the History of Difference," 29–54.

48. "This antagonistic structure acts out the tensions of a conflictual culture that defines itself through racial ideologies." Young, *Colonial Desire*, 19.

49. Indeed, Chomatianos's descriptions of Latins, such as they exist, concern their theological commitments rather than their cultural practices. For more on the way that theological concerns shifted the parameters of ethnography during the Byzantine period, see Anthony Kaldellis, *Ethnography after Antiquity: Foreign Lands and Peoples in Byzantine Literature* (Philadelphia: University of Pennsylvania Press, 2013), esp. 56–72.

50. Like the racial theorists of the eighteenth century who were trying to explain why Africans and Asians are "similar to but different from" Europeans, Chomatianos develops a grammar of theological difference that prohibits the middle space—prohibits the ecclesiastical hybrid. In addition to the evidence of Greek/Latin harmony on Athos prior to 1204 and the proliferation of Greek/Latin marriage among the aristocratic classes that occurred after 1204, there is also evidence of Greek aristocrats who willingly adopted Western liturgical rites and affiliation. Some examples are offered by Page, *Being Byzantine: Greek Identity before the Ottomans, 1200–1420* (Cambridge: Cambridge University Press, 2008), 199.

51. A great deal of scholarly research has explored the aristocratic connections and ever-changing factionalism during this period. See, for example the many illuminating essays in Benjamin Arbel, Bernard Hamilton, and David Jacoby, eds., *Latins and Greeks in the Eastern Mediterranean after 1204* (London: Routledge, 1989); and Donald Nicol, "Symbiosis and Integration"; and "Mixed Population and Local Patriotism in Epiros and Western Macedonia during the Fourth

Crusade," in *XVe congrès international des études byzantines, Rapports: 1 Histoire* (Athens, 1976), 1–33. Studies of *The Chronicle of Morea* are particularly well positioned to examine this material. Of recent, note Teresa Shawcross, *The Chronicle of Morea: Historiography in Crusader Greece* (Oxford: Oxford University Press, 2009). See also Page, *Being Byzantine*, 177–242.

52. The thirteenth-century chronicles by Niketas Choniates and George Akropolites are especially relevant. Note, for example, the way that Akropolites describes Theodore I Laskaris's efforts to marry off his daughters to secure political alliances with the Latins. Theodore also takes a Latin bride for his third wife, sister of the Latin emperor of Constantinople, Robert. Akropolites, *Historia*, in *Georgii Acropolitae Opera*, ed. A. Heisenberg and P. Wirth (Stuttgart: Teubner, 1978); English translation: *George Akropolites: The History—Translated with an Introduction and Commentary by Ruth J. Macrides* (Oxford: Oxford University Press, 2007), paragraph 15.

53. On this score, it is illuminating to contrast Chomatianos's efforts to drive a wedge between the Greek and Latin populations against the picture of the interethnic cooperation and religious indifference in *The Chronicle of Morea*, which is a fourteenth-century pro-Frankish chronicle of the Villehardouin dynasty of the Peloponnese of the thirteenth century. What is especially noteworthy is that many of the same personalities of *Ponemata* 22 are included in the *Chronicle*. For a detailed examination of this aspect of the *Chronicle*, see Shawcross, *Chronicle of Morea*, esp. 211–37 as well as the final chapter of this volume.

54. It is important to note, however, that Theodore Doukas's interest in Greek/Latin theological difference was largely utilitarian. When it suited his purposes to do so, he was perfectly willing to align himself with papal agents, effectively establishing a temporary ecclesiastical union. The same was true of Manuel Doukas, Theodore's brother and successor. See Nikolaos Chrissis, *Crusading in Frankish Greece: A Study of Byzantine-Western Relations and Attitudes 1204–1282* (Turnhout: Brepols, 2012), 94–95.

55. To be sure, this is not the first Byzantine text to raise questions about the efficacy of marriage outside of the *ethnos*. Emperor Constantine VII Porphyrogenitos, writing in the middle of the tenth century claimed that just as animals mate with their own kind, so too the Romans were a distinct group that should stick to their own—specifically, he was critiquing a marriage between a Roman (i.e., a Byzantine) and a Bulgar. Constantine, *De administrando imperio*, ed. C. Moravcsik and R. J. H. Jenkins (Washington: Dumbarton Oaks Center for Byzantine Studies, 1962–67), 13.175–81. The same text, however, recognizes that marriages between the imperial court of Constantinople and the Franks were taking place. See Price, *Being Byzantine*, 43–45; and Ruth J. Macrides, "Dynastic Marriages and Political Kinship," in *Byzantine Diplomacy* ed. J. Shepard and S. Franklin (Aldershot, U.K.: Variorum, 1992), 263–80.

56. See, especially, the work of David Jacoby, including "Les Vénitiens naturalisés dans l'Empire Byzantin: un aspect de l'expansion de Venise en Romanie du XIIIᵉ au milieu du XVᵉ siècle," *Travaux et Mémoires* 8 (1981): 217–35; and "After the Fourth Crusade: The Latin Empire of Constantinople and the Frankish States," in *The Cambridge History of the Byzantine Empire c.500–1492*, ed. Jonathan Shepard (New York: Cambridge University Press, 2009), 759–78.

57. The majority of the surviving sources describe the role of the *gasmoules* as sailors in the Byzantine navy. For a summary of the historiographical debate concerning their identity, see Thekla Sansaridou-Hendrickx, "The Gasmules in the 13th and the 14th Centuries: Social Outcasts or Advocates of Cultural Integration?," *Acta Platristica et Byzantina* 8 (1997): 135–43. On the Latin side, most of the proscriptions came from the Venetians. The Franks, by contrast, made it a policy to intermarry with daughters of Greek aristocrats.

58. I would argue, in fact, that Eastern Christian thought since the crusades has been haunted by a set of insecurities born of subjugation and defeat and that all contemporary Eastern Christian discourse seeks to compensate for these embedded anxieties in one way or another.

59. Page, *Being Byzantine*. Kaldellis provides an even more succinct articulation of ways in which Byzantine authors after the crusades felt the destabilizing effects of a Latin "gaze" that upended their cultural sensibilities, confidence, and identity. Kaldellis, *Ethnography after Antiquity*, 168–72.

60. By way of contrast, "orthodoxy" was far less often identified as a constituent marker of Roman identity for the elite circles of the Nicaean Empire that recaptured Constantinople in 1261.

61. In the year 1484, the Church of Constantinople (likely under pressure from the Ottoman government) passed a conciliar decree officially adopting Balsamon and Chomatenos's restriction against sharing the Eucharist with Latins. For more on the nineteenth- and twentieth-century story, see Demacopoulos "'Traditional Orthodoxy' as a Postcolonial Movement."

5. George Akropolites and the Counterexample(s)

1. The text itself offers few internal indications of the date of composition apart from the fact that it is situated after Michael VIII Palaiologos took Constantinople in 1261.

2. For a cursory summary of his civil positions and career more generally, see "George Akropolites" in *The Oxford Dictionary of Byzantium* (New York: Oxford University Press, 1991). For a more thorough biography, see Ruth Macrides's introduction to *George Akropolites: The History—Translated with an Introduction and Commentary by Ruth J. Macrides* (Oxford: Oxford University Press, 2007), 3–104, especially 19–28 concerning his public career.

3. Concerning his family pedigree, see Alexander Kazhdan and Silvia Ronchey, *L'aristocrazia bizantina dal principio dell'XI alla fine del XII secolo* (Palermo: Sellerio, 1997), 104; and Macrides, *George Akropolites: The History*, 6–7.

4. Macrides, *George Akropolites: The History*, 8, esp. note 26, which references Gregory of Cyprus's claim that secondary education in Nicosia was in Latin and proposes that the same might have been the case in Constantinople.

5. Akropolites, *Historia*, 32.2. Several editions of the Greek text of the *Historia* are in existence, the most recent being that of P. Wirth (who reprints and corrects A. Heisenberg's 1903 edition); see *Georgii Acropolitae Opera* (Stuttgart: Teubner, 1978). Ruth J. Macrides, *George Akropolites: The History*, offers an English translation.

6. Each of the letters is from Theodore to George. None of George's letters to the emperor survive. In response to the gift of the collection, the emperor prepared an encomium for Akropolites. For the letters, see N. Festa, ed., *Theodori Ducae Lascaris Epistulae CCVII* (Florence, 1898), 67–116. For the encomium, see Aloysius Tartaglia, ed., *Theodorus II Ducas Lascaris opuscula rhetorica* (Munich: K. G. Saur, 2000), 96–108, esp. 105.225. For an overview, see Macrides, *George Akropolites: The History*, 9–11.

7. Akropolites, *Historia*, 49. See Macrides, *George Akropolites: The History*, 11–12.

8. Akropolites, *Historia*, 66 and 68.

9. Akropolites, *Historia*, 72 and 82. See Macrides, *George Akropolites: The History*, 12.

10. Interestingly, Akropolites was one of the very few close associates of Emperor Theodore to survive the purge that followed the change in dynasty in 1259. Of course, at the time of Michael VIII's rise to power, George was in a prison in Epiros.

11. See Macrides, *George Akropolites: The History* 12–14.

12. Macrides, *George Akropolites: The History*, 13–14.

13. Gregory was patriarch of Constantinople from 1283 to 1289 and famously led the eventual Byzantine repudiation of the Second Council of Lyon in 1285. Given that Lyon had been largely orchestrated by Akropolites, we can see Gregory's efforts as a repudiation of his teacher's theological and diplomatic work.

14. According to Macrides, Akropolites continued fulfilling many of his duties as *megas logothete*, particularly his judicial role. In 1273, Michael VIII appointed Akropolites to sit among the senators who were judging John Bekkos (then *chartophylax*) for his opposition to Michael's policies regarding union with the West. Convicted in this trial, Michael imprisoned Bekkos but the latter ultimately changed his mind and went on to become one of the century's most important theological advocates of union with the West.

15. It is unknown what the precise nature was of the relationship between George's wife, Eudoxia, and Michael VIII. The marriage occurred prior to 1256, thus before Michael's rise to power. See Macrides, *George Akropolites: The History*, 17–18.

16. Among other things, the Second Council of Lyon (which is considered an ecumenical council in the Roman Catholic Church) was the first general council to declare the *filioque* dogmatically binding. The literature on this council and its aftermath in Byzantium is extensive. For an overview, see Henry Chadwick, *East and West: The Making of a Rift in the Church—From Apostolic Times until the Council of Florence* (Oxford: Oxford University Press, 2003). For a precise account of the *filioque* debates in this context, see A. Edward Siecienski, *The Filioque: History of a Doctrinal Controversy* (Oxford: Oxford University Press, 2010).

17. More than anything else, Akropolites's "capitulation" to the Roman Church's primacy was (and remains) a source of great consternation to Orthodox apologists.

18. For an overview of Michael's struggles to enforce the union with the West, see Chadwick, *East and West*, 246–58; A. Edward Siecienski, *The Papacy and the Orthodox: Sources and History of a Debate* (Oxford: Oxford University Press, 2017), 293–309 and, especially, Aristedis Papadakis, *Crisis in Byzantium: The Filioque Controversy in the Patriarchate of Gregory II of Cyprus (1283–1289)* (Crestwood, N.Y.: St. Vladimir's Seminary Press, 1997).

19. George's son Constantine noted in his own will that his father had "collided with the church and the traditions of the church, having given most to the master and the emperor." See Macrides, *George Akropolites: The History*, 19.

20. For an assessment of the theological teaching of these tracts and how we might reconcile them with his advocacy of union at the Council of Lyon, see Gerhard Richter, "Des Georgios Akropolites Gedanken über Theologie, Kirche und Kircheneinheit," *Byzantion* 54 (1984): 276–99.

21. Like Anna Komnena and George Pachymeres, Akropolites identifies just two responsibilities for the historian—to be impartial and to relate events that might otherwise be consigned to oblivion. See Macrides, *George Akropolites: The History*, 30; and, also, Macrides, "The Thirteenth Century in Byzantine Historical Writing," in *Porphyrogenita: Essays on the History and Literature of Byzantium and the Latin East in Honor of Julian Chrysostomides*, ed. Charalambos Dendrinos, et al. (Aldershot, U.K.: Ashgate, 2003), 63–76.

22. Akropolites was one of only four thirteenth-century Greek chroniclers. He and George Pachymeres provide the most extensive accounts of the thirteenth century—Akropolites covers the period between 1203 and 1261 and Pachymeres covers 1255 to 1308. Niketas Choniates, whose *Chronike diegesis* spans 1118–1206, provides the single best Greek account of the events of 1204 (he was in resident in Constantinople at the time), but offers few details of the lingering impact of

the Latin conquest on Greek communities or the Nicaean Empire more generally, which is the primary thrust of Akropolites account. Theodore Skoutariotes provides an additional thirteenth-century voice, but his chronicle adheres more closely to the "one world genre" attempting to record the entirety of history beginning with creation. More importantly, Skoutariotes relies heavily on Akropolites for his coverage of the Latin Empire of Byzantium. Thus, Akropolites's *Historia* is effectively the only primary historical account of the Greek Christian community in exile during the Latin Empire of Byzantium. For an overview of where Akropolites fits within the thirteenth-century chroniclers, see Macrides, *George Akropolites: The History*, 4–5. For a summary of the historiographical and scholarly debates surrounding Choniates's life and work, see the many studies by Alicia Simpson, including *Niketas Choniates: A Historiographical Study* (Oxford: Oxford University Press, 2013) and *Niketas Choniates: A Historian and Writer* (Geneva: La Pomme d'Or, 2009). A. Heisenberg identified Skoutariotes with the anonymous author of the *Synopsis chronike* preserved in the Marcan Library of Venice (*Marc. gr.* 407), which begins with creation and continues until 1261. See Macrides, *George Akropolites: The History*, 5n11.

23. According to Akropolites, the Epirotes are not Romans; they are a "Western race" (80); they break oaths (25, 38, 49); they usurp power (21, 26, 40); and they are ignorant of Roman traditions (21). Such accusations, of course, reflect the continued question of Nicaean versus Epirote claims to legitimacy vis-à-vis the reclamation of the Byzantine throne. But it is important to recall that this very demarcation, between Nicaeans and Epirote claims, is the consequence of the Latin colonization of Byzantium and the inability of indigenous community to rally around a single mode of resistance.

24. Akropolites, *Historia*, 36; trans. Macrides, *George Akropolites: The History*, 200.

25. John III Vatatzes was the emperor of Nicaea from 1222–54.

26. The alliance lasted less than a year as the Bulgarians soon pulled their support for the Latins in Constantinople. See Macrides, *George Akropolites: The History*, 202nn2–5; Richard Spence, "Gregory IX's Attempted Expeditions to the Latin Empire of Constantinople: The Crusade for the Union of the Latin and Greek Churches," *Journal of Medieval History* 5 (1979): 163–76; and Nikolaos Chrissis, *Crusading in Frankish Greece: A Study of Byzantine-Western Relations and Attitudes 1204–1282* (Turnhout: Brepols, 2012), 106–13.

27. Akropolites, *Historia*, 36; Macrides, *George Akropolites: The History*, 200. He goes on to note that the Nicaeans were able to weather a siege at the town of Tzouroulos, despite being greatly outnumbered, and that Asan returned to the Nicaeans when he learned of the death of his wife and child, which he took to be a sign of divine retribution for his disloyalty. Akropolites, *Historia*, 36; Macrides, *George Akropolites: The History*, 201.

28. Both paragraph 37 and paragraph 76 include acknowledgments of ongoing hostility between the Latins and the Romans but in less striking ways. Paragraph 76, for example, chronicles the emergence of Michael VIII Palaiologos at a time of multiple threats to the empire and acknowledges that there is a contingent of the "Latin race" within the electoral body of the Empire of Nicaea that is separate from those who rule Constantinople.

29. See, for example, Akropolites, *Historia*, 15; Macrides, *George Akropolites: The History*, 149. See Macrides commentary in the introduction at 89–91, where she observes that Akropolites made similar claims about the Bulgarians.

30. For more on the complicated meaning of the word *Rhomaikos* in Akropolites's text, which can mean the soldiers of the true Romans (i.e., the Nicaeans) or the Greek population more broadly, see the analysis by Gill Page, *Being Byzantine: Greek Identity before the Ottomans, 1200–1420* (Cambridge: Cambridge University Press, 2008), 99–107.

31. Akropolites, *Historia*, 16; Macrides, *George Akropolites: The History*, 153.

32. Akropolites, *Historia*, 17; Macrides, *George Akropolites: The History*, 154.

33. Akropolites, *Historia*, 17; Macrides, *George Akropolites: The History*, 155.

34. Akropolites, *Historia*, 17; Macrides, *George Akropolites: The History*, 155.

35. Akropolites, *Historia*, 17; Macrides, *George Akropolites: The History*, 155.

36. In paragraph 16, Akropolites is summarizing his view of emperor Henry. In paragraph 17, he chronicles the sad state of affairs under the legate, Pelagus, and the efforts of the "inhabitants of the city" to speak to Henry.

37. The battle occurred in 1223 or 1224 and served as the first of a series of skirmishes that drove the Latin Empire out of most of Asia Minor. When the two brothers were captured, they were blinded for their treason. Akropolites, *Historia*, 22; Macrides, *George Akropolites: The History*, 165–69; see especially the helpful notes by Macrides.

38. As noted, Akropolites composed two tracts against the Latin teaching of the procession of the Holy Spirit, which largely reflect the Byzantine position of his era. It is generally assumed that he composed these treatises while in prison in Arta. See Richter, "Des Gregorios Akropolites Gedanken," for an assessment.

39. Akropolites, *Historia*, 50; Macrides, *George Akropolites: The History*, 259–68. At issue was the potential treason of Michael Komnenos Palaiologos (the future emperor Michael VIII) near the end of the reign of John III in 1253. The specifics of the charges need not concern us. The significance, for our purposes, lies with the startling testimony that the Nicaean court chose to pursue jousting between two aristocrats as a means of obtaining a divine judgment about which of the two was telling the truth. Not surprisingly, this episode has drawn a considerable amount of scholarly attention. For an overview, see Macrides's helpful notes in *George Akropolites: The History*, 263–68.

40. For a survey of the medieval (Western) concept of trial by fire, see Robert Bartlett, *Trial by Fire and Water* (Oxford: Clarendon Press, 1986).

41. Akropolites presents the future emperor Michael VIII as willing to endure the contest to prove both his innocence and his faith in God. But it is the presiding metropolitan bishop who decries the practice as alien to the Church and the Roman way of life. Akropolites, *Historia*, 50; Macrides, *George Akropolites: The History*, 262.

42. As noted, he does opine that Pelagius's responsibility to lead Constantinopolitan Greeks to accept papal authority was "reasonable."

43. Akropolites, *Historia*, 15; Macrides, *George Akropolites: The History*, 148–53.

44. Akropolites, *Historia*, 15; Macrides, *George Akropolites: The History*, 148–53.

45. Akropolites, *Historia*, 18; Macrides, *George Akropolites: The History*, 157–59. According to Orthodox canon law and Byzantine imperial law (which are often one and the same), one cannot marry into a family with which one is already spiritually joined through the sacraments of baptism or marriage. See, among other things, Angeliki Laiou, *Mariage amour et parenté à Byzance aux XI–XIII siècles* (Paris: De Boccard, 1992); and Laiou, "Marriage Prohibitions, Marriage Strategies, and the Dowry in Thirteenth-Century Byzantium," in *La Traduisissions du Patrimoine: Byzance et l'aire méditerranéen* (Paris: De Boccard, 1998), 129–60.

46. Donald Nicol argued that the emperor Michael VIII not only arranged marriages with Latins in order to improve diplomatic relations with them, but also may have married off the daughters of Theodore II as a way to prevent them from marrying Byzantine aristocrats who might have challenged his claim to the throne. See Donald Nicol, "The Price of Survival," in *The Last Centuries of Byzantium 1261–1453* (New York: Cambridge University Press, 1993).

47. As we have seen in several chapters, crusader accounts of the Christian East reflect a series of Orientalizing characteristics and their account of the conquest of the East often incorporates a sexual dimension.

48. See, especially, his opening pages where, even though his chronicle will focus exclusively on the period of the Nicaean Empire, he connects the Palaiologan dynasty and the Empire of Nicaea to the Ancient Roman tradition mediated in the East through the Roman emperor Constantine. Akropolites, *Historia*, 1; Macrides, *George Akropolites: The History*, 105–07. For more on the ways that Byzantine writers on the Middle Byzantine period connected themselves to the Ancient Roman tradition, see Athanasios Markopoulos, "Roman Antiquarianism: Aspects of the Roman Past in the Middle Byzantine Period (9th–11th Centuries)," in *Proceedings of the 21st International Congress of Byzantine Studies*, ed. E. Jeffreys (Aldershot, U.K.: Ashgate, 2006), 277–97. For the period in which Akropolites

is writing, see Kaldellis, *Hellenism in Byzantium: The Transformations of Greek Identity and the Reception of the Classical Tradition* (Cambridge: Cambridge University Press, 2007), 360–68, and Page, *Being Byzantine*, 94–137.

49. Some examples of Byzantine historiography bringing Roman traditions and emperors down to the present day that were in place by the thirteenth century include Michael Psellos's *Historia Syntomos* and John Zonaris's *Epitome* and, of course, Anna Komnene's *Alexiad*. On the connection to Anna's *Alexiad* and other sources, see Macrides, *George Akropolites: The History*, 46–51.

50. With respect to the Franks of the Peloponnese, it is noteworthy that Akropolites never challenges their right to rule it, even though other texts claiming to reproduce the Palaiologan view (such as *The Chronicle of Morea*) will repeatedly assert that the Byzantines refused to accept Frankish rule in the Peloponnese.

51. Akropolites, *Historia* 15 and 17; Macrides, *George Akropolites: The History*, 148 and 155.

52. Akropolites, *Historia* 16; Macrides, *George Akropolites: The History*, 153.

53. Akropolites, *Historia* 17; Macrides, *George Akropolites: The History*, 155.

54. Kaldellis's premier entry into all of these questions is his magisterial *Hellenism in Byzantium*.

6. *The Chronicle of Morea*

1. The Morea, also known as Achaea in the ancient and medieval world, is typically known as the Peloponnese today. The other Latin vassal states were the Kingdom of Thessalonika and the Duchy of Athens. Initially, the Principality of the Morea was in vassalage to the Kingdom of Thessalonika. When the latter was conquered by the despot of Epiros in 1224, the principality became the most powerful Latin realm in Greece.

2. In 1259, William II Villehardouin was captured by forces aligned with Michael VIII Palaiologos at the Battle of Pelagonia. After Michael recaptured Constantinople in 1261, William was able to negotiate his release from prison in exchange for the castles of Mistra, Monemvasia, and Grand Maine.

3. The specific arrangement allowed William to continue as "prince" and effective ruler of the Peloponnese for the remainder of his life. At the time of his death, control of the principality passed to William's eldest daughter, Isabelle, who was married to one of Charles's younger sons.

4. As Teresa Shawcross notes, "It is surely neither insignificant nor accidental that it was precisely at that time at which it faced its greatest threat that Moreot identity came to receive its most uncompromising expression." Teresa Shawcross, *The Chronicle of Morea: Historiography in Crusader Greece* (Oxford: Oxford University Press, 2009), 238.

5. In her own assessment of the *Chronicle*, Shawcross affirms the colonial conditions that gave rise to *The Chronicle of Morea* and acknowledges the ways

that colonial and postcolonial discourse have framed scholarly assessments of the *Chronicle*; however, she does not ever explicitly employ postcolonial critique as a means of interpretation.

6. As the Franks went from town to town (fortress to fortress) in the Peloponnese, local aristocrats were given the option of choosing between conflict (which could result in total annihilation of their lands and privilege) or allegiance (which allowed the lords to retain all property and privilege in exchange for feudal loyalty). For example, see *Chronicle*, vv. 1480–1505, 2015–2105. For an English translation, see Harold Lurier, *Crusaders as Conquerors: The Chronicle of Morea translated from the Greek with Notes and Introduction* (New York: Columbia, 1964), 112 and 130–32. Specifically, the *Chronicle* notes that the indigenous population was permitted to retain its laws, customs, and religion in exchange for feudal loyalty (vv. 2080–2105; Lurier, *Crusaders as Conquerors*, 132).

7. Charles of Anjou is introduced around line 5930 (out of 9219) of the Greek verse account, but he and his heirs do not gain full control of the Morea until the death of William II, which occurs at line 7820.

8. Of the four Greek manuscripts, there are two distinctive branches. The oldest is Ms. Havniensis 57, which has a near copy in Ms. Taurinensis B.II.I. A subsequent Greek text, Ms. Parisinus graecus 2898, dates to the fifteenth or sixteenth century and itself has two copies. The Old French text is catalogued as Royal Library of Belgium no. 15702. The Italian and Aragonese are both derivative of the Greek accounts.

9. For a summary of current scholarship on the manuscript issues, see Shawcross, *Chronicle of Morea*, 31–52. See also Lurier, *Crusaders as Conquerors*, 32–61; and J. J. Schmitt, ed., *The Chronicle of Morea, A History in Political Verse, Relating to the Establishment of Feudalism in Greece by the Franks in the Thirteenth Century, Edited in Two Parallel Texts from the Mss of Copenhagen and Paris, with Introduction, Critical Notes, and Indices* (London: Methuen, 1904).

10. Shawcross contends that the core of the original text was in circulation by the 1320s (some scholars had previously believed it to be earlier than this) and that it was continued (whether by the same author or another is unknowable) into the 1340s. Shawcross, *Chronicle of Morea*, 47.

11. Of the surviving texts, the most hostile to Byzantines is the Havniensis manuscript, which also happens to be the oldest. Subsequent Greek manuscripts reverse much of the editorial bias and it is generally assumed that this editorial change reflects the shifts in political fortunes of the Morea and the willingness of a Greek-speaking audience in a post-Frankish world to continue to see the *Chronicle* as part of its own history. See Shawcross, *Chronicle of Morea,* 187–88, for the ways that this distinction plays out in the coverage of the Battle of Prinitsa in 1262.

12. Lurier, *Crusaders as Conquerors*, 60–61. Throughout his treatment of the question, Lurier is responding to Schmitt, who had insisted that the original could not have been in French.

13. Shawcross, *Chronicle of Morea*, 49–52.

14. It is worth noting that the *Chronicle* is especially hostile to those Greeks who first align with but later betray Frankish interests. Note, for example, that when the Greek population in the region around modern-day Tripoli switches sides in the middle of the war with the Byzantines in the late 1260s, Prince William II orders his Turkish mercenaries to slaughter the population and burn their villages.

15. For more on the alliance between Peloponnesian Greeks and the Franks, see Shawcross who offers multiple examples of the ways that Greek acceptance of the Franks was purchased. Shawcross, *Chronicle of Morea*, 204–06.

16. Perhaps the most surprising error in this respect is the fact that the text actually describes Geoffrey's capture of the castle of Corinth, even though it later asserts that Corinth was one of the castles that resisted Frankish rule.

17. Shawcross observes that there is a subtle "us versus them" employed by the use of pronouns in the oldest surviving manuscripts (both Greek and French) of the *Chronicle*. For example, first-person plural pronouns ("our") for the Franks are often juxtaposed to third-person plural pronouns ("them") for the Greeks. This linguistic distinction, she argues, appears more frequently in the French manuscript. Shawcross, *Chronicle of Morea*, 191–93.

18. For Shawcross's assessment of this aspect of the *Chronicle*, see 193–200.

19. Theodore led the Byzantine troops at the Battle of Pelagonia where William was captured. Theodore was also William's brother-in-law.

20. The entire dialogue runs from vv. 4100–55; Lurier, *Crusaders as Conquerors* 192–95, quotation at 193.

21. What is more, William had marched into northern Greece (where he was ultimately captured) under honorable pretext in order to extend his fame and fortune.

22. Accusations of Byzantine treachery in the context of 1204 run from v. 587 to v. 900; see Schmitt, *Chronicle*; Lurier, *Crusaders as Conquerors*, 85–93.

23. "Behold the iniquity and sin which the wretch committed, to strangle his lord, to seize his sovereign power; who will hear of it and say that men who keep neither to the truth nor to an oath believe in God? Why, the unbaptized races, should they make you an oath, according to the customs which they have and to the law which they adhere to, would receive death rather than commit perjury. But the Romans, who say that they believe in Christ, the more they swear to you and affirm their oaths, the more they plot against you to deceive you, to take of your possessions or to slay you. Alas, and what do they gain by sinning against God? And how completely has the sin which they commit dazzled them, that it

has plucked them out of their estates and they have become slaves all over the world. What other people exists in the world today that is sold as slaves other than the Romans [i.e., Byzantines]? But as each man does, so shall he receive." Schmitt, *Chronicle*, vv. 1245–62; Lurier, *Crusaders as Conquerors*, 103–4. As Lurier notes, a portion of this is omitted in the later pro-Greek manuscript.

24. Schmitt, *Chronicle*, vv. 7132–90; Lurier, *Crusaders as Conquerors*, 273–74.

25. Schmitt, *Chronicle*, vv. 3934–39; Lurier, *Crusaders as Conquerors*, 187. For the practice of "brother-making" as an aristocratic pledge in Byzantium, see Claudia Rapp, *Brother-Making in Late Antiquity and Byzantium: Monks, Laymen, and Christian Ritual* (Oxford: Oxford University Press, 2016).

26. See Shawcross, *Chronicle of Morea*, 201.

27. Shawcross identifies a series of earlier texts that emphasize the theme of Greek effeminacy, including *Gesta Francorum,* Odo of Deuil's *De Profectione Ludovici VII in Orientem, Itinerarium Peregriorum*, and especially Walter Map's *De Nugis Curialium*. See Shawcross, *Chronicle of Morea*, 196–97.

28. Schmitt, *Chronicle*, vv. 4915–70 at vv. 4939–4; Lurier, *Crusaders as Conquerors*, 215.

29. Schmitt, *Chronicle*, vv. 5127–30; Lurier, *Crusaders as Conquerors*, 220–21.

30. Schmitt, *Chronicle*, vv. 4040–70; Lurier, *Crusaders as Conquerors*, 190–91. Another example of the Byzantines employing arrows but not engaging the field is vv. 1070–81, which describes the skirmishes between Franks and Byzantines in the initial years after 1204.

31. A clear example is the story of the Battle of Prinitsa where three hundred knights (supposedly consisting entirely of Frankish descent) defeated thousands of soldiers of mixed identity under Byzantine command. Schmitt, *Chronicle*, vv. 4666–60; Lurier, *Crusaders as Conquerors*, 208–10, see also Lurier's note (208n4), which suggests that the entirety of the passage is a historical fiction.

32. The pope is mentioned only once, in the context of Charles of Anjou who defended the papacy (and St. Peter) by waging war against the Hohenstaufens and the Ghibellines, who are framed as the "tyrannizers of the church." Schmitt, *Chronicle*, vv. 6803–15; Lurier, *Crusaders as Conquerors*, 264–65.

33. Schmitt, *Chronicle*, ca. v. 2090; Lurier, *Crusaders as Conquerors*, 129.

34. Schmitt, *Chronicle*, vv. 7770–7800; Lurier, *Crusaders as Conquerors*, 289–90.

35. Schmitt, *Chronicle*, vv. 755–840; Lurier, *Crusaders as Conquerors*, 89–91.

36. As elsewhere, this particular invective against the Byzantines finds its most expansive form in the Havniensis manuscript. See Shawcross, *Chronicle of Morea*, 198–99.

37. For example, see Schmitt, *Chronicle*, vv. 765–68; Lurier, *Crusaders as Conquerors*, 89.

38. Schmitt, *Chronicle*, vv. 4670; Lurier, *Crusaders as Conquerors*, 208.

39. For this line of interpretation, I am appreciative of the insight of Sharon Kinoshita, whose postcolonial reading of Robert de Clari was instrumental in my thinking about *The Chronicle of Morea*. Shawcross offers an alternative (albeit not unrelated) assessment of the *Chronicle* as the "idyll of a lost age," by which she means that it seeks to present a fictitious past, a fantasy, as a historical truth (*Chronicle of Morea*, 247–49).

40. The entire episode runs from vv. 2100–10; Lurier, *Crusaders as Conquerors*, 132–41. The plot is first introduced at v. 2105.

41. For a detailed account of the difference between the *Chronicle*'s narrative of events and a more plausible historical reconstruction based upon other evidence, see Lurier's long footnote, *Crusaders as Conquerors*, 133–34n66.

42. Schmitt, *Chronicle*, vv. 2351–2410; Lurier, *Crusaders as Conquerors*, 140–41.

43. Schmitt, *Chronicle*, vv. 2472–2628; Lurier, *Crusaders as Conquerors*, 144–48.

44. The entire story makes little sense historically, including of course the notion that Robert would have attempted a marriage alliance with the king of Aragon in the 1220s. See Lurier, *Crusaders as Conquerors*, 144n89. For her part, Shawcross rightfully understands how we should treat sources like this—the importance does not lie solely with the "facts" that they convey, but with the attitudes, ideas, and ideologies they seek to convey. Shawcross, *Chronicle of Morea*, 23–24.

45. Schmitt, *Chronicle*, vv. 4100–4325; Lurier, *Crusaders as Conquerors*, 192–97.

46. Schmitt, *Chronicle*, vv. 5524–40; Lurier, *Crusaders as Conquerors*, 232.

47. Schmitt, *Chronicle*, vv. 5740–5921; Lurier, *Crusaders as Conquerors*, 237–41.

48. The text, in fact, offers one of its most profound prebattle speeches: Schmitt, *Chronicle*, vv. 3952–4015; Lurier, *Crusaders as Conquerors*, 188–89.

49. Schmitt, *Chronicle*, vv. 4030–95.

50. On William's advising Charles of strategy, see Schmitt, *Chronicle*, vv. 6922–7007; Lurier, *Crusaders as Conquerors*, 267–69; on implementing a strategy of deception, see Schmitt, *Chronicle*, vv. 7030–90.

51. Schmitt, *Chronicle*, vv. 6951–56; Lurier, *Crusaders as Conquerors*, 268.

52. Schmitt, *Chronicle*, vv. 5120–5470; Lurier, *Crusaders as Conquerors*, 220–30.

53. Schmitt, *Chronicle*, vv. 5632–70; Lurier, *Crusaders as Conquerors*, 234–35.

54. On the effort to account for this rupture, see especially Schmitt, *Chronicle*, vv. 4450–4513.

55. Schmitt, *Chronicle*, vv. 6264–70; Lurier, *Crusaders as Conquerors*, 250–52.

56. On the arrangement with Charles, see Shawcross, *Chronicle of Morea*, 241–44.

57. For a summary of the origins of hybridity in postcolonial critique, see Robert Young, *Postcolonialism: An Historical Introduction* (Oxford: Blackwell Publishing, 2001), especially "India III: Hybridity and Subaltern Agency," which explore the insights of Anish Nandy and Homi Bhabha 337–59. For a more in-depth genealogy of "hybridity" as a category of cultural identity, see Robert J. C. Young, *Colonial Desire: Hybridity in Theory, Culture, and Race* (London: Routledge, 1995).

58. In such a setting, hybridity, like ambivalence, can reveal an inherent disconnect between the ideology of colonial mastery and the reality of the colonial experience.

59. On *archondes*, see Shawcross, *Chronicle of the Morea*, 16, who details the independence of certain key families (Chamaretos and Sgouros) from Byzantine imperial rule. On the Chameteros family, see also Paul Magdalino, "A Neglected Authority for the History of the Peloponnese in the Early 13th Century: Demetrios Chomatianos, Archbishop of Bulgaria," *Byzantinische Zeitschrift* 70 (1977): 316–23. On the long history of the word "archon" from its ancient Greek use to its contemporary use in the Orthodox Christian Church, see Milton Efthimiou and Matthew Briel, *Titles, Offices, and Ranks in the Byzantine Empire and Orthodox Church* (New York: Order of St. Andrew the Apostle, 2016).

60. While many of the land-owning Byzantine aristocrats (i.e., archons) of the Peloponnese had established a semiautonomy from the imperial government in Constantinople in the previous century, the formation of an independent Frankish Morea constituted the first time in which these men entered into what we might call feudal contracts according to Western standards with respect to a specific number of days per year of military service and the requirement to field a specific number of dependent knights and soldiers.

61. See, for example, the speech by William Champenois: Schmitt, *Chronicle*, v. 1810 and again at 1838; Lurier, *Crusaders as Conquerors*, 123.

62. Schmitt, *Chronicle*, vv. 2140; Lurier, *Crusaders as Conquerors*, 134.

63. Schmitt, *Chronicle*, vv. 7533, 7621, 7698, etc.

64. Schmitt, *Chronicle*, vv. 1410–12; Lurier, *Crusaders as Conquerors*, 141. And the chronicler's decision to put the phrase "Basileus of Glory" into the mouth of Charles of Anjou as a reference to God further indicates the extent to which he and his readership have appropriated Byzantine ideas to make them their own. Schmitt, *Chronicle*, vv. 6456–58; Lurier, *Crusaders as Conquerors*, 256.

65. Schmitt, *Chronicle*, vv. 970–88; Lurier, *Crusaders as Conquerors*, 95. Interesting, the *Chronicle* also adds that the Lombards, who had lobbied for the election of the Marquis of Montferrat rather than Baldwin, continued in their dissent after the coronation. Robert de Clari, by contrast, maintains that everyone accepted the decision of the electors.

66. Schmitt, *Chronicle*, vv. 2720–54; Lurier, *Crusaders as Conquerors*, 151–52. The monastery in question is St. James at Andravida, which did contain a family mausoleum. See Lurier, *Crusaders as Conquerors*, 152n1.

67. Schmitt, *Chronicle*, vv. 2746–48. I have changed several of Lurier's terms here (including "psalters" instead of "cantors") to better reflect the Greek, and "ages of ages" instead of "eons to eons" to better reflect contemporary English translations of the Orthodox funeral service.

68. On their bilingualism, see Shawcross, *Chronicle of Morea*, 200–01. An example of their appropriation of the Roman kiss is Schmitt, *Chronicle*, vv. 8882–85; Lurier, *Crusaders as Conquerors*, 317.

69. See, for example, Schmitt, *Chronicle*, vv. 2020–75; Lurier, *Crusaders as Conquerors*, 130–32.

70. Schmitt, *Chronicle*, vv. 3952–4015; Lurier, *Crusaders as Conquerors*, 188–89.

71. Schmitt, *Chronicle*, vv. 5730–36; Lurier, *Crusaders as Conquerors*, 237.

72. Shawcross, *Chronicle of Morea*, 240–41.

73. Shawcross, *Chronicle of Morea*, 255–59.

74. Schmitt, *Chronicle*, vv. 4334–38; Lurier, *Crusaders as Conquerors*, 198. Here we can likely isolate one of the most pronounced differences between the original (now lost) prototype and the subsequent Havniensis manuscript. Whereas the initial description of the baptism is passed over without editorial comment, a later passage in the Havniensis manuscript decries Michael's subsequent behavior against William on the basis of their supposed sacramental bond.

Conclusion

1. See Demacopoulos, "'Traditional Orthodoxy' as a Postcolonial Movement," *Journal of Religion* 97 (2017): 475–99; and Demacopoulos and Aristotle Papanikolaou, "Orthodox Naming of the Other: A Postcolonial Approach," in *Orthodox Constructions of the West*, ed. Demacopoulos and Papanikolaou (New York: Fordham University Press, 2013), 1–22.

2. Kallistos Ware, *Eustratios Argenti: A Study of the Greek Church under Turkish Rule* (Eugene, Ore.: Wipf & Stock, 1964).

INDEX

The word "Greek" is used in the index to refer to people also called Eastern, Byzantine, and Orthodox Christians in the text, and the word "Latin" to Western, Frankish, German, and Venetian Christians.

ORTHODOX CHRISTIANITY AND CONTEMPORARY THOUGHT

SERIES EDITORS
Aristotle Papanikolaou and Ashley M. Purpura

George E. Demacopoulos, *Colonizing Christianity: Greek and Latin Religious Identity in the Era of the Fourth Crusade.*

Brian A. Butcher, *Liturgical Theology after Schmemann: An Orthodox Reading of Paul Ricoeur.* Foreword by Andrew Louth.

Ashley M. Purpura, *God, Hierarchy, and Power: Orthodox Theologies of Authority from Byzantium.*

Lucian N. Leustean (ed.), *Orthodox Christianity and Nationalism in Nineteenth-Century Southeastern Europe.*

John Chryssavgis (ed.), *Dialogue of Love: Breaking the Silence of Centuries.* Contributions by Brian E. Daley, S.J., and Georges Florovsky.

George E. Demacopoulos and Aristotle Papaniklaou (eds.), *Christianity, Democracy, and the Shadow of Constantine.*

George E. Demacopoulos and Aristotle Papaniklaou (eds.), *Orthodox Constructions of the West.*

John Chryssavgis and Bruce V. Foltz (eds.), *Toward an Ecology of Trans-figuration: Orthodox Christian Perspectives on Environment, Nature, and Creation.* Foreword by Bill McKibben. Prefatory Letter by Ecumenical Patriarch Bartholomew.

Ecumenical Patriarch Bartholomew, *In the World, Yet Not of the World: Social and Global Initiatives of Ecumenical Patriarch Bartholomew*. Edited by John Chryssavgis. Foreword by Jose Manuel Barroso.

Ecumenical Patriarch Bartholomew, *Speaking the Truth in Love: Theological and Spiritual Exhortations of Ecumenical Patriarch Bartholomew*. Edited by John Chryssavgis. Foreword by Dr. Rowan Williams, Archbishop of Canterbury.

Ecumenical Patriarch Bartholomew, *On Earth as in Heaven: Ecological Vision and Initiatives of Ecumenical Patriarch Bartholomew*. Edited by John Chryssavgis. Foreword by His Royal Highness, the Duke of Edinburgh.

CPSIA information can be obtained
at www.ICGtesting.com
Prinfed in the USA
JSHW011316271119
2674JS00001B/13